MW01624482

LIVING IN THE
LIGHT

LIVING IN THE LIGHT

A Guide to Personal and Planetary Transformation

SHAKTI GAWAIN

WITH LAUREL KING

Whatever Publishing, Inc.
San Rafael, California

Published by Whatever Publishing, Inc.
58 Paul Drive, San Rafael, CA 94903

87 88 89 12 11 10 9

Cover design by Kathleen Vande Kieft
Back cover photo by Russ Fischella

ISBN 0-931432-14-6

To the Universe

ACKNOWLEDGMENTS

I want to acknowledge Laurel King, who played an important role in helping me to create this book. She has assisted me in leading workshops for years, and is thoroughly familiar with my work. She collected and organized a great deal of material from tapes of my workshops, wrote large portions of several of the chapters, and created many of the meditations and exercises. Most importantly, her bright spirit and sparkling creativity made working on the book fun!

I would also like to express my appreciation to my editor, Kim Peterson, for her many valuable suggestions and contributions. I want to thank my partners at Whatever Publishing, Marc Allen and Jon Bernoff, for their support. For years, Marc has tried in every conceivable way to get me to write this book. I'm glad his efforts are finally being rewarded!

Special thanks to my dear friend Dean Patyk for his constant love and support. I acknowledge gratefully the support of my wonderful friends and family who have participated in my growth and in the creative process that went into this book. I also want to thank Michael Kayden for being an important friend and mirror to me in this process.

And I thank you, my readers, clients, students, and friends who give me so much love, encouragement, and appreciation.

CONTENTS

INTRODUCTION

The Beginning of My Journey

I have always had a burning desire to understand how the universe works, what life is all about, and the meaning and purpose for which I am here. In retrospect, I can see that my entire life has been devoted to my search for truth and understanding.

I was brought up in a very intellectual, well-educated, nonreligious family. My parents were essentially atheists and very early on I remember having the attitude that a belief in God was a human fabrication, a fantasy, a superstition created to help people feel better about the totally unexplained, and unexplainable, predicament we seem to find ourselves in. Human existence or any other kind of existence was simply an accident of nature and had no particularly fathomable meaning. I preferred to admit that I didn't know how we got here or why, rather than to adopt some simplistic explanation merely to gain a sense of security. I believed that truth was rational and anything that couldn't be proved scientifically didn't exist. I also felt somewhat condescending toward people who were weak enough to have to make up a god to believe in.

The positive side of this up-bringing was that I didn't get a lot of the rigid and deeply negative programming about right and wrong, heaven and hell, and sin that so many people receive in their early religious training. Also, I had parents who really loved me and in some way deeply saw me as a bright, intelligent, and powerful being. Although they were divorced when I was less than two years old, I received a lot of support from them, especially from my mother, whom I lived with.

My mother is a very open-minded and adventurous person. She doesn't seem to have many of the fears that so many people in her generation have, so I never got the programming that the world is a dangerous and scary place. My mother loves to explore new places and we traveled a lot when I was a child—all over the U.S., to the West Indies, Mexico, Hawaii, Europe. We also moved frequently. Until I was about fifteen, I had never lived in one place longer than two or three years. My mother loves to try new things, too, and for me she was a great role model of fearlessness and pioneer spirit. She had been one of the first educated American women in her generation to have natural childbirth. I was the first baby her doctor had ever delivered without an anesthetic; I was blessed with a very fortunate birth.

My mother's family had been Quakers and we still used the "plain language" when speaking to my grandmother (saying 'thee' rather than 'you' for the Quakers is an acknowledgment of the god within each person). So, on a deep level, I absorbed the profound respect for spirit and concern for humanity that is woven into the fabric of the Quaker religion.

When I was thirteen years old I went through an emotional crisis. Triggered initially by the collapse of my first romance (with an 'older' man of 19, I was sure no one would ever compare), it snowballed into a deep and long-lasting existential despair. I took a long hard look at life and recognized that there really was no point or meaning to it. Already I could see that all the things that were supposed to provide significance in life—education, success, relationships, money—were in themselves ephemeral, meaningless, and empty. There didn't seem to be anything else to fill the void. I was deeply disillusioned and depressed and basically remained in that state for several years.

In retrospect, I can see that I was going through a place that all of us must pass through at one time or another—what mystics call the piercing of the veil of illusion. It's the point where we truly recognize that our physical world is not the ultimate reality and we begin to turn inward to discover the true nature of existence. At these times we usually feel emotionally that we are hitting bottom, but as we actually hit the bottom we fall through a trap door into a bright new world—the realm of spiritual truth. Only by moving fully into the darkness can we move through it into the light.

New Experiences

Over the next few years I began to have new experiences, openings, a growing awareness that did not fit into my former rational framework. In college I studied psychology and got involved in some encounter groups and sensitivity training groups, which, in addition to allowing me to release old emotional pain, led me to new feelings of love, joy, and oneness with all. I smoked some marijuana and experimented a little with LSD; these were very positive experiences in gaining new levels of awareness and insight. I studied dance and discovered that when I was dancing I would often have an exhilarating feeling, as if some higher force had taken over and was moving me in an abandoned and thrilling way.

I had always been interested in Eastern philosophy, so I read books about Buddhism and Hinduism. I practiced yoga and meditation and found that they helped me to feel more centered, relaxed, and in tune with myself. After college I spent two years traveling around the world, living for several months in India, where I gained a deep awareness of the eastern mystical tradition. My travels were a powerful experience for me because with little money and no real plans, I lived by following my intuition. I had set off originally for a vacation in Italy and ended up making a two-year journey around the world. I learned that I could live happily with virtually no possessions and move safely into unknown places.

Getting Conscious

When I returned to this country I was hooked on something called "consciousness." I couldn't define what it was but I knew that I wanted more of it and I knew that compared to it, nothing else mattered. What was the point of pursuing a career, money, or relationships when I realized that if I got more "consciousness" I would automatically have all these other things as well?

I moved to the San Francisco Bay Area, which I recognized as the forefront of the pursuit of consciousness. I plunged myself into this pursuit. I took classes and workshops, avidly read new books, meditated, and talked constantly to others involved in the same process. After reading *Handbook To Higher Consciousness* by Ken Keyes, I went to live at his center in Berkeley where we worked on our consciousness intensely, day and night, for a year. After that I continued to live communally for several years with others who were involved in an intensive personal growth process. I did whatever I could to make enough money to live on—housework, office work, odds and ends—while I focused on my *real* work—my inner work.

That was ten years ago and since that time my life has been totally dedicated to my growth and evolution as a conscious being. Although I wanted lots of things, I realized that they would all come to me as a result of learning to live fully and freely in accordance with the true principles of the universe. And so my strongest passion became my journey into the light.

My Name

People are always asking me about my name so I thought I'd tell you about it.

While in India, I became very fascinated with the Hindu religion and began to study it. Because I had not been raised as a religious Christian, Christianity had never held much interest for me. I liked some of the ideas in Buddhism a lot, but it seemed a bit intellectual to me. The myths, symbols, and deities in the Hindu religion touched me in a deeper place in my soul. It is a very complex religion and I don't even pretend to understand it, but I grasped a few things.

In the Hindu religion there is a trinity of three main deities that symbolize the three aspects of life. Brahma is the creator, Vishnu is the preserver, and Shiva is the destroyer. Shiva represents the constant changing of the universe, the flow of life, the fact that everything must constantly be destroyed in order to be reborn. He reminds us that we must constantly let go of everything we hold on to, in order to flow with the motion of life. Many of his fervent devotees give up home and possessions and wander freely, abandoning themselves to following and trusting the energy of the universe. Shiva is also known as the Lord of the Dance and they say that it is his dance that keeps the universe in motion. He is depicted as a very beautiful and powerful man with long flowing hair (it is said that his hair is the holy Ganges river). I felt irresistibly drawn to him.

Shakti is the feminine aspect of Shiva. The word "shakti" means "energy"—the energy that everything in the universe is made of. It is the energy of life—the life force running through our bodies. It also means "female energy." In the Hindu practice of Tantra there are techniques for enlightenment through channeling one's sexual energy. In this practice the man is referred to as Shiva and the woman as Shakti.

When I returned from India I met, and for several years lived with, my friend Marc Allen. He didn't think my previous name fit me and, knowing of my "love affair" with Shiva, he began calling me Shakti. I liked it and began using it.

At the time I don't think I realized how powerful the name was, but I certainly realize it now. I feel that the vibration of the name is helping me to emerge into my full power.

Gawain is my given last name. It is the same name as Sir

Gawain in the King Arthur legends. According to one dictionary definition, it means "battle hawk," which I think is a wonderful image. To me, Shakti represents my female aspect, and Gawain my male aspect.

Creative Visualization

One of the earliest workshops I took was the Silva Mind Control Course. At that time I was still rather skeptical about this sort of thing and probably would never have gone to it except that my mother had taken the course and highly recommended it to me. I will never forget her description of a technique in which you can picture in your mind what you want to have happen and it will happen. My mind felt doubtful about this but my heart made a leap and I remember thinking, "Ever since I was a child, I always *knew* that there was magic. That somehow, somewhere magic really exists. This sounds like the closest thing to that that I have ever heard of."

I took the course and I was amazed! We started slowly and easily with simple techniques that anyone could accept and do and gradually we worked our way into more unexplainable but very powerful processes. After five days I had a strong psychic experience in which, for a period of several hours, I was able to consistently pick up specific information that I had no way of knowing except through my intuition. That experience began to dissolve some of my former limits on what I thought was possible.

The most important technique I learned in that course was the basic technique of creative visualization—relaxing deeply and then picturing a desired goal in your mind exactly the way you want it to be. I started to practice this technique and found that it was amazingly effective. Quite often the things I was picturing came true quickly and in unexpected ways. I became fascinated with the possibilities and took some other classes and workshops on similar subjects. I began to use creative visualization techniques in my life regularly and to teach them to my friends. I read the Seth book, *The Nature of Personal Reality* by Jane Roberts and was powerfully affected by the idea that we all create our own reality. Soon I began to lead workshops and do private counseling and eventually I wrote *Creative Visualization.*

When I got the idea to write the book, I just wanted to put all the ideas and techniques down on paper in a comprehensive way. I thought it would be a little booklet I could give to friends and perhaps sell to my clients and a few interested people. As I wrote it I was filled with self-doubt: "Who am I to be writing a book like this? I'm no expert." However, some force inside of me kept pushing me to do it, so I did. I used creative visualization techniques to help create the book. I got a friend to design the cover. Then I hung the cover up on my wall and kept imagining and affirming that the book was already finished. I found writing it was fairly effortless (except for my nagging doubts) and before I knew it, it had turned into a real book, which some friends and I published together.

What I didn't fully realize at the time was that the book was being channeled from a higher source within me. On a personality level, I had doubts and fears, but because of my inner commitment to myself I was willing to go ahead and follow the creative energy anyhow. Because I had a natural ability to think and write clearly, was really interested in these ideas, had a good background in the subject, and was willing to take some risks, the universe could use me as a channel.

The publishing process was similar. My friends, Marc Allen and Jon Bernoff, and I knew very little about business or publishing and had no money at all, but we had a desire to create our own books and music. By trusting our feelings and being willing to risk acting on them, we found that we were led step by step in what we needed to do. We made many mistakes in the process (mostly when we *didn't* follow our inner guidance) and some of them were painful and extremely expensive, but today through many miracles, we have a successful publishing company (Whatever Publishing, Inc.) and a record company (Rising Sun Records).

Creative Visualization has been successful way beyond any wild fantasy I might have had at the time I wrote it. Although it was never marketed or publicized in any significant way, other than through word of mouth, at the time of this writing it is rapidly nearing the half-million mark in copies sold. It has been translated into several foreign languages. I have received many letters and calls from people all over the world saying it has helped them to transform their lives. All this is quite gratifying, I must say, especially because I can see that it is the higher power of the universe at work. I feel like a proud mother, watching my child out there in the world doing its work and making its fortune, knowing that it is mine and yet not mine. It came through me and I helped to form it and yet it is a being, an entity of its own, with its own destiny and its own connection to the creative source.

Surrendering to the Universe

When I first discovered the techniques of creative visualization and found that they worked, I was excited because I felt that through using them I could create whatever I wanted in my life. I was elated by the feeling that I could have everything I desired!

This was an important step for me as it took me out of the essentially powerless attitude that I had had previously—the attitude that life is something that happens to you and that all you can do is make the best of it. It was basically a victim position—giving power to people and things outside of myself. Using creative visualization, I began to realize that the power rested in me, that I could choose to create my life the way I wanted it to be. It was very empowering and very freeing.

As I explored the process of creating my own reality I gradually began to realize that the creative power I was feeling was coming from some other source than my personality/ego self. For one thing, some of the things I *thought* I wanted didn't manifest and in retrospect I could see that it was for my highest good that they hadn't happened. Other things occurred so miraculously that it was as if some unseen force was putting everything into place. Sometimes I would have flashes of insight and awareness, or future visions, that were highly accurate and they seemed to come from some source deep within myself. I became more and more interested in discovering what this creative force was all about and how it worked. I began to realize that "it" (my higher self) seemed to know more than "I" (my personality self) did about a lot of things. I saw that it would probably be smart to try and find out what that inner guidance was telling me and follow it. Every time I did that it seemed to work.

Eventually I lost interest in trying to control my life, to make things happen in a way that I thought I wanted them to be. I began to practice surrendering to the universe and finding out what "it" wanted me to do. I discovered that in the long run it really wasn't that different. The universe always seems to want me to have everything I want, and it seems to know how to guide me in creating it better than I would know how to do so myself. The emphasis is different though. Instead of figuring out what I want, setting goals, and trying to control what happens to me, I began to practice tuning in receptively to my intuition and acting on what it told me without always understanding why I was doing what I was doing. It was a feeling of letting go of control, surrendering, and allowing the higher power to be in charge.

About this time I met a woman named Shirley Luthman who became a very important teacher to me. She led a group each week and I began to go to it faithfully and continued to do so for five years. She taught me a great deal about how to surrender and become a conscious channel for the universe. Many of the ideas in *Living in the Light,* including the concept of male and female the way I use it, were inspired by Shirley and I am deeply grateful for what she taught me. She has authored a book called *Collection* (published by Mehitabel & Co., P.O. Box 151, Tiburon, CA 94920) which readers might be interested in.

Trusting Myself

After several years with Shirley, I found myself confronting the age-old problem of how to let go of the guru. I loved and respected Shirley so much, and what I had received from her had been so invaluable, that it was very difficult to face the time when I knew that I could not look to her for answers anymore.

As I underwent the process of strengthening and learning to trust my channel, Shirley served as a mirror for me, reflecting the power of my inner female. In a sense, she was the metaphysical mother who gave me the support and security I needed until I was ready to trust myself completely.

Eventually my inner guidance told me I had to stop relying on her. The time had come for me to fully trust the power of my channel. It has been both terrifying and liberating to realize that I have my own path and there is no one ahead of me to show me the way. My life is a daily adventure, a moment-by-moment journey of discovery, with only the universe as my guide.

Living in the Light

Since writing *Creative Visualization,* a great many people have been asking me to write another book. About two years after *Creative Visualization* was published I began to have strong feelings that I *would* write another book. One day as I was walking in the woods, I was thinking about my new book and I wondered idly what I should call it. Suddenly my attention was drawn to a patch of woods near the path where a ray of sunlight was filtering brightly through the trees and shining on the green leaves. It was a beautiful sight and as I gazed, the words "Living in the Light" came to me. I knew immediately that it was the title of my next book and I remember the feeling that I hadn't really thought of it myself but that I had "received" it. I even had the impression that I didn't have much choice about it . . . that I was being directed to use that name!

I felt very inspired, began to make some notes and told

people that I was working on my new book. My publisher had a cover designed and began to do some preliminary promotion. But after awhile, I noticed that I hadn't actually written anything. I kept thinking it was going to happen, but it didn't. The truth was, I was not feeling the energy to actually sit down and write, and no amount of thinking that I "should" do it was making it happen. By this time in my life I was quite committed to the philosophy that life doesn't have to be a struggle. I knew that when it was ready to happen it would happen easily. I wasn't willing to do it if it felt like hard work; I felt that the moment would come when the energy would be so strong that I wouldn't be able *not* to write.

Several years went by, and I became involved with many other things. People continued to ask for my new book and I kept reassuring them that it would be along eventually. Privately, I sometimes had my doubts, and I had to accept the fact that it was possible that it wouldn't happen. Still, I felt that it would.

Writing this book was a little like being pregnant. I could feel something forming and growing inside of me and I knew that I was creating even though nothing seemed to be happening externally. The baby would emerge when it was fully formed and ready.

Now is the time. The book has flowed easily and, working with Laurel, the writing process has been exciting and relatively effortless. Although I am involved in an enormous number of other projects, I seem to have found the time here and there to write.

To those of you who have asked me for this book I say thank you for your encouragement. And to all of you I say, "I hope you enjoy reading it as much as I have enjoyed writing it. . . . "

Love,
Shakti

PART ONE

THE PRINCIPLES

1

A NEW WAY OF LIFE

We are living in a very exciting and powerful time. On the deepest level of consciousness, a radical spiritual transformation is taking place. I believe that, on a worldwide level, we are being challenged to let go of our present way of life and create an entirely new one. We are, in fact, in the process of destroying our old world and building a new world in its place.

The old world was based on an external focus — having lost our fundamental spiritual connection, we have believed that the material world was the only reality. Thus, feeling essentially lost, empty, and alone, we have continually attempted to find happiness and fulfillment through external "things" — money, material possessions, relationships, work, fame, good deeds, food, or drugs.

The new world is being built as we open to the higher power of the universe within us and consciously allow that creative energy to move through us. As each of us connects with our inner spiritual awareness, we learn that the creative power of the universe is within us. We also learn that we can create our own reality and take responsibility for doing so. The change begins within each individual, but as more and more individuals are transformed, the mass consciousness is increasingly affected.

My observation that a profound transformation of consciousness is taking place in our world at this time is based on the changes I see within myself, those around me, and in our society. It is affirmed by feedback I receive from thousands of people I work with all over the world.

Living in the Light is about this transformation of consciousness within each individual and in the world. My use of the terms "old world" and "new world" throughout the book refer to the old way of life that we are leaving behind and the new one that we are creating.

For many people, this time may be distressing, because the world situation and/or our personal lives may seem to be going from bad to worse. It's as if many things that used to work are not working any more. I believe things *are* falling apart and will continue to do so with even greater intensity, but I do not feel this is negative. It will only be upsetting to the degree that we are emotionally attached to our *old way of living* and steadfastly follow old patterns, rather than trying to open our eyes to the profound changes that are occurring.

Paradoxical as it may seem, these changes are the most incredible blessing that any of us could possibly imagine. The simple truth is that the old way of life that we have been following for centuries does not work. It has never brought us the deep fulfillment, satisfaction, and joy that we have always sought. Of course some people have led relatively happy lives (although far more, I'm afraid, have led relatively disillusioned, painful, and unfulfilling lives). Even the happiest of lives in the old world cannot compare to the depth of fullness and bliss that will be possible at the higher level of consciousness available in the new world.

It's as if we've been in school for our entire lives, receiving an education that teaches the exact opposite of the way the universe actually functions. We try to make things work as we've been taught, and we may even enjoy some degree of success, but for most of us things never seem to work out as well as we had hoped. That perfect relationship never materializes, or if it does, it soon sours or fades away. Or it may seem as though there is never quite enough money; we never feel truly secure or abundant. Perhaps we don't get the appreciation, recognition, or success that we want. Even if we do achieve some of these things, we still may suffer from a vague sense that there must be something more, some deeper meaning. Some of us may actually connect with that deeper meaning and feel increasingly fulfilled and expanded by a growing spiritual awareness. Nevertheless, there are stubborn and sometimes puzzling old patterns and areas of life, where the light just doesn't seem to have dawned.

Thus, our first task in building the new world is to admit that our "life education" has not necessarily taught us a satisfying way to live. We must return to kindergarten and start to learn a way of life that is completely opposite of the way we approached things before. This may not be easy for us, and it will take time, commitment, and courage. Therefore, it's very important to be compassionate with ourselves, to continually remind ourselves how tremendous this task is that we are undertaking.

Just as a baby learns to walk by falling down repeatedly, we must remember that we are babies in the new world. We will learn by making lots of mistakes and often we may feel ignorant, frightened, or unsure of ourselves. But we would not get angry at a baby every time he fell down (if we did, he'd probably never learn to walk with full confidence and power), so we must try not to criticize ourselves if we are not able to live and express ourselves as fully as we wish immediately.

We are now learning to live in accordance with the true laws of the universe. Living in harmony with the universe is living totally alive, full of vitality, joy, power, love, and abundance on every level. So, although letting go of the old world may seem difficult at times, it is well worth whatever it takes to make the transition into the new world.

Meditation

Sit or lie down, relax, close your eyes, and take a few deep breaths. As you exhale, imagine that you are letting go of everything that you don't want or need. Easily, without effort, let any frustrations, tiredness, or worries melt away. This is a time to release an old way of life that no longer works for you. Imagine that your old ways, your old patterns, and all the obstacles to achieving what you want are leaving your body with each breath. Every time you release a breath, and release a little of your old limitations, you create more space inside of you for something new.

After doing this for a few minutes, begin to imagine that every time you inhale you are breathing in life energy, the life force of the universe. Within this life energy is everything you need and desire — love, power, health, beauty, strength, abundance. Breathe it in with each inhalation. Imagine a new way of life opening up, filling you with aliveness, vitality, and energy. Pretend your life is exactly the way you want it to be. Imagine this new life is here, now, and savor it. Let go of the old and live in the new.

When the meditation feels complete, gently open your eyes and come back into the room. See if you can retain that sense of newness in yourself. Remember that you are now in the process of creating a new life for yourself.

2

THE HIGHER POWER WITHIN US

The foundation for life in the new world is built on the understanding that there is a higher intelligence, a fundamental creative power, or energy, in the universe which is the source and substance of all existence. The words and concepts that have been used to describe this power are innumerable; some currently being used in our culture are:

God	The Universe	Source
Spirit	Higher Self	Cosmic Intelligence
Higher Power	I Am	Inner Guidance
The Light	The Force	Christ Consciousness

These terms are attempts to express an experience or knowingness that is difficult to convey in words and rational concepts. Each of us has this experience within us; the words we choose to describe it are merely the labels that suit us best.

I seldom use the word God, as it has so many confusing connotations. Frequently, people associate it with early religious training which is no longer meaningful to them. Some may think of God as *someone* or *something* outside of themselves: the "old man in the sky with the long white beard." I prefer terms such as higher power, the universe, spirit, your higher self, or the light. In this book, I will use these terms interchangeably to refer to that highest creative intelligence and power within us. If any of these terms are not particularly meaningful to you, please feel free to substitute whatever word you prefer.

For the first twenty years of my life I had no conscious experience of, or belief in, a higher power of any sort. I have had to move through many levels of doubt, skepticism, disbelief, and fear in order to arrive at the great trust I now have in the higher power of the universe that is within me and within everyone and everything that exists. I have not accepted anything on blind faith, so in a sense I have had to "prove" everything to myself through my life experiences. As I've learned to place absolute trust in the higher power of the universe and to live in accordance with universal principles, the changes I have felt and seen in my life are truly miraculous.

Those of you who have felt a deep spiritual awareness throughout your lives already have a solid foundation to build upon. For those of you who have felt spiritually "disconnected" as I have, I hope my words will support and encourage you to find this inner connection for yourselves.

The universe has both personal and impersonal aspects: as I surrender and trust more, I find my relationship with this higher power becoming more personal. I can literally feel a presence within me, guiding me, loving me, teaching me, encouraging me. In this personal aspect the universe can be teacher, guide, friend, mother, father, lover, creative genius, fairy godmother, even Santa Claus. In other words, whatever I feel I need or want can be fulfilled through this inner connection. I seldom feel truly alone anymore. In fact, it is in physical aloneness that I often find the most powerful communion with the universe. At such times, the previously empty places inside of me are filled with the light. Here I find a constant guiding presence that tells me which move to make next and helps me to learn the lesson that lies in taking each step along my path.

Meditation

Sit or lie down in a comfortable position. Close your eyes and take a few deep breaths. Each time you exhale, relax your body more and more. Then take a few more deep breaths and each time you exhale relax your mind. Let your thoughts drift by without holding onto any of them. Allow your mind to go out of focus. Relax your consciousness into a deep place within you.

Imagine that there is a very powerful presence within you and all around you. This presence is totally loving, strong, and wise. It is nurturing, protecting, caring for, and guiding you. It is also very light, joyful, and playful. As you get to know and trust it, it will make your life exciting and fun.

You may get an image or a feeling or a physical sensation that represents this higher presence. Even if you don't see or feel a thing, assume it is there anyhow.

Relax and enjoy the feeling or thought that you are being totally taken care of by the universe. Say this affirmation to yourself silently or aloud, "I feel and trust the presence of the universe in my life."

3

INTUITION

Once we acknowledge the higher power of the universe, the obvious question arises: "How can we contact this power or gain access to it?" After all, if there is a superior wisdom or a deeper knowledge than we normally experience, by tapping into it, we should be able to receive valuable guidance in how to live well in this confusing world. This realization began to dawn on me a few years ago as I undertook my journey toward the light. I have since discovered that the knowingness that resides in each of us can be accessed through what we usually call our intuition. By learning to contact, listen to, and act on our intuition, we can directly connect to the higher power of the universe and allow it to become our guiding force.

This is where we find ourselves in total opposition to life as we've been taught to live it in the old world. In western civilization, we have learned to respect and even worship the rational, logical aspect of our being, and to dismiss, depreciate, or deny our intuition. We do acknowledge the ability of animals to seemingly understand things that are way beyond their rational capacity; we call this instinct. But it's a mystery that defies *logical* explanation, so we shrug our shoulders and dismiss it as something vastly inferior to the magnificent human ability to reason.

Our culture's entire value system is firmly based on this belief that the rational principle is superior and, in fact, constitutes the highest truth. The western scientific tradition has become our religion. We are taught from a young age to try to be reasonable, logical, and consistent; to avoid emotional, irrational behavior; and to suppress our feelings. At best, feelings and emotions are considered foolish, weak, and bothersome. At worst, we fear that they may threaten the very fabric of civilized society.

Our established religious institutions support this fear of the intuitive, nonrational self. Once based on a deep awareness of the universal creative principle in every being, many religions only pay lip service to that idea now. Instead, they seek to control the behavior of their devotees, using elaborate rule structures purported to save people from their deep, irrational, and basically "sinful" natures. And according to many psychological disciplines, the dark and dangerous instinctive nature of man must be controlled. From this perspective, it is only the rational part of us that is capable of harnessing this mysterious force and channeling it into healthy, constructive modes.

Generally, less technically developed societies approach life with a deep awareness of and respect for the intuitive element of existence. Every nuance of their daily lives is guided by a strong sense of connection with the creative force. However, it is their very lack of technical development that has contributed to their gradual destruction or subversion into modern civilization. Two examples relevant to most Americans are the native American and African cultures. Both of these groups were devastated by their contact with "Western" culture. However, a deep respect and appreciation for native Americans has begun to surface in our awareness in recent years. And the African culture, forcibly brought to this continent, has probably done more than any other culture to keep the intuitive power alive in our country through its strong spirit.

In human evolution it seems that as our rational capacity has evolved, we've grown increasingly fearful of the intuitive aspect of our natures. We've attempted to control this "dark force" by creating authoritative rule structures that define right and wrong, good and bad, and appropriate and inappropriate behavior in a very heavy-handed way. We justify this rigid approach to life by blaming everything on our nonrational nature — from our personal emotional dramas to social ills such as drug and alcohol addiction, crime, violence, and war.

However, once we accept the reality of the higher power operating in the universe that is channeled to us through our intuition, it becomes clear that our personal problems and the ills of the world are actually caused by *not* following our inner intuitive knowingness. The more we distrust and suppress our inner self, the more likely it is to eventually burst out in distorted ways. In other words, such problems are not an example of our emotional, nonrational nature running wild and uncontrolled; instead, both personal and social problems are the result of fear and suppression of our intuition.

Our rational mind is like a computer — it processes the input it receives, and calculates logical conclusions based on this information. But the rational mind is finite; it can only compute with the input it has received directly. In other words, our rational mind can only operate on the basis of the direct experience each of us has had in this lifetime.

The intuitive mind, on the other hand, seems to have access to an infinite supply of information. It appears to be able to tap into a deep storehouse of knowledge and wisdom, the universal mind. It also is able to sort out this information and supply us with exactly what we need, when we need it. Though the messages may come through a bit at a time, if we learn to follow this supply of information piece by piece, the necessary course of action will unfold. As we learn to rely on this guidance, life takes on a flowing, effortless quality. Our life, feelings, and actions interweave harmoniously with those of others around us.

It is as if each of us played a unique instrument in a huge symphony orchestra, conducted by a universal intelligence. If we play our part without regard for the conductor's direction or the rest of the orchestra, then we have total chaos. If we try to take our cues from those around us, rather than the conductor, it will be impossible to achieve harmony — there are too many people, all playing different things. Our intellect is not able to process so much input and decide on the best note to play at each moment. However, if we watch the conductor and follow his direction we can experience the joy of playing our unique part, which can be heard and appreciated by everyone, and at the same time we will experience ourselves as part of a greater harmonious whole.

When we apply this analogy to our lives, we see that most of us have never realized a conductor was present. We have lived the best we can, using only our intellect to understand our lives, to figure out the best course of action. If we are honest with ourselves, we will readily admit that we are not making great music under the guidance of our rational mind alone. The dissonance and chaos in our lives and in the world certainly reflect the impossibility of living this way.

By tuning into the intuition and allowing it to become the guiding force in our lives we allow the conductor to take his rightful place as the leader of the orchestra. Rather than losing our individual freedom, we will receive the support we need to effectively *express* our individuality. Moreover, we will enjoy the experience of being part of a larger creative channel.

I don't fully understand how the intuition functions in such an amazing way, but I definitely know, through direct experience and through observation and feedback from the many people I have worked with, that it does. And I find that the more I trust and follow this inner "voice," the easier, fuller, and more exciting my life becomes.

Meditation

Sit or lie down in a comfortable position in a quiet place. Close your eyes and relax. Take several slow, deep breaths, relaxing your body more with each breath. Relax your mind and let your thoughts drift, but don't hold onto any thought. Imagine that your mind becomes as quiet as a peaceful lake.

Now focus your conscious awareness into a deep place in your body, in the area of your stomach or solar plexus. It should be the place in your body where you feel that your "gut feelings" reside. This is the physical place where you can most easily contact your intuition.

Imagine that you have a wise being living inside there. You might have an image of what this wise being looks like, or you might just sense that it is there. This wise being is really a part of you — your intuitive self. You can communicate with it by silently talking to it, making requests, or asking questions. Then relax, don't think too hard with your mind, and be open to receiving the answers. The answers may come in words or in feelings or images. The answers are usually very simple, they relate to the present moment (not the past or future), and they "feel right." If you don't receive an immediate answer, let go and go about your life. The answer will come later, either from inside of you in the form of a feeling or idea, or from outside through a person, a book, an event, or whatever.

For example, you might say, "Intuition, tell me what I need to know here. What do I need to do in this situation?"

Trust the feeling that you get and act on it. If it is truly your intuition, you will find that it leads to a feeling of greater aliveness and power, and more opportunities begin to open up for you. If it doesn't seem right, you may not have been truly acting from your intuition but from some ego voice in you. Go back and ask for clarification.

It takes practice to hear and trust your intuition. The more you do it, the easier it will become. Eventually you will be able to contact your intuition, ask yourself questions, and know that in that "wise being" within you, an incredible source of power and strength is available to answer your questions and guide you. As you grow more sensitive to this guidance from the intuitive feelings within, you will gain a sense of knowing what you need to do in any situation. Your intuitive power is always available to guide you whenever you need it. It will open to you as soon as you are willing to trust yourself and your inner knowledge.

4

BECOMING A CREATIVE CHANNEL

To whatever degree you listen to and follow your intuition, you become a creative channel for the higher power of the universe. When you willingly follow where your creative energy leads, the higher power can come through you to manifest its creative work. When this happens, you will find yourself flowing with the energy, doing what you really want to do, and feeling the power of the universe moving through you to create or transform everything around you.

In using the word *channeling* I am *not* referring to the psychic process of trance channeling. Trance channeling involves a medium who goes into a trance state and allows another being to speak through him or her. (One of the best-known examples of trance channeling is Jane Roberts, who served as a channel for a being named Seth.) By channeling, I mean being in touch with and bringing through the wisdom and creativity of your own deepest source. Being a channel is being fully and freely yourself and consciously knowing that you are a vehicle for the highest creativity of the universe.

Every creative genius has been a channel. Every masterwork has been created through the channeling process.

Great works are not created by the ego. They *arise* from a deep inspiration on the universal level, and are then expressed and brought into form *through* the individual ego and personality.

A person may have great technical skill, but without the ability to channel, his work will be uninspiring. The difference between a technician and a channel was clearly demonstrated in the movie *Amadeus.* Salieri knew how to write music but he didn't know how to tap into the creative source. Mozart — one of the most amazing channels who ever lived — wrote music that was both technically perfect and wonderfully inspired, and he did so easily, spontaneously, without thought or effort. From his early childhood on, music just seemed to bubble up and overflow from within him. I'm sure he had no idea how it happened and could not have explained to anyone else how to do it.

Such genius has always seemed mysterious and unexplainable, a god-given talent possessed by only a few. It seems to come and go at will — sometimes it's there, sometimes it's not. Because of this, many creative people fear their talent will suddenly disappear. They don't know how they got it so they have no idea how to recover it if it vanishes.

Creative people usually function as channels in only one area of their lives (such as art, science, or business) and have no idea how to do it in the rest of their lives. Thus, their lives are often terribly out of balance. (See the section on Highly Intuitive People in the chapter Trusting Intuition.)

I believe we are all geniuses — each in our own unique way. We will discover the nature of our particular genius when we stop trying to conform to our own or other people's models, learn to be ourselves, and allow our natural channel to open. Through trusting and acting on our intuition, it's possible to learn to live as a channel at every moment, in every area of our lives.

When I speak of a channel, I have an image of a long, round pipe with energy flowing through it. It's somewhat like the pipe in a pipe organ, with the music coming through.

This channel image has three important features:

1. It is open and unobstructed inside so that the energy can move through freely.

2. It has a definite physical form; a structure surrounds the open space so that the energy is directed in a particular way. Without this structure, the energy would be free-floating, without any form.

3. It has a power source — something which moves energy through the channel.

In a pipe organ, the power source (the organ) sends energy through the open pipes. The particular combination of open space inside each pipe and the structure — the size and shape of the pipe — causes a certain note to be sounded. The power source is the same for all the pipes and the energy moving through them is the same, but because each one is a different size and shape, each one makes a unique sound.

We can think of ourselves as channels similar to these pipes. We have a common power source (the universe) and the same creative energy flows through each of us. Our body and personality form the structure that determines the unique direction and function of each of us as a channel. It is up to us to keep our channel open and clear and to build and maintain a strong, healthy, beautiful body/personality structure as a vehicle for our creative energy. We can do this by constantly tuning in, asking where the energy wants to go, and moving with it.

A strong body/personality structure is not created by eating certain foods, doing certain exercises, or following anybody's rules or good ideas. *It is created by trusting your intuition and learning to follow its direction.* When your inner voice tells you what to eat, how to exercise, or anything else, you can trust that this advice will strengthen your ability to channel, no matter how different it might seem from any previous ideas you had about what's good for you.

All of us are already channels to some extent, unconsciously and sporadically. The following true story is a good example of this. A friend was in a pet shop recently where she saw a beautiful parrot for sale at a very reasonable price. She had always wanted a parrot, but had never been able to afford one, especially now, as she did not even have all the money she needed to pay her rent.

She left the pet shop regretting her inability to take advantage of the good deal. She tried to forget the entire thing, but try as she might, she could not get the parrot out of her mind. The idea of even considering such a purchase seemed ludicrous. Nevertheless, two days later, she went back to the pet store and paid all the money she had for rent as a down payment on the bird, seriously questioning her sanity all the while.

On the way to the pet store she felt certain that if her decision was not right, someone else would have already purchased the bird. This thought was so compelling that she practically raced to the store to get her money down before it was too late. The next day, while she dropped in to visit the bird, the manager said, "It's a good thing you came in when you did yesterday. An hour later, someone else came in to buy the parrot."

Later that same day, she met with a client who unexpectedly advanced her the same amount of money that she had paid for the bird the day before: And when she returned home, her husband told her their landlady had called to tell them to wait on paying the rent for a couple of weeks as she was going away on vacation!

And as if these things were not affirmation enough that she had been right to follow her intuition about the bird, the next day she got a new job, with an advance payment that not only enabled her to pay the rent, but to pay off the balance on the bird as well. My friend told me that after all this had happened, she felt full of enormous power and confidence. She said, "I wish I could feel this way all the time, about everything going on in my life!"

This is an excellent example of spontaneous channeling. You may have had a similar experience, where following your intuition about something proved so fruitful and fulfilling. If so, the next step is to become more conscious of the process so you can recognize when you are channeling, as opposed to blocking, fighting, or trying to control the energy. The more willing you are to surrender to the energy within you, the more power can flow through you.

I am learning to follow the spirit within me wherever it wants to take me. Every moment I check in, feeling the energy inside me and letting it direct me. I find this a wonderful way to live. When I do this, I experience joy, power, love, peace, and excitement, just as my friend did when she responded to her intuition and bought the parrot. But following this higher power takes a commitment to my intuition. I must allow my gut feeling to tell me what I want or don't want, and then act on this information. When I am willing to do this, power flows through me, increasing in strength all the time.

I know we've all had experiences at certain times when we've felt the light and power flow through us; when it almost seems as if we've had a preview of being enlightened. We get a brief glimpse and then it goes away again. When it goes away, we feel lost and unsure of ourselves.

As you practice and learn to trust your intuition this will change. Increasingly, you will feel the flow until it's there all the time. Then you will find yourself right where you want to be at every moment. You'll be where the energy is the greatest for you, doing what you want to do, and watching miracles being accomplished. You will channel energy that transforms others. For example, you might walk into a room and suddenly everyone present will feel more connected with themselves. Or people passing you on the street will feel a sudden shift in their energy without even knowing why.

Because of the commitment to trust yourself, everything in your life changes rapidly. At first, when you make the choice to let go of your old patterns, it may appear that things in your life are falling apart. If you decide to go all the way in this process, you will eventually let go of everything you've been attached to. But this will be a joyful experience, because your true happiness comes from your connection with the universe. All of the material aspects of life are just a bonus, icing on the cake, a fun game that you play as a channel for the universe.

We can learn to live in the world of form — our physical bodies, personalities, and physical surroundings — without being attached to it. Up until now, most people have only let go of their attachment to form by leaving their bodies at the time of death. A few have attempted to transcend attachment by removing themselves from the temptations of the world — by entering a monastery or engaging in a spiritual practice that separates them from the world.

I'm suggesting that we can have everything the world has to offer — all the relationships, wealth, beauty, power, and fun we might want, yet be willing to let go of it at any moment. The universe within us is rich and powerful, and intuitively we know this; we already know we have everything we need, so there really is no need to be attached to anything. Our body/ego self, however, feels it will die without certain things, and thus our attachment is perpetuated. But as we learn to live as a channel, the body/ego self discovers that aliveness and fulfillment come from connection with our inner universe, not from externals. Gradually the ego loosens its hold and we truly transcend attachment.

Maintaining Your Focus

An important part of becoming a channel is staying focused on your relationship with the universe. This focus allows your channel to remain open to the energy flowing through. It's so easy to lose our focus, to get lost in other people, external goals, and desires. And the problem is, we do exactly that: we lose our connection with the universe inside ourselves. As long as we focus on the outside there will always be an empty, hungry, lost place inside that needs to be filled.

When I keep my focus on the universe inside, I can have everything: money, success, and fulfilling relationships, as well as that incredible connection inside myself.

If I'm in love with someone and begin to think of him as my source of joy, then I lose myself. I have to remind myself that the source of joy and love is already within me, that I am experiencing love externally only because it is inside me. I try to keep the focus on the universe within and at the same time see the universe coming through my lover to me.

I do the same thing when people tell me they love what I do in my workshops. I thank them and then take their appreciation back to the universe within me. If I were caught up in trying to control everything, the universe couldn't move through me to them.

For me, it's a constant discipline to remember to go back inside to connect with my intuition. I'll remind myself regularly during the day to do this. If I find myself getting lost in my outer activities, I'll check back inside to see if I'm being true to my feelings. This keeps the flow of the universe moving through me.

Living as a Channel

Channeling works in two ways: energy either flows through you to others, or from others to you. For example, as I write my book, I focus on the energy flowing from the universe through me to others. Then, when people say to me, "I just love your book; it's changed my life," I am conscious of appreciation coming from them to me and back to the universe.

As you become increasingly conscious of the flow of the universe moving through you and through everything and everyone else, your body will become capable of channeling more energy. The more energy you are willing to receive, the more you'll be able to give.

To become a clear channel for the universe presents the

highest challenge and offers the greatest potential joy and fulfillment for every human being. Being a channel means living fully and passionately in the world, having deep relationships, playing, working, creating, enjoying money and material possessions, totally being yourself, yet never for one moment losing your profound connection with the power of the universe within you.

Then you can watch the universe create through you; it can use you to do its work. Living as a channel is an experience that's available to anyone who is willing to make the inner commitment.

Group Channeling

As we learn to trust and follow our intuition, we are learning to open and strengthen our individual channel so we can bring more power, creativity, and love through us. When we come together in a relationship or in a group, each individual channel becomes part of a bigger channel. A group channel is created which is more powerful than any of us individually can be.

When many bodies and minds are willing to surrender, open up, and grow, these combined energies create a very strong, open structure that allows a lot more energy to come through from the universe. The process intensifies tremendously and everyone gets a powerful "hit" of the energy which is capable of pushing each of us to the next level of our growth. Even though we may all be in somewhat different places and going through different things, each person receives the inspiration, the support, the push, or whatever is needed to enable them to take the next step on their journey. A group channel can open us up to a deeper level of awareness, and in the process we share more of ourselves and find that we are healed of things that have held us back.

This is one reason I love teaching workshops and working with groups. My friends call me an "energy junkie" because I'm always attracted to situations where the energy is most intense and expansive. I love the way my personal growth process is speeded up by the intensification that happens in groups.

I no longer follow a specific format or structure in my workshops. I prefer to create a group channel and then allow the universe to take over and guide the group as a whole. As a facilitator, my job is to share my process of learning to become a channel, and encourage others to undertake this practice as well.

As everyone surrenders and opens up, the group channel is formed. This process can be confusing and chaotic at times because the leader is not "in control" in the usual sense of the word. It can arouse my fears and everyone else's, but I find that when I'm willing to move through the fears, something very powerful and beautiful emerges through the group channel. The universe leads us into new places and new discoveries which we would not have had an opportunity to experience if we had stayed within a more formal structure. I find the process of group channeling very exciting and rewarding.

In a sense, everyone living on this planet is a part of one gigantic group channel — the mass consciousness of humanity. This world as it is now is the creation of the group channel. As each one of us individually surrenders to the power of the universe and allows that power to transform and enlighten us, the group channel is affected accordingly. The mass consciousness becomes more and more enlightened. This is how I see our world being transformed.

Meditation

Sit or lie down in a comfortable position. Close your eyes. Take a deep breath and relax your body. Take another deep breath and relax your mind. Take another deep breath and let everything go. As you relax you find yourself in a deep, quiet place inside. This is the deepest part of yourself. Allow yourself to just rest in that place for a few moments, with nothing you need to do or think about.

From this deep, quiet place, ask for the spirit of the

universe to come through you. Affirm your willingness to be a channel for the universe. Feel the power, wisdom, and creativity within you.

You are a channel. See your energy moving through you to others. Know that as you follow your inner guidance your creativity is manifested in the world. Get an image of what this is like for you. Stay open to any image that may come to you. Imagine what it would feel like if this were happening right now.

You are an open channel for the universe. You are filled with the light and power that flows through you into your life and toward others.

Channel Exercise

Everyone is a channel for the universe. In this exercise I ask you to feel and acknowledge this for an entire day. As you practice doing this, it will become easy for you to do on a daily basis.

As you start your day, before you get out of bed, spend a few minutes seeing yourself as a channel for the universe. Feel the energy in your body and be aware of your ability to channel the light toward others. With each person you meet and each exchange you have, realize the light of the universe is moving through you to them. In reverse, focus on the channel in each person you're with and see that every exchange you have with them is the universe talking to you. As you acknowledge your own true power and that of others the light will grow. You will begin to see the light and the gift in every situation.

5

THE WORLD AS OUR MIRROR

The physical world is our creation: we each create our own version of the world, our particular reality, our unique life experience. Because my life is being created through my channel, I can look at my creation to get feedback about myself. Just as an artist looks at his latest creation to see what works well and what doesn't, we can look at the ongoing masterwork of our lives to appreciate who we are and to recognize what we still need to learn.

We're creating our lives as we go along; therefore, our experiences and needs give us an instant, ongoing reflection of ourselves. In fact, the external world is like a giant mirror which reflects both our spirits and our forms clearly and accurately. Once we have learned how to look into it and perceive and interpret its reflection, we have a fabulous tool.

The Mirror Process

The mirror process is a technique that can help us see the world as a mirror. Viewed in this way, the external world can teach us about hidden aspects of ourselves that we can't see directly. The process is based on two premises:

1. I assume that *everything* in my life is my reflection, my creation; there are no accidents or events that are unrelated

to me. If I see or feel something, if it has any impact on me, then my being has attracted or created it to show me something. If it didn't mirror some part of myself I wouldn't even be able to see it. All the people in my life are reflections of the various characters and feelings that live inside of me.

2. I try never to put myself down for the reflections I see. I know that nothing is negative. Everything is a gift that brings me to self awareness; after all, I'm here to learn. If I was already perfect I wouldn't be here. Why should I get angry at myself when I see things I've been unconscious of? It would be like a first grader getting frustrated because he wasn't in college yet. I try to maintain a compassionate attitude toward myself and my learning process. To the extent that I can do this, the learning process becomes fun and really quite interesting.

I am learning to view my life as a fascinating and adventurous movie. All the characters in it are parts of me played out on the big screen so that I can clearly see them. Once I see them and recognize their various feelings and voices inside myself, it is easy to choose which characters to keep and expand, and which ones to let go of or transform.

If the movie portrays problems, hassles, or struggles, I know I must check inside to find out where I'm not being true to myself. I also know that when I'm trusting and being myself as fully as possible, everything in my life reflects this by falling into place easily, often miraculously.

Problems are Messages

If there are problems in your life, that's the universe trying to get your attention. It's saying, "Hey, there's something you need to be aware of, something that needs to be changed here!" If you pay attention to the small signals, you will learn from them, but if you don't, the problems will intensify until you get the message and start to pay attention. If you accept that every time a problem occurs the universe is showing you something, you will make rapid progress on your journey of self-discovery.

When something "negative" happens, it's tempting to say, "Why does this happen to me? I'm doing the best I can but nothing seems to be going right. I can't understand why I keep having this problem." If you find yourself doing this, try to open up to another way of looking at things. Go inside and say to the universe, "I know you're trying to show me something. Help me understand what it is."

After you do this, let go of focusing on it, but stay open to the message that will be coming through. It may come in the form of an inner feeling or awareness, some words from a friend, or something unexpected that happens to you. The message may come through immediately or it may take quite awhile. One of my clients was fired, quite unexpectedly, over two years ago. At first, he was devastated, but after a month of "getting his bearings," he went into business on his own. His business is now doing very well, but it was only a few weeks ago that he finally "got" the message that his firing reflected. As he was talking to a friend about working for other people, he suddenly realized that the firing incident was trying to tell him that he was much better off being in business for himself, rather than working for other people. For him, this realization not only affirmed his present course in life, but it also finally resolved the sense of incompleteness about being fired that had lingered with him since the incident.

Interpreting the Reflection

The trickiest part of using the mirror process is learning how to interpret the reflection you see. Once you do get a message, but you're not quite sure what it is, how do you find out?

It will not help to analyze and think about it with your rational mind. It is far more effective to turn to your inner self, to ask the universe for help. Simply sit quietly, take a few deep breaths, and focus your awareness within — to the wise being within you who is in touch with the wisdom of the universe. Ask this being, either silently or out loud, for guidance or help in understanding the message. As you tune into your gut feeling and get a sense of what feels right in the moment, act on this feeling.

After acting on the feeling, try to be aware of the external and internal feedback from your actions. The external feedback is how well things work. Do things seem to fall into place and work easily? Then you're surely in tune with your inner guidance. If you're struggling to do something that doesn't happen easily, it's a message to let go and check back in to find out what you really want to be doing.

Internal feedback will come to you as feelings. If you feel empowered, more alive, then it's right. The ultimate key is *aliveness*. The more the universe moves through you, the more alive you feel. Conversely, every time you don't follow your inner guidance you feel a loss of energy, loss of power, a sense of spiritual deadness.

In being true to yourself you will feel more alive, but you may also feel uncomfortable. This is because you are risking change! As you undergo certain changes you may experience intense emotions. Allow these emotions expression; after all, your inner voice has to move through years of accumulated unconsciousness, doubt, and fear. So simply let these feelings come up and flush through you — they are being cleaned out and healed by the light.

External feedback may also mirror these feelings: your doubts and fears will often be reflected in the reactions of those around you. If your friends and family question or judge the changes in you, recognize that they are simply mirroring the doubting, fearful voices in you, such as, "What if I'm doing the wrong thing? Can I really trust this process?"

Respond to such feedback from others in whatever way you feel is appropriate: reassure them, ignore them, argue with them, whatever. The important thing is to recognize that you are *really* dealing with your inner fears. Affirm that you are learning to trust yourself more and more. You will be amazed to see how others immediately mirror your increasing self-trust and confidence by responding to you with trust and confidence.

Remember:

If you judge and criticize yourself, others will judge and criticize you.

If you hurt yourself, others will hurt you.

If you lie to yourself, others will lie to you.

If you are irresponsible to yourself, others will be irresponsible in relation to you.

If you blame yourself, others will blame you.

If you do violence to yourself emotionally, others will do violence to you emotionally, or even physically.

If you don't listen to your feelings, no one will listen to your feelings.

If you love yourself, others will love you.

If you respect yourself, others will respect you.

If you trust yourself, others will trust you.

If you are honest with yourself, others will be honest with you.

If you are gentle and compassionate with yourself, others will treat you with compassion.

If you appreciate yourself, others will appreciate you.

If you honor yourself, others will honor you.

If you enjoy yourself, others will enjoy you.

Changing Old Patterns

It's very important to realize that you may not be able to change your old patterns overnight. Sometimes things seem to change rapidly, once you've recognized the message, but sometimes it seems like you keep doing the same old thing and getting the same unpleasant results long after you feel you know better. It takes time for the ego to change its habits, so you have to watch the same lousy movie repeat itself a few times.

If you feel your progress is too slow, ask the universe for help, and remind yourself that it *will* change soon. Change happens not by trying to *make* yourself change, but by becoming conscious of what's *not* working. You can then ask your higher self for help in releasing the old and bringing in the new pattern. Remember, the darkest hour is just before the dawn — change often occurs just when you've given up, or when you least expect it.

Using the Mirror Process

In using the world as your mirror, you must deal with the external realities of your life in whatever way you need to handle them. But as soon as possible, before, during, or after you deal with the externals, check inside to find out what is being shown to you.

For example, if someone is angry at you and blames or criticizes you, you may need to say to them, "Stop blaming me. I don't want to hear your judgments and criticisms of me. If you can talk about your own *feelings* I'll be glad to listen, but if you keep attacking me, I'm going to leave." If they take more responsibility for their feelings (for example, "I felt hurt and angry when you didn't call me yesterday."), then you will probably be able to continue the conversation on a more productive level. If they continue to blame and focus on your "problems," you probably need to support yourself by walking out of the room and refusing to continue the conversation until they stop their attack.

Either way, you have handled the *external* situation. Now, as soon as you get a chance, check inside yourself and ask, "I wonder what this person's anger is mirroring in me?" You may realize that you have been feeling very angry and critical toward yourself lately. Or perhaps you will discover that your inner self is upset because you haven't been paying enough attention to yourself. When other people want more from you, it's usually an indication that you want more from yourself.

A friend of mine discovered that her boyfriend had been seeing another woman and lying to her about it. She was very hurt and angry, particularly to discover his dishonesty. She expressed her feelings and asked him to leave her alone for awhile to sort things out on her own.

When she was alone, she asked herself, "Is there some way I'm lying to myself, some way I'm not being totally truthful and honest with myself, that would cause me to attract a dishonest man?" She let go of thinking about it and went to work. By the end of the day she realized she had often felt this man was not fully present with her, was not being real with her. But in the past, she had denied and covered up these feelings because she was afraid to confront him with what she felt and intuitively knew. Thus, she effectively lied to herself and supported him in his deceptions as well.

She realized this was a lesson in learning to trust her feelings more and to have the courage to express and support them. She started to do this more with her boyfriend, and they eventually worked out an honest, communicative relationship. She might also have chosen not to continue the relationship. What matters is that she received the gift from it — learning to trust and express her feelings.

If you are emotionally triggered by something a person does, the two of you are probably mirrors for each other. It may appear that you have opposing viewpoints, but internally you are probably very similar. One of you is acting out one side of the internal conflict, while the other one plays out the other side.

For example, one person may want more commitment in a relationship, while the other wants more freedom. They become extremely polarized on this issue and truly believe that they want opposite things. However, if one person suddenly switches their position (the one who wanted commitment suddenly wants freedom) the other person almost always swings to the opposite polarity. The reason for this is that they are attempting to resolve an inner conflict they *both* have — the desire for closeness and security and the fear of entrapment.

Once people look inside and become more aware of their feelings, they often recognize that they have simply projected their inner conflict onto the outside world so that they could recognize and deal with it. If a person truly and unequivocally wants a committed relationship, he will simply attract another person who wants the same thing. If someone feels completely clear about wanting to explore being with many partners, he simply does it. By using the mirror process, you can recognize what you really feel and learn to be more honest with yourself. Once you recognize an internal conflict, you can ask the universe for help in resolving it and integrating your feelings.

Seeing the world as your mirror also gives you wonderful opportunities to receive positive feedback. Think of everything that you like and enjoy about your life right now. You created these things — they are also your mirrors. Think of the people you know whom you love, enjoy, respect and admire. They are your mirrors. They couldn't even be in your life if they didn't reflect you: you would not be able to recognize their positive qualities if you didn't have similar ones. Think of the people and animals that love you. They are a mirror of how you love yourself. If you have a home that you love, or a particular spot in nature that is very beautiful to you, it is a mirror of your own beauty. When you see beauty anywhere, it's a reflection of yourself.

There are mirrors everywhere. Whoever you have a connection with is a mirror for you, and the deeper the connection, the stronger the mirror. Part of the fun in using the mirror process is discovering who we are through these external reflections. The key is always to go back inside to discover the meaning of the reflection for you. The more you are willing to do that without either rationalizing away what you see or blaming yourself for it, the faster you can move toward reaching your fullest potential.

Meditation

Relax and close your eyes. Take a few deep, slow breaths and move into a deep place inside of you. Bring to your mind a person or thing in your life and ask him/her/it what it is mirroring to you. Stay open to receiving the answer, whether it comes in words, feelings, or images.

Exercises

1. Think of a person you especially love or admire. List all their positive qualities. Think about how those qualities mirror you. In some cases, they may be qualities you have not yet fully developed in yourself. Recognize that this person is here to teach and inspire you by his or her example.

2. Make a list of all the things and people you like in your life. Praise and appreciate yourself for creating and attracting these mirrors.

6

SPIRIT AND FORM

Spirit is the essence of consciousness, the energy of the universe that creates all things. Each one of us is a part of that spirit — a divine entity. So the spirit is the higher self, the eternal being that lives within us.

Form is the physical world. As an individual, my form is my physical body, my mind, and my personality. It is also my self-concept — my ego/identity structure: "My name is Shakti Gawain. I was born on September 30, 1948. I'm 5′ 9″ tall and weigh 130 pounds. I'm intelligent and have a generally outgoing personality." This is all information about my form.

We, as spiritual beings, created the physical world as a place to learn. It's our school, our playground, our artist's studio. I believe that we're here to master the process of creation — to learn how to consciously channel the creative energy of spirit into physical form.

Physicists are now discovering what metaphysicians have claimed for thousands of years: seemingly solid physical matter is, in reality, made of energy. If we look through a powerful microscope at anything "solid," we see an infinite number of little vibrating particles. If we closely examine one of these particles, we discover that it is made of even smaller particles, and so on. The fact is that everything physical is made of "energy" — which we can also call "spirit" or "the universe." So modern science supports the ancient metaphysical truth that form is created out of spirit.

When our spirit decides to manifest as physical form, the first thing it creates is a physical body in which to house itself. We choose a life situation and create a body in accordance with what we feel will best serve and teach us in this lifetime. Ultimately, our goal is to create a body/personality that can fully express our divine creative spirit, a form that can do everything our spirit wants to do easily, skillfully, and beautifully.

However, the physical world still exists at a relatively primitive level of creation compared to the consciousness of our spirits. I read recently in a scientific article that the human body/mind has evolved very little since prehistoric times. Thus, we have very evolved beings embodied in relatively simple, unevolved forms. These forms have a certain consciousness of their own which revolves around basic survival issues — how to get enough food, shelter, and emotional nurturing; how to protect oneself from danger; and how to make sure reproduction takes place and offspring survive.

After we are born into the body, we forget who we really are and why we came here. We take on the "survival" consciousness of the physical world and we get lost in the world of form. We forget our spirits, believing we are just our personalities. We lose touch with our true power and feel lost and helpless. Life becomes a tremendous struggle to find meaning and satisfaction.

We may spend many lifetimes caught up in this cycle. Certainly, most of us have spent many years in this lifetime looking outside of ourselves, trying to find fulfillment in the world of form. Eventually we realize that it's not working: no matter what we do in the world, we don't find happiness. We become unwilling to spend one more lifetime, one more year, or even one more minute in futile struggle. In frustration and hopelessness, we give up.

This is usually a painful and frightening place in a person's life — it feels like hitting bottom. It is a time of ego death, when the body/mind form recognizes the hopelessness of trying to live this way and surrenders its fight. It would rather die than keep trying. So at this time a person often has thoughts and feelings of death, or may experience the death of a close friend or family member (or several of them). Some people create a serious illness, accident, or other major crisis at this time, and some contemplate or even attempt suicide.

But the darkest hour *is* truly just before the dawn. When we finally give up the struggle to find fulfillment "out there," we have nowhere to go but within. It is at this moment of total surrender that the light begins to dawn. We expect to hit bottom, but instead we fall through a trap door into a bright new world. We've rediscovered the world of our spirit.

This is like being reborn. We are infants in this new world and have no idea how to live since none of our old ways work here. We feel uncertain and out of control because our ego is not in control any more. Yet hope is reborn with us, and power and vision start to come through. From this point we become gradually more "enlightened."

Ram Dass has a beautiful analogy for this process. He likens it to a clock, where 12:00 is the starting point. From 12:00 to 3:00 life is totally lost in the illusion of form. From 3:00 to 6:00 is gradual "disillusionment" with the world, and 6:00 is where you hit bottom. You feel that you lose everything, but as you pass through 6:00 you are actually waking up to the spirit. From 6:00 back up to 12:00 is ever-increasing enlightenment. As individuals, we are at various stages in this process. By the time we have enough awareness to be talking about this, we are all well into the light. I have a sense that we each have one major cycle of this type lasting over many physical lifetimes, and we also have an infinite number of minor cycles — sometimes almost daily!

I also have the feeling that the mass consciousness in this world is just passing through 6:00.

When we, as individuals, first rediscover our spirit, we are usually drawn to nurture and cultivate this awareness. This often involves one degree or another of withdrawing from the world and going within. For some people this takes the form of spending time in nature; for some it involves practicing meditation, going to retreats, and so forth; for some it may be simply finding time to be alone and quiet. Often it's a time of partial or complete withdrawal from relationships, work, and/or other attachments which tend to pull us outside of ourselves. For some beings, this phase may last a whole lifetime or more; for others it might last only a few weeks or months. Each entity is unique, so we all experience this move within in different ways. In one form or another, we learn to go within and be in that quieter place in ourselves for awhile. There we find a deeper and deeper connection with our spirit.

While we are feeling deeply connected with ourselves in this way, we often find that we have a feeling of clarity, vision, wisdom, power, and love. This is because our spirits are already highly evolved. They are already immersed in the truth and the light. So as soon as we make that contact we get a temporary "high" — an experience of momentary enlightenment.

The problem is that our form hasn't evolved yet. It's just given up its old way, died, been reborn, and is now in an infantile state, not knowing what to do. If we take it by the hand and start to guide and teach it, it will learn very fast how to live in a new way. However, it still has all the old memories, patterns, and programs from the old world, and it keeps trying to revert back to them.

So here we have the dilemma in which we all currently find ourselves — a great discrepancy between our spirit and our form. The spirit is very powerful and creative and has a lot of things it would like to do to express itself in the physical world, but it needs to have the form as a vehicle in which to do it. The form is willing but isn't yet able to go where the spirit wants to go. It has to be educated and transformed through the power and wisdom of the spirit.

Dealing with the Discrepancy

Being a very evolved spirit in a relatively unevolved form is quite uncomfortable. It accounts for most of the problems we are having. It's as if we are gods and goddesses living in little mud hovels and driving around in clunky, funky, old jalopies. It can be frustrating and demeaning — especially when nobody even recognizes who we are! When we were oblivious of who we were it wasn't so bad; we just accepted it as our lot in life. But now that we remember our true identity, we may feel like we're trapped in an alien world.

This understanding can explain a lot of things that many of us are experiencing in our lives. Why is it that we have wonderful moments of consciousness and clarity, and then find we have completely lost our perspective and become immersed in fear and pain again? How is it that we can feel so loving, wise, and accepting one day and the next day feel so angry, foolish, and judgmental? Why did we feel like we'd really "gotten it" at a workshop and then seem to "lose it" the next day? How is it that we can feel so peaceful and unattached when we are meditating, yet often our relationships seem like a worse mess than ever? And how come we have such a trust in the abundance of the universe but we're still having financial problems?

The answer is simple — we are dealing with the discrepancy between spirit and form. This is a very difficult thing to confront, and we are facing a real challenge. Many people reach this point and have a hard time going any further.

On the traditional spiritual path we remain more or less withdrawn from the world. In this way we can be true to our spirit and avoid dealing with the attachments and patterns of our form. Unfortunately, the form never has an opportunity to develop and we eventually just leave the body in order to move into other realms. The physical world remains untransformed.

In order to create the new world, we are being challenged to move back into the world of form with full spiritual awareness. We need to recognize the discrepancy between our spirit and our form and then allow the spirit to transform the physical body, the mind, and the personality into a powerful and beautiful channel through which it can fully express itself.

Integrating Spirit and Form

The first step in the process of consciously transforming your form to match your spirit is to be able to *recognize* and *feel* both the consciousness of your spirit and the consciousness of your form (personality/mind/ego). It's a bit like living with two people inside of you. You may be accustomed to feeling only one of them most of the time, with occasional flashes of the other. Or you may flip back and forth frequently between the two perspectives. It's as if one takes control of the body for awhile and you see things from that viewpoint. Then the other one takes over and suddenly everything looks quite different.

For example, I frequently get inspiring, creative ideas for a new project I want to do. I get a very strong vision of how wonderful it will be and how it can work. All this is coming from my spirit, of course. I get very excited and jump into the project, making all kinds of plans and initiating many actions in that direction. A few days or weeks later I find myself feeling totally overwhelmed, overworked, frustrated, and ready to throw the whole thing out of the window. My spirit had a true vision, but I was trying to achieve it faster than my form was able to go. At this point I have to stop and consider what's realistic for me, then set the project aside for awhile, or allow it to take longer and develop more slowly. My spirit tends to race ahead, so it has to learn to go at the pace my form can handle.

The second step is to *love* and *accept* both aspects of yourself. They are both beautiful and vital parts of you. Without your spirit you wouldn't be alive — you'd only be a dead body! Without your form you wouldn't be able to be in this world — you'd be existing in some other realm of consciousness.

It may be frustrating at times to see that your form can't do all that your spirit wants to yet. But it's important to appreciate it as it is now and allow the integration to take place at its own pace.

For example, a few years ago I was living with a man and we had an "open relationship" — in other words, we were free to be with other lovers. I had a very strong spiritual ideal that I could love someone deeply and allow him to be free to follow energy he might feel with someone else, while I was free to do likewise. Sometimes I was able to do this, and I had some beautiful moments where I felt an expansive and exhilarating unconditional love, a deep intimacy with my lover; I sometimes even felt a love toward his other lovers! But most of the time I was wracked with jealousy and emotional pain. I finally realized that I was not emotionally ready to live my ideal at that time. I had enough respect for my feelings to change the situation.

I still feel that I will someday be secure enough in myself to have that balance of depth and freedom in relationships if I want it, but I am allowing myself to move toward that very slowly, at the pace that I can handle emotionally (more on this in the chapter on Relationships).

The basic key to integrating spirit and form is learning to listen to your intuition and act on it. The more you do this, the more your mind, personality, and body have an opportunity to learn to trust and rely on the spirit. The more the form surrenders to and moves with the spirit, the more enlightened and empowered it will become.

Here is a very important point: you cannot force your form to trust and follow the spirit through *will.* You must allow it to educate itself through conscious observation.

In other words, you can't force yourself to always follow your intuitive feelings, even though you desire to live that way. Sometimes it may seem like too big a risk; even though your spirit knows it would work out, your form is too afraid to do it. Don't push yourself past what you are ready to do. Simply observe the process and be honest with yourself about how it feels and what happens. Then the change will happen naturally and spontaneously.

For example, suppose you are with a friend and there's something you want to say but you are afraid to do so for fear your friend will get hurt or angry and reject you. If you find you do have the courage, go ahead and say what you feel. Then observe what happens and how you feel as a result. Chances are good that you will feel energized and empowered by the experience.

If, on the other hand, you are too afraid to speak the truth, don't try to push yourself past your fear. Again, simply observe yourself being with your friend and not being totally yourself. Notice that you feel a deadness and loss of energy; you may also feel resentful toward your friend. *Try not to judge yourself for your lack of action.* Remember: this is a learning process.

The spirit always tends toward expansiveness, depth, greater energy, and aliveness. The form (ego/personality) always tends toward what it perceives to be safety, security, and the status quo, which is usually a deadening experience.

If you are able to observe yourself without rationalization or judgment you will begin to notice that when you trust yourself and follow your energy fully, you feel better. Conversely, when you follow your old patterns of fear and holding back, you feel worse. After awhile, your form gets the message clearly and begins to *spontaneously* follow the energy instead of the old pattern because it knows it will feel better. Eventually you have a form that automatically goes for the light in every situation, without having to think about it and control it.

In this process of learning to trust yourself, many old feelings and deep emotional patterns will come to the surface to be healed and released. This is a very important part of it, and must be allowed to happen. Old memories and experiences may be triggered. Feelings of sadness, fear, pain, guilt, and rage may come up. Allow yourself to feel all of it, allow it to wash through you; it will be released. It is being cleaned out of your form. As the light of spirit penetrates every cell of your body, it dispels the darkness.

As you learn to consciously observe the transformation process, you will watch yourself repeating a lot of old patterns long after you seemingly know better. Spiritually and intellectually, you realize there is another way, but emotionally, you are still clinging to the old habits. This is a difficult time, but try to be patient and compassionate with yourself. When you recognize the futility of an old pattern so clearly, it's about to change! A short time later, you will suddenly begin to respond differently, in a more positive way.

The enlightenment of the form happens through a miraculous process. As the ego surrenders to trusting the universe, the spirit penetrates every cell of the body, transforming the darkness into light.

You will see your physical body change and become lighter, stronger, more clearly defined, healthier, and more beautiful. There is a translucent quality — as if you can actually see the light shining through. Because your life is your creation and the mirror of your transformation, all the forms in your life — your work, money, car, house, relationships, community, the world — will increasingly express the power and beauty of your spirit.

Meditation

Get comfortable, relax, and close your eyes. Take a few deep breaths and relax your body and mind completely. Allow your conscious awareness to move into a deep, quiet place within you.

Imagine that there is a beautiful golden light radiating from a place deep within you. It begins to grow and expand until it fills your entire body. It's very powerful, and as it fills you, it penetrates into every cell of your body, literally waking up each molecule to the light. Imagine your entire body glowing and radiating with this light. Then see and feel your body being transformed — becoming healthier, stronger, and more beautiful. Imagine everything else in your life being similarly transformed.

Exercise

See if you can observe yourself nonjudgmentally and notice when you are able to listen to your intuitive feelings and act on them, and when you are not. Observe how you feel and what happens in each of these situations. Ask your spirit to help you learn to trust and follow your energy more and more.

7

THE MALE AND FEMALE WITHIN

Each of us has male *and* female energies within us. I believe that one of the most important challenges we have in this world is to develop these energies fully, so they can interact in harmony with each other.

The eastern philosophies have always included the concept of yin (feminine/receptive) and yang (masculine/active) and have said that everything in the universe is made up of these two forces. In the west, Carl Jung did pioneering and exciting work with his concept of the anima and the animus. He explained that men have a feminine side (anima) and women have a masculine side (animus), that most of us have strongly repressed these aspects of ourselves, and that we must learn to come to terms with them. He and his followers have done wonderful work using dreams, myths, and symbols to help men and women reclaim the lost, denied parts of themselves. Many other philosophers, psychologists, poets, playwrights, and artists have expressed the ideas of masculine and feminine energies within ourselves and within everything.

As I mentioned earlier in the book, the person who helped me the most to understand the male and female within was Shirley Luthman. Her ideas in this area were so clear, simple, and profound they literally began to revolutionize my life. I found that this concept provided me with a powerful tool — I could look at just about anything in my life or in the world from the perspective of male/female energies and understand so much better what was really going on! I began to adapt and reinterpret the ideas I'd learned from eastern philosophy, Jung, and Luthman in my own way and incorporate them into my own metaphor. I have found that wherever I go, when I start to share this metaphor with people, they really light up. They have the same reaction I did — it makes so many things so clear.

Some people have resistance to the words "female" and "male" because in our culture we have so many preconceived ideas about what those words mean, so much emotional "charge" associated with them. If it's more comfortable for you, substitute the words "yin" and "yang," or any other words that appeal to you.

Male and Female

I think of our female aspect as being our intuitive self. This is the deepest, wisest part of ourselves. This is the feminine energy, for men or women. It is the *receptive* aspect, the open door through which the higher intelligence of the universe can flow, the receiving end of the channel. Our female communicates to us through our intuition — those inner promptings, gut feelings, or images that come from a deep place within us. If we don't pay conscious attention to her in our waking life, she attempts to reach us through our dreams, our emotions, and our physical body. She is the source of higher wisdom within us, and if we learn to listen carefully to her, moment by moment, she will guide us perfectly.

The male aspect is action — our ability to do things in the physical world — to think, to speak, to move our bodies. Again, whether you are a man or a woman, your masculine energy is your ability to act. It is the outflowing end of the channel. The feminine receives the universal creative energy and the masculine expresses it in the world through action; thus, we have the creative process.

Our female is inspired by a creative impulse and communicates it to us through a feeling, and our male acts on it by speaking, moving, or doing whatever is appropriate.

For example, an artist might awaken with an inspired idea for a painting (an image communicated from his female) and immediately go into his studio, pick up his brush, and begin painting (action taken by his male).

A mother might feel sudden concern for her child (a warning from her inner female), and run into the other room and pull the child away from a hot stove (action taken by her male).

A businessperson might have an impulse to contact a certain associate (guidance from his or her female), make a call (action taken by his or her male), and launch a new deal.

In each case where the male and female within were in creative union there was a creative result — a painting, saving the child, a business enterprise. Even the simple sequence of feeling hungry, going into the kitchen, and fixing a meal illustrates the same process.

The union of feminine and masculine energies within the individual is the basis of all creation. Female intuition plus male action equals creativity.

In order to live a harmonious and creative life you need to have both your inner female and male energies fully developed and functioning correctly together. To fully integrate the inner male and female you need to put the female in the guiding position. This is her natural function. She is your intuition, the door to your higher intelligence.

Your male listens to her and acts on her feelings. The true function of male energy is absolute clarity, directness, and a passionate strength based on what the universe inside of you, coming through your female, tells you.

The female says, "I feel this." He says, "I hear your feelings. What would you like me to do?" She says, "I want that." He says, "You want that? OK great, I'll get it for you."

And he goes directly to get it for her, trusting totally that in her desire is the wisdom of the universe.

Remember now that I am talking about an *internal* process in each of us. Sometimes people externalize this idea and think I'm saying that men should let women tell them what to do! What I'm actually saying is that we *each* need to let our intuition guide us, and then be willing to follow that guidance directly and fearlessly.

The nature of the feminine is wisdom, love, and clear vision expressed through feeling and desire. The male nature is all-out risk-taking action in service to the feminine, much like the chivalrous knight and his lady.

Through his surrender to her and his action on her behalf, our male energy builds a personality structure within us that protects and honors the sensitive energy of our intuitive female. I often imagine my male as underneath or behind my female — supporting, protecting, and "backing her up." For a man, the image might be reversed — you might see your female as within or behind you — guiding, empowering, nurturing, and supporting you. When these two energies are thus in harmony and working together, it's an incredible feeling: a strong, open, creative channel, with power, wisdom, peace, and love flowing through.

The Old Male and the Old Female

Unfortunately, we have not learned how to allow our male and female energies to function naturally, in the proper relationship with each other.

In our culture, we have used our male energy (our ability to think and act) to suppress and control our feminine intuition, rather than to support and express her. This traditional use of the male energy I call the "old male" and it exists equally in men and women, although it is often more obvious and external in men, more subtle and internal in women.

The old male is that part of us that wants to keep control. He is terrified of our feminine power because he doesn't want to surrender to the power of the universe. He is afraid that if he surrenders, he will lose his individual identity. Another word for the old male is the *ego:* its function is to hold onto individuality and separateness at any cost. Therefore, it denies the power of the feminine, which is a force moving toward union and oneness.

In relationship with the old male, the female is helpless in the world. Her power cannot move directly into the physical world without the support of the male's action. Her power is suppressed, and must come out indirectly through manipulative patterns or physical symptoms, or in sudden, unfocused ways — emotional outbursts or even (in extreme cases) acts of violence.

You can see that men and women have played out these roles externally. In the traditional male role, men are taught to deny and suppress their inner female, to be machine-like, unemotional, totally in control, and suppressive toward women (secretly, they may be terrified of women because women remind them of the power of their inner woman, whom they are busy denying). Because they are cut off from their internal power source, they really feel very alone and lost.

In the traditional female role a woman also learns to use her male energy to deny and suppress her feminine power. This leaves her helpless, dependent on men, emotionally unbalanced, and able to express her power only indirectly, through manipulation (she may be afraid that if men found out how powerful she really is, they would abandon her, so she carefully keeps her power hidden).

It's important to realize that *both* the old male and the old female exist in each sex. A woman who is expressing herself in the traditional way described above has a controlling, macho, old male inside her, suppressing her. She will tend to attract men who mirror this male personality and will act it out in their behavior toward her. This behavior may range from paternalistic and chauvinistic to verbally or physically abusive, depending on how the woman treats herself and what she believes she deserves. Once she begins to trust and love herself more and starts to use her internal male energy to support herself, the behavior of the men in her life will reflect that shift. They will either change dramatically and continue to change as she does, or they will disappear from her life, to be replaced by men who are supportive and appreciative of her, who will mirror her new attitude toward herself. I've seen this happen over and over again.

The traditional macho man has a helpless, hysterical female voice inside of him desperately trying to be heard. He will tend to attract women who have a low self-image and are clingy and needy, or who express their power indirectly through manipulation — little girl "cuteness," sexual seductiveness, "cattiness," or dishonesty. These women reflect his lack of trust and respect for his inner female by not trusting and respecting themselves. By opening to and trusting his own feminine nature, he'll find within himself the nurturing, support, and connection he's been lacking. The women in his life will mirror this shift by becoming stronger, more independent, more direct and honest, and more genuinely loving and nurturing.

The New Male and the New Female

The feminine power, the power of spirit, is always within us. It is up to the ego — our male energy — to determine how we relate to that power. We can either fight it, block it, attempt to control it, and try to keep ourselves separate from it, or we can surrender and open to it, learn to support it, and move with it.

Individually and collectively, we are shifting from a position of fear and control into surrender and trust of the intuitive. The power of the feminine energy is on the rise in our world. As she emerges within us and we acknowledge and surrender to her, the old male within us is transformed. He re-emerges, birthed through the female, as the new male — the one who goes all out in his trust and love for her. He must grow to become her equal in power so that they can be the lovers they are meant to be.

I believe that the new male has been truly birthed in our consciousness only within the last few years. Before that we had little experience in our bodies of the true male energy. Our only concept of male was the old male — an energy completely divorced from the feminine.

The birth of the new male is synonymous with the birth of the new age. The new world is being built within us and mirrored around us as the new male (physical form) emerges in all his glory from the feminine power (spirit).

An Image

Every now and then I do a visualization process in which I ask for an image of my male and female. Each time I do it, I receive something a little different which teaches me something new. I'm sharing with you one of the most powerful images, because it is such a dramatic illustration of one aspect of the relationship between inner female and male.

My female energy appeared as a beautiful, radiant queen, overflowing with love and light. She was being carried through the streets on a litter borne by several carriers. The people were lining the streets, waiting for an opportunity to see her. She was so beautiful, open, and loving that as she passed by, waving, smiling, and throwing kisses to people, they were instantly healed of any pain or limitation.

By her side walked a samurai warrior carrying a sword. This was my male energy. It was well understood by everyone that if anyone made a threatening move toward the queen, he would instantly raise his sword and ruthlessly cut down the offender. Knowing this, naturally, no one dared to harm her.

He was willing to be absolutely unhesitating in his trust of his own judgment and his own response, which left her completely safe and protected. Feeling totally safe, having no need to hide or defend herself, she was free to be completely open, soft, and loving and to give her gifts freely and generously to all around her.

Meditation

Sit or lie down in a comfortable position and close your eyes. Take a few deep breaths and relax your body and mind completely. Allow your conscious awareness to move into a quiet place within you.

Now bring to your mind an image that represents your inner female. This image could be of an actual person, an animal, or it could be something more abstract — a color or shape. Spontaneously take whatever comes to you.

Take a look at your female and get a sense or a feeling of what she represents to you. Notice some of the details of the image. Notice the colors and the textures. Notice how you feel about her.

Ask her if she has anything she would like to say to you right now. Allow yourself to receive her communication, which may or may not be in words. You may also ask her any questions you have. There may be something you want to know from her. Again, receive her communication to you, whether it comes in words, a feeling, or an image.

Once you have allowed yourself to receive her communication, and you feel complete for this moment, then take a deep breath and release her image from your mind. Come back to a quiet, still place.

Now draw to mind an image that represents your male self. Again, take what image comes to you. It could be an image of an actual man or it could be some abstract symbol or color. Explore his image. Begin to notice the details of it. Notice its colors and texture. Notice how you feel about him. Then ask him if he has anything to communicate to you at this time. Be receptive to receiving his communication, whether it is in words or some other form. If you have anything you want to ask him, do this now. Be open to any words or images you may receive. If an answer doesn't come to you immediately, know that it will come later.

Once you feel complete with your communication with him, release his image from your mind. Come again to a quiet place inside.

Now, ask for the images of both your male and female to come to you at the same time. See how they relate to one another. Are they in relationship with one another or are they separate? If they are in relationship to one another, how do they relate? Ask them if they have anthing they would like to communicate to one another or to you. Stay open to what comes to you in words, images, or feelings. If you have anything you'd like to say to them or ask them, do that now.

When you feel complete, once again take a deep breath and release their images from your mind. Come back to a quiet, still place inside.

Exercise

Close your eyes and contact your female intuitive voice.

Ask her what she wants; is there a gift she desires or something she wants to say or do? When she has told you what she wants, see your new male as supporting her desire. See him as taking whatever necessary action to honor her need and desire.

When you open your eyes, do your best to follow whatever you feel your female wants you to do.

8

MEN AND WOMEN

We all instinctively understand the basic functions of feminine and masculine energies, but we may not realize that they both exist in each person. More often we tend to associate male and female energies with their respective body types.

Thus, women have become the symbols of female energy. Traditionally, women have developed and expressed receptivity, nurturing, intuition, sensitivity, and emotion. They have more or less repressed assertiveness, direct action, intellect, and the ability to function effectively and strongly in the world.

Likewise, men have become the symbols of male energy. Traditionally, they have developed their ability to act in the world strongly, directly, assertively, and aggressively. They have developed their intellect. And to a large extent they have repressed and denied their intuition, emotional feelings, sensitivity, and nurturing.

From this perspective, each person is only half a person, dependent on the other half for its very existence. As we cannot live in the world without the full range of masculine and feminine energies, each sex has been helplessly dependent on the other for its survival. Men have desperately needed women to provide them with the nurturing, intuitive wisdom, and emotional support without which they unconsciously know they would die. Women have been dependent on men to take care of them and provide for them in the physical world, where they haven't known how to take care of themselves.

It might seem like a perfectly workable arrangement — men help women, women help men — except for one underlying problem: as an individual, if you don't feel whole, if you feel your survival depends on another person, you are constantly afraid of losing them. What if that person dies or goes away? Then you die, too, unless you can find another such person who is willing to take care of you. Of course, something might also happen to *that* person. Thus, life becomes a constant state of fear in which the other person is merely an object for you — your supply of love or protection. You must control that source at any cost: either directly, by force or superior strength; or indirectly using various manipulations. Generally, this happens subtly — "I'll give you what you need so you will be just as dependent on me as I am on you, so you will keep giving me what I need."

So our relationships have been based on dependency and the need to control the other person. Inevitably, this leads to resentment and anger, most of which we repress because it would be too dangerous to express it and risk losing the other person. The repressing of all these feelings leads to dullness and deadness. This is one reason why so many relationships start off exciting ("Wow! I think I've found someone who can really fulfill my needs!"), and end up either filled with anger or relatively dull and boring ("They aren't fulfilling my needs nearly as well as I had hoped, and I've lost my own identity in the process, but I'm afraid to let go for fear I'll die without this person.").

Finding the Balance

In recent times, of course, the strongly separated roles of men and women have begun to shift. In the last two generations, increasing numbers of women are exploring and expressing their abilities to act in the world. At the same time, a growing number of men have been looking within themselves and learning to open to their feelings and intuition.

I believe this is happening because we have reached a dead-end street with our "old world" relationships and externalized concepts of masculine and feminine. The old models and ways of doing things are too limiting for us now, and we have not yet evolved effective patterns to take their place. It's a period of chaos and confusion, pain and insecurity, but also of tremendous growth. We *are* making a leap into the new world. I believe that every form of relationship, from the most traditional marriage to open relationships or homosexual or bisexual relationships, represents each being's attempt to find their feminine/masculine balance within.

Women have traditionally been in touch with their female energy but they haven't backed her up with their male energy. They have not acknowledged what they know inside. They have always acted as if they were powerless when they are really very powerful. They have gone after external validation (from men especially), rather than internally validating themselves for what they know and who they are.

Many women, like myself, have had a strongly developed male energy but have used it in the "old male" way. I was very intellectual, very active, and drove myself very hard to shoulder the responsibilities of the world. I also had a very strongly developed female, but I didn't put her in charge. In fact, I ignored her a lot of the time. I basically protected my sensitive, vulnerable feelings by erecting a tough outer shell.

I've had to learn to take that powerful male energy and use it to listen to, trust, and support my female. This allows her the safety and support to emerge fully. I feel and appear softer, more receptive, and more vulnerable, but I am really much stronger than before.

Women are now learning to back themselves up and validate themselves, instead of abandoning the responsibility and trying to get a man to do it for them. However, it's a deep-seated pattern that has endured for centuries, and it takes time to change it in the deepest layers. The key is to just keep listening to, trusting, and acting on our deepest feelings.

The qualities that women have looked for in men — strength, power, responsibility, caring, excitement, romance — must be developed inside of ourselves. A simple formula is this — just treat yourself exactly the way you would want to be treated by a man!

The interesting thing is that what we create within us is always mirrored outside of us. This is the law of the universe. When you have built an inner male who supports and loves you, there will always be a man, or even many men, in your life who will reflect this. When you truly give up trying to get something outside yourself, you end up having what you always wanted!

For men, of course, the principle is exactly the same. Traditionally, men are disconnected from their female energy; thereby disconnected from life, power, and love. They've been out there in the world secretly feeling helpless, alone, and empty, although they pretend to be in control and powerful. (War is a good example of the old male energy lacking the wisdom and direction of the female.) Men seek nurturing and internal connection through women but once they have connected with their own inner female, they will receive her incredible love from within themselves.

For men, all the qualities you've wanted from a woman — the nurturing, softness, warmth, strength, sexuality, and beauty — already exist in your inner female. You will feel this when you learn to listen to your inner feelings and support them. You need to totally respect and honor your inner female energy by acting on your feelings for her. Then, every woman, every person, in your life will mirror that integration. They will have the qualities you've always wanted, and they will also receive love, warmth, nurturing, and strength from you.

Many men, especially in recent times, have chosen to connect deeply with their feminine energy and in doing so have disconnected from their male. They've rejected the old macho image and have no other concept of male energy to relate to. These men are usually so afraid of their male energy, fearing that it will burst forth with all the old mindlessness and violence they equate with maleness, that they reject the positive, assertive male qualities, as well.

I feel it's very important for these men to embrace the concept of the new male — one who allows his spontaneous, active, aggressive male energy to flow freely, knowing that the power of his feminine is in charge, wisely directing him. This requires a deep trust that the inner female knows what she's doing and won't allow anything destructive or harmful to happen.

New World Relationships

A new idea of relationships is emerging which is based on each person being whole within him- or herself. Internally, each person is a fully balanced feminine/masculine being with a wide range of expression from softest receptivity to strongest action.

Externally, most people's style of expression will certainly be determined strongly by which type of body they are in — male or female.

When people hear these ideas they sometimes express the fear that we will all become outwardly androgynous — men and women all appearing pretty much the same. The reverse is actually true. The more women develop and trust their male aspect to support them and back them up internally, the safer they feel to allow their soft, receptive, beautiful feminine aspect to open up. The women I know who are going through this process (myself included) seem to become *more* feminine and beautiful even while they are strengthening their masculine qualities. Men who are surrendering and opening fully to their female energy are actually reconnecting with the inner feminine power which enhances and strengthens their masculine qualities. Far from becoming effeminate, the men I know who are involved in this process seem more secure in their maleness.

In the new world, when a man is attracted to a woman, he will recognize her as a mirror of his feminine aspect. Through her reflection he can learn more about his own female side and move through whatever fears and barriers he may have to come to a deeper integration within himself. When a woman falls in love with a man, she is seeing her own male reflected in him. In her interactions with him she can learn to strengthen and trust her masculine side.

If you know on a deep level that the person you're attracted to is a mirror of yourself, you cannot be too dependent on him or her because you know that everything you see in your partner is also in you! You recognize that the reason you're in the relationship is to learn about yourself and deepen your connection with the universe. So healthy relationships are based not on neediness but on the passion and excitement of sharing the journey into becoming a whole person.

Gay Relationships

My own experience in relationships is heterosexual, so I can hardly consider myself much of an expert on gay relationships. However, from talking and working with quite a few gay and lesbian friends and clients, I do have a strong sense that on a spiritual level, homosexual and bisexual relationships are a powerful step that some beings take to break through old, rigid roles and stereotypes to find their own truth.

For some people, being in a close, intense relationship with a person or persons of the same sex is the most powerful mirroring process they can find. Two women, for example, often seem to find a depth of connection with each other that they don't find with a man. They use this intuitive feminine connection to create a strong foundation and safe environment for each of them to practice building their internal male. They totally reflect and support each other in becoming whole and balanced.

A man sometimes seems to find a matching male intensity with another man — an ability to go all out that he wouldn't find with a woman. He may also find in another man a support for moving into and exploring his feminine self without feeling he has to fulfill the old, stereotyped male role.

I think many of these things are mysteries that we will understand only in retrospect. I believe that every being chooses the life path and relationships that will help him or her to grow the fastest.

As we continue to evolve, I believe we will gradually stop categorizing ourselves and our relationships with any particular labels such as gay, straight, monogamous, open, and so on. I foresee a time when each person can be a unique entity with his or her free-flowing style of expression. Each relationship will be a unique connection between two beings, taking its individual form and expression. No categories are possible because each one is so different and follows its own flow of energy.

Exercise

Think of some of the most important women in your life. What are their strongest or most attractive qualities? Be aware that they mirror some aspects of your own female energy (whether you are a woman or a man).

Now think of some of the most important men in your life. What qualities do you most like, admire, or appreciate about them? Recognize that they reflect similar aspects of your own male energy (again, this applies to you whether you're a man or woman).

If you have trouble seeing that some of the things you admire in others are in you as well, it may be because you have not yet developed those qualities in yourself as strongly as they have. In this case, try the following meditation.

Meditation

Get in a comfortable position. Close your eyes, relax, take a few deep, slow breaths and move your consciousness into a deep, quiet place inside.

Bring to mind one person whom you admire or are attracted to. Ask yourself what qualities you find most attractive in this person. Do you see those same qualities in yourself? If not, try imagining that you possess those same qualities. Imagine how you would look, talk, and act. Picture yourself in a variety of situations and interactions.

If you feel these are qualities you want to develop more within yourself, continue to do this visualization regularly for awhile.

9

EAST AND WEST: A NEW CHALLENGE

I have a strong feeling that in my last life I was a spiritual ascetic, perhaps in India, and probably living in meditation on a mountaintop somewhere. That way of life has a comfortable familiarity to it, and there is a longing somewhere within me to continue to live in that blissful simplicity! However, I know that this time I have chosen to take it to the next level — to create a body and a world that can match and express my spirit.

It is interesting to look at the world from the perspective of male and female; in doing so I have discovered some fascinating things. In a sense, the East can be seen to represent the female. Most of the Eastern cultures (India, Tibet, China, Japan, and many others) have an ancient and powerful spiritual tradition. Until recently, their strength and development have been primarily in the intuitive and spiritual realms, at least in comparison with the Western world. They have lacked development in the physical realm and, as a result, they have experienced a great deal of poverty, chaos, and confusion.

The energy in the West (Europe and the U.S.) is more masculine. It has been focused primarily on developing the physical realm while all but ignoring spiritual development. As a result, we have made incredible technological progress but we are experiencing a terrible poverty of spirit, a feeling of disconnection from our source.

These two worlds are drawn to one another just as men and women are — with a certain amount of fear and distrust, but an overwhelming attraction nonetheless. Eastern spiritual teachings are flooding the West, and Western technology is gravitating toward the East. We are each hungry for what the other has.

One of my favorite mental pictures from my travels in India is this: I was standing in a bazaar. In front of me were two booths. One booth had beautiful traditional handcrafted items for sale. A group of Europeans and Americans were crowded around it, eagerly bargaining for the lovely treasures. The other booth proudly displayed a variety of plastic items — bowls, kitchen utensils, even plastic shoes. A long line of Indians patiently waited their turn to purchase these precious things. Naturally, neither one of the groups cast even a second glance at the other booth!

East and West can learn from each other, but like woman and man, they must ultimately find within themselves that which they admire in each other. Hopefully, the developing Third World countries will learn from our mistakes and develop a technology that is more harmoniously attuned to the spirit and the environment. And we must develop a spiritual path that helps us to deal with the physical world.

The Eastern spiritual traditions (and our earlier Western spiritual traditions, for that matter) are based on removing oneself as much as possible from the world in order to connect more deeply with the spirit. The world with its temptations and distractions is a very difficult place to maintain a focus and commitment to inner truth.

Thus, most serious spiritual paths have involved some degree of renunciation of the world — relationships, money, material possessions, pleasures, and luxuries have been given up. The ideal has been to withdraw to a monastery or mountaintop and pursue a life of quiet contemplation, giving up all attachment to the world. Even those who choose to remain householders with families and jobs have usually followed strong rules and restrictions that are designed to keep them as separate from the world as possible.

This contemplative spiritual orientation has been a necessary and powerful step, but it is reflective of the split we have maintained between spirit and form, between the female and male within us. To be a spiritual seeker we have had to leave the physical world. "Enlightenment" has been the reason for reclaiming spirit by denying the body — transcending form by leaving it. Thus, individual beings have become "enlightened" in the sense that they have fully realized their spiritual nature, but they have not fully enlightened their form. When they have eventually left their bodies, the world remained largely untransformed. These masters have supported and preserved the intuitive principle in our world and have paved the way for us to take the next step — the enlightenment of the form and the subsequent transformation of our world.

Those of us who choose to be spiritual seekers and transformers must now move *into* the world *with the same degree of commitment* to our spiritual selves as we would have if we renounced the world. This path is much more difficult! We are now challenged to totally surrender to the universe, to follow unquestioningly its guidance and to do so *while* having deep, passionate relationships, dealing with money, business, families, creative projects, and so many other "worldly" things. Rather than avoiding our attachments to the world, the time has come to confront them on the deepest, cellular levels of our bodies. We must move *into* the challenging situation, move into, recognize and own all the feelings and attachments, and allow them to be dissolved and transformed through the spiritual power within us.

Meditation

Relax, close your eyes, and take a few deep breaths. With each breath drop more deeply into a quiet place inside yourself. From this place of calm start to see a new image of yourself in the world. Your focus is on the universe and you follow unquestionably its guidance. You trust yourself. You feel strong and courageous. You carry a sense of knowingness with you into the world. Because of this trust and focus within yourself, what you create on the outside is beautiful. Your world is nourishing to yourself and others. You are having deep, passionate relationships, dealing with people, money, your career, your body, and everything around you.

You are able to be in the world and enjoy all "worldly" things, yet keep your commitment to the universe within yourself. This commitment is reflected in the amazing light and power around you.

PART TWO

LIVING THE PRINCIPLES

10

TRUSTING INTUITION

Most of us have been taught from childhood not to trust our feelings, not to express ourselves truthfully and honestly, not to recognize that at the core of our being lies a loving, powerful, and creative nature. We learn very easily to try to accommodate those around us, to follow certain rigid rules of behavior, to suppress our spontaneous impulses, and to do what is expected of us. Even if we rebel against this, we are trapped in our rebellion, doing the opposite of what we've been told in a knee-jerk reaction against authority. Very seldom do we receive any support for trusting ourselves, listening to our own sense of inner truth, and expressing ourselves in a direct and honest way.

When we consistently suppress and distrust our intuitive knowingness, looking instead for authority, validation, and approval from others, we give our personal power away. This leads to feelings of helplessness, emptiness, a sense of being a victim; eventually to anger and rage, and, if these feelings are also suppressed, to depression and deadness. We may simply succumb to these feelings, lead a life of quiet numbness and desperation, and die. We may overcompensate for our feelings of powerlessness by attempting to control and manipulate other people and our environment. Or we may eventually burst forth with uncontrolled rage which is highly exaggerated and distorted by its long suppression. None of these are very positive alternatives.

The true solution is to re-educate ourselves to listen to and trust the inner truths that come to us through our intuitive feelings. We must learn to act on them, even though it may feel risky and frightening at first, because we are no longer playing it safe, doing what we "should" do, pleasing others, following rules, or deferring to outside authority. To live this way is to risk losing everything that we have held onto for reasons of external (false) security, but we will gain integrity, wholeness, true power, creativity, and the *real* security of knowing that we are in alignment with the power of the universe.

I am not attempting to disregard or eliminate the rational mind by suggesting that our intuitive awareness is the guiding force in our lives. The intellect is a very powerful tool, best used to support and give expression to our intuitive wisdom, rather than to suppress our intuition as we now use it. Most of us have programmed our intellect to doubt our intuition. When an intuitive feeling arises, our rational minds immediately say, "I don't think that will work," "nobody else is doing it that way," or "what a foolish idea," and the intuition is disregarded.

As we move into the new world, it is time to re-educate our intellect to recognize the intuition as a valid source of information and guidance. We must train our intellect to listen to and express the intuitive voice. The intellect is by nature very disciplined and this discipline can help us to ask for and *receive* the direction of the intuitive self.

What does it mean to trust your intuition? How do you do it? It means tuning in to your "gut feelings" about things — that deepest inner sense of personal truth — in any given situation, and acting on them, moment by moment. Sometimes these "gut messages" may tell you to do something unexpected or inconsistent with your previous plans; they may require that you trust a hunch that seems illogical; you may feel more emotionally vulnerable than you are used to;

you may express thoughts, feelings, or opinions foreign to your usual beliefs; perhaps follow a dream or fantasy; or take some degree of financial risk to do something that feels important to you.

At first you may fear that trusting your intuition will lead you to do things that seem somewhat hurtful or irresponsible to others. For example, you may hesitate to break a date, even though you need time for yourself, because you fear hurting your date's feelings. I've found that when I really listen to and trust my inner voice, in the long run, everyone around me benefits as much as I do.

People may sometimes be temporarily disappointed, irritated, or a bit shaken up as you change your old patterns of relating to yourself and others. But this is simply because the people around you are being pushed to change as well. If you trust, you will see that the changes are also for their highest good. (If you *do* break that date, your friend may end up having a wonderful time doing something else.) If they don't want to change, they may move away from you, at least for a while; therefore, you must be willing to let go of people. If there is a deep connection between you, chances are that you will be close again in the future. Meanwhile, everyone needs to grow in their own way and their own time. As you continue to follow your path, you will increasingly attract people who like you as you are and want to relate to you in a new way.

Practicing a New Way of Living

Learning to trust your intuition is an art form, and like all other art forms, it takes practice to perfect. You don't learn to do it overnight. You have to be willing to make "mistakes;" to try something and fail, and then try something different the next time; sometimes even to embarrass yourself or feel foolish. Your intuition is always one-hundred percent correct, but it takes time to learn to *hear it* correctly. If you are willing to risk acting on what you believe to be true, and risk making mistakes, you will learn very fast by paying attention to what works and what doesn't work. If you hold back out of fear of being wrong, learning to trust your intuition could take a lifetime.

It is often hard to distinguish the "voice" of our intuition from the many other "voices" that speak to us from within: the voice of our conscience, voices of our old programming and beliefs, other people's opinions, fears and doubts, rational head trips, and "good ideas."

People frequently ask me how to differentiate the true voice or feelings of the intuition from all the others. Unfortunately, there's no simple, sure-fire way at first. Most of us are in touch with our intuition whether we know it or not, but we're usually in the habit of doubting or contradicting it so automatically that we don't even know it has spoken. The first step is to pay more attention to what you feel inside, to the inner dialogue that goes on within you.

For example, you might feel, "I'd like to give Jim a call." Immediately, the doubting voice inside says, "Why call him at this time of day? He probably won't be home," and you automatically ignore your original impulse to call. If you had called, you would have found him at home, and discovered he had something important to say to you.

Another example: you might get a feeling in the middle of the day that says, "I'm tired, I'd like to take a rest." You immediately think, "I can't rest now, I have a lot of work to do." So you drink some coffee to get yourself going and work the rest of the day. By the end of the day you feel tired, drained, and irritable, whereas if you had trusted your initial feeling, you might have rested for a half hour and continued about your tasks, refreshed and efficient, finishing your day in a state of balance.

As you become aware of this subtle inner dialogue between your intuition and your other inner voices, it's very important not to put yourself down or diminish this experience. Try to remain a somewhat objective observer. Notice what happens when you follow your intuitive feelings. The result is usually increased energy and power, and a sense of things flowing. Now, notice what happens when you doubt, suppress, or go against your feelings. Invariably, you will observe decreased energy, powerless or helpless feelings, and emotional and/or physical pain. Either way, you'll be learning something, so try not to condemn yourself when you don't follow your intuition (thus adding insult to injury!). Remember, it takes time to learn new habits; the old ways are deeply ingrained. I've been working intensively on my own re-education for a number of years, and while the results I'm enjoying are wonderful, there are still many times that I don't yet have the courage or awareness to be able to trust myself completely and do exactly what I feel. I'm learning to be patient and compassionate with myself as I gain the courage to be true to myself.

One important step in learning to hear and follow your intuition is simply to practice "checking in" regularly. At least twice a day, and much more often, if possible (once an hour is great), take a moment or two (or longer, if you can) to relax and listen to your gut feelings. Cultivate this habit of talking to your inner self. Ask for help and guidance when you need it and practice listening for answers which may come in many forms: words, images, feelings, or even through being led to some external source such as a book, a friend, a teacher who will tell you just what you need to know. Your body is a tremendous helper in learning to follow your inner voice. Whenever it is in pain or discomfort, it is usually an indication that you have ignored your feelings. Use it as a signal to tune in and ask what you need to be aware of.

As you learn to live from your intuition, you give up making decisions with your head. You act moment by moment on what you feel and allow things to unfold as you go. In this way, you are led in the direction that is right for you. Decisions are made easily and naturally; you don't need to try to make big decisions concerning future events. Focus on following the energy in the moment and you'll find that it will all get handled in its own time and way. If you *must* make a decision related to something in the future, follow your gut feeling about it at the time the decision needs to be made.

Remember, too, that although I sometimes speak of following your inner voice, most people do not literally experience it as a voice. Often it's more like a simple feeling, an energy, a sense of "I want to do this" or "I don't want to do that." Don't make it into a big deal, a mysterious mystical event, a voice from on high! It's a simple, natural human experience that we have lost touch with and need to reclaim.

The main sign that you are following your intuition in your life is increased aliveness. It feels like more life energy is flowing through your body. Sometimes it may even feel a little overwhelming, like more energy than your body can handle. You may even have the experience of feeling tired from *too much* energy coming through you. You won't bring through more energy than you can deal with, but it may stretch you a little! Your body's expanding its capacity to channel the universal energy. Simply relax into it and rest when you need to. Soon you'll feel more balanced and you'll even begin to enjoy the increasing intensity.

At first you may find that the more you act on your intuition, the more things in your life seem to be falling apart — you might lose your job, a relationship, certain friends, or your car might even stop working! You're actually changing fast and shedding the old things in your life that don't fit you anymore. As long as you didn't let go of them, they imprisoned you. Now, as you continue on this path, following the energy moment by moment as best you can, you will see new forms begin to be created. It will happen easily and effortlessly. Things will just fall into place, and doors will open in a seemingly miraculous way. You will just go along doing what you have energy to do, and not doing what you don't have the energy to do, and having a wonderful time, and you will literally be able to watch the universe creating new forms through you. You're starting to experience the joy of being a creative channel!

Specific Examples

Here are a few examples from my life, and the lives of my friends and clients, of the types of situations you might be confronted with in following your intuition. Notice that the words in parentheses are the thoughts and feelings that might have held you back or stopped you from trusting your intuition in the past.

— Leaving a party or meeting because you realize you really don't want to be there (even though you're afraid of what others might think or you don't want to miss something good).

— Telling someone that you are attracted to him, or that you would like to get to know him, or that you love him, or whatever it is that you're feeling, because it feels good to be open and tell the truth (even though you're afraid of being rejected, and it makes you feel very vulnerable, and anyway, you're just not supposed to do that).

— Deciding not to write your thesis because you really don't feel very interested in it; every time you think about it it feels like a terrible chore (even though you spent five years working for it, and your parents will be upset if you don't get your degree, you'd really like to have the prestige, and you think you could get a better job with it).

— Taking singing lessons, music lessons, a dance class, or whatever, because you have a fantasy that you would love to be able to sing, play an instrument, or dance (even though you don't think you have any talent, you're too old to learn now, or you might look foolish).

— Not going to work one day just because you feel like you want a quiet day to yourself to hang around home, lie in the sun, take a walk, or even just lie in bed (even though you *always* go to work and think it's terribly irresponsible not to if you're not actually sick, or you're afraid you might lose your job, or you think it's silly or frivolous).

— Quitting your job because you hate it and you realize that you don't really need to do something that you don't like (even though you're not really sure what you're going to do next and you'll only have enough money to last you for a short time, and you feel scared about not having the security of a regular income).

— Not doing a favor for someone who's asked you to because you really don't want to and you know you'd feel resentful if you did (even though you're afraid you're selfish, or you might lose a friend or antagonize a co-worker).

— Spending a little money on something special for yourself or someone else, on impulse, just because it makes you feel good (even though you're normally very frugal, and you really feel maybe you can't afford it).

— Telling someone your opinion about something because you're tired of just pretending to agree with others (even though you normally wouldn't dare to express yourself that way).

— Telling your family that you're not cooking dinner because you just don't feel like it (even though you're afraid you're being a bad wife and mother and they all might find out they don't need you anymore and your whole identity will be shot).

— Not making a decision about something because you're not sure yet what you really feel about it (even though it makes you feel uncomfortable and off balance to be in a state of indecisiveness).

— Starting your own business because you have a strong feeling inside that you can do it (even though you've never done anything like that before).

Well — you've got the idea. Trusting your intuition means tuning in as deeply as you can to the energy you feel, following that energy moment to moment, trusting that it will lead you where you want to go and bring you everything you desire. It means being yourself, being real and authentic in your communications, being willing to try new things because they feel right, doing what turns you on.

Highly Intuitive People

Many people are already highly developed intuitively — they are very much in touch with their intuition, but are afraid to act on it in the world. Often, these people will follow their intuitive promptings in one specific area of their lives, but not in others. Many artists, musicians, performers, and other highly creative people fall into this category. They strongly trust and spontaneously act on their intuition within the bounds of their art form; thus, they are extremely creative and often very productive, but they don't have the same degree of self-trust and willingness to back their feelings with action in other areas of their lives, particularly in their relationships and in matters of business and money. Thus, we have the classic case of the artistic type who is chaotic and unbalanced emotionally, and/or inept or even exploited financially.

A classic example of this problem was seen in the movie *Lady Sings the Blues,* based on the life of the great singer Billie Holliday. In one scene she is traveling with her show on a grueling tour of the country. She is feeling exhausted and depleted and yearns to go home to see her husband and to rest. She resolves to cancel her tour and follow her heart. However, her business managers succeed in convincing her that this move would ruin her career, that she *must* continue on the road. Shortly after giving in to their arguments, she begins to indulge heavily in drugs. From that point on her life takes a downward and tragic course.

Naturally one such incident does not ruin an entire life, but this movie provides a graphic illustration of the way that many artists and performers give away their authority to other influences around them and suffer the resulting inner conflict, pain, and loss of power. In order to come into balance, these people must learn to trust their intuition and assert themselves in *all* areas of their lives.

Psychics also experience this problem. They are very open, receptive, and intuitive, and do not block these qualities as many of us have done. They may even give their intuition free reign in their work or under certain conditions. Once again, the problem is that they don't fully trust and back their intuition in every moment of their lives, especially in the area of personal relationships. They are too wide open to other people's energies and often do not know how to stay connected to their own individual feelings and needs; how to assert themselves and how to set boundaries. From my experience, these highly sensitive people often have problems with their bodies — either weight problems or chronic illness. These problems are healed when they learn to balance their receptive, intuitive nature with an equally developed willingness to act on their feelings and assert themselves in personal relationships.

Many spiritual seekers who have spent a good deal of time meditating, becoming very sensitive and attuned to their inner energy, also have problems of imbalance. The seeker has a strong mental image of what it is to be "spiritual" — loving, open, and centered. He or she wants to act out this model at all times and thus is afraid to act spontaneously or honestly express feelings for fear that what comes out may be harsh, rude, angry, selfish, or unloving.

None of us are fully enlightened yet, so as we risk expressing ourselves more freely and honestly, some of what comes out will be unpolished, distorted, foolish, or thoughtless. As we learn to act on our inner feelings, all the ways we've blocked ourselves in the past are cleared out, and in that process a lot of old "stuff" comes to the surface and is released. A lot of old beliefs and emotional patterns are brought to light and healed. In this process we have to be willing to face and reveal our unconsciousness (by the time we can see it, it's already changing anyway). If we pretend to be more "together" than we really are, we will miss the opportunity to heal ourselves. I have found this to be a very vulnerable and out-of-control feeling. I can't worry too much about how I'm presenting myself or how I look to others or whether I'm doing the right thing. I just have to be myself as I am now, as best I can, accepting the mixture of enlightened awareness and human limitation that is what I am right now.

It isn't necessary to be perfect to be a channel for the universe. You just have to be real — be yourself. The more real, honest, and spontaneous you are, the more freely the creative force can flow through you. As it does so, it cleans out the remnants and pieces of old blockages. What comes out may sometimes be unpleasant or uncomfortable, but the energy moving through will feel great! The more you do this, the clearer your channel gets, so that what comes through is an increasingly perfect expression of the universe.

Remember, too, that some of our spiritual models reflect our "good ideas" more than they reveal an accurate picture of enlightenment. The picture that many people have of wanting to be mellow, positive, and loving all the time is really an expression of their ego's need to feel in control, good, and right. The universe has many colors, moods, speeds, styles, and directions; furthermore, they are all constantly changing. Only by letting go of our ego's control and risking moving fearlessly with this flow will we get to experience the ecstasy of being a true channel.

Exercise

1. Write down all the reasons you can think of for not trusting and following your intuition. Include on the list any fears you have about what might happen to you if you trust your intuition and act on it all the time.

2. Review the meditation at the end of the third chapter (the chapter on Intuition, see page 13).

3. At least twice a day (more often if you can remember), take a minute to relax, close your eyes, and "check in" with your gut feeling to see if you are doing what you feel you want to be doing.

4. For one day, or one week, assume that your intuitive feeling about things is always one-hundred percent right, and act as if that is so.

11

FEELINGS

One of the most common problems I encounter in my work is that so many people are out of touch with their feelings. I recognize this as my mirror, so working with others to help them feel and express their feelings has helped me to be much more in touch with my own. When we have suppressed and closed off our feelings, we cannot contact the universe within us, we cannot hear our intuitive voice, and we certainly can't enjoy being alive.

It seems that many of us did not get much real emotional support when we were growing up. Our parents didn't know how to support their own feelings, much less ours. Perhaps they were too overwhelmed with the difficulties and responsibilities in their lives to be able to give us the emotional response and care we needed.

Whatever the causes, if we don't feel anyone is there to listen to us and care about our feelings, or if we get a negative response when we do express ourselves, we soon learn to suppress our emotions. When we bottle up our feelings, we close off the life energy flowing through our bodies. The energy of these unfelt, unexpressed feelings remains blocked in our bodies, causing emotional and physical discomfort and eventually illness and disease. We become numb and somewhat deadened.

Every day I encounter people in my workshops and private counseling practice who have been stuffing their feelings throughout their lives. Many people are afraid to feel their so-called "negative" emotions — sadness, hurt, anger, fear, despair. They are afraid that if they open up to experiencing these feelings, the emotions will be overwhelming. They are terrified that if they get into the experience they'll remain stuck there forever.

In fact, the opposite is true. When you are willing to fully experience a particular feeling, the blocked energy releases quickly and the feeling dissolves. When counseling someone who has blocked emotion, I support them in moving into the feeling and allowing it to overwhelm them. Once they've felt it completely and expressed it, it's usually dissipated within a few minutes. It's amazing to watch people who have suppressed a painful feeling for thirty, forty, or fifty years release it within a few minutes and experience peacefulness in its place.

Once you have experienced and released blocked emotions from the past, a greater flow of energy and vitality will enrich your life. It is important to learn to be in touch with your feelings as they arise: in this way they can continue to move through and your channel will remain clear.

Emotions are cyclical in nature and, like the weather, they are constantly changing. In the course of an hour, a day, or a week we may move through a wide range of feelings. If we understand this, we can learn to enjoy all our feelings and simply allow them to keep changing. But when we are afraid of certain feelings, like sadness or anger, we will put on our emotional brakes when we start to feel them. We don't want to feel it completely, so we get stuck halfway into it and never get through it.

Often, the people who come to my workshops want to learn how to "think positively" so they won't feel so stuck in their negative feelings. They are surprised when I urge them to feel their negative feelings more, not less! It's only by loving and accepting all parts of ourselves that we can be free and fulfilled.

We tend to think of certain feelings as "painful" and therefore we wish to avoid them. However, I have discovered that pain is actually *resistance to a sensation.* Pain is a mechanism in our physical body which helps us to avoid physical harm. If you touch a hot stove you will feel pain; this is resistance to the sensation of heat that you are experiencing. It causes you to pull your hand away and thus avoid damaging your body.

So on the physical level, pain is a useful mechanism in that it keeps us out of danger. However, if a sensation isn't really dangerous, you can relax into it and the pain will diminish and dissolve. For example, if you stretch a muscle farther than usual, it will at first feel painful, but as you continue to relax gently and steadily into the stretched position, the pain will be released. In childbirth, if a woman resists the intense sensation she is experiencing, she will have pain. The more she is able to relax into the sensation, the less painful it will be.

On the emotional level, it is our *resistance to a feeling that causes us pain.* If, because we are afraid of a certain feeling, we suppress it, we will experience emotional pain. If we allow ourselves to feel it and accept it fully, it becomes an intense sensation, though not a painful one.

There are no such things as "negative" or "positive" feelings — we make them negative or positive by our rejection or acceptance of them. To me, all feelings are part of the wonderful, ever-changing sensation of being alive. If we love all the different feelings, they become so many rainbow colors of life.

Here are some of the emotions that people seem to be most afraid of, with some explanation of how to handle them:

Fear — It's most important just to acknowledge and accept your fears. If you accept yourself for feeling afraid, and don't try to push yourself past your fears, you will start to feel more secure, and the fear will lessen.

Sadness — Sadness is related to the opening of your heart. If you allow yourself to feel sad, especially if you can cry, you will find that your heart opens more and you can feel more love.

Grief — This is an intense form of sadness, related to the death or ending of something. It is very important to allow yourself to grieve fully and not to cut this process short. Grief can sometimes last a long time, or recur periodically for a very long time. It's necessary to accept it and give yourself as much support as you need to go through it, whenever it comes up.

Hurt — Hurt is an expression of vulnerability. We tend to mask it with defensiveness and blame so we won't have to admit how vulnerable we really feel. It's important to express feelings of hurt directly and, if possible, in a nonblaming way (in other words: "I felt really hurt when you didn't ask me to go with you," as opposed to "You don't care about my feelings. How could you be so insensitive." and so on).

Hopelessness — This is related to surrender. When you feel hopeless, your ego is giving up; you are recognizing that none of your old patterns are working. If you allow yourself to really give up and feel the hopelessness completely, it will be followed by peace and a new level of surrender to the universe.

Anger — When we suppress our true power and allow other people to have undue power over us, we become angry. Usually we suppress this anger and go numb. As we start to get back in touch with our power, the first thing we feel is the stored-up anger. So for many people who are growing more conscious, it's a very positive sign when they begin to get in touch with their anger. It means they are reclaiming their power.

If you have not allowed yourself to get angry much in your life, you will start to set up situations and people that trigger your anger. Don't focus much on the external problem, just allow yourself to feel the anger and recognize that it is your power. Visualize a volcano going off inside of you and filling you with power and energy.

Often people are very frightened of their anger — they fear it will cause them to do something harmful. If you have this fear, allow yourself to feel it fully and create a safe situation where you can express it — either alone, or with a counselor or a trusted friend. Allow yourself to rant and rave, kick and scream, throw a temper tantrum, throw or hit pillows — whatever you feel like doing. Once you've done this in a safe environment (you may need to do it regularly), you will no longer be afraid of doing something destructive and you will be able to handle the situations in your life more effectively.

If you are a person who has felt and expressed a lot of anger in your life, you need to look for the hurt that is underneath it and express that. You are using anger as a defense mechanism to avoid being vulnerable.

An important key in transforming anger into an acceptance of your power is learning to assert yourself. Learn to ask for what you want and do what you want to do without being unduly influenced by other people. When you stop giving your power away to other people you won't feel angry any more.

Acceptance of our feelings is directly related to becoming a creative channel. If you don't allow your feelings to flow, your channel will be blocked. If you've stored up a lot of emotions, you have a lot of screaming, whimpering voices inside of you which don't allow you to hear the more subtle voice of your intuition.

Often people need help in experiencing and releasing old emotional blocks and learning to live in a more feeling way. If you believe you need some help with this, find a good counselor or therapist, or a group that practices peer counseling techniques (where participants counsel each other). In seeking a therapist, ask people you know for referrals and don't hesitate to interview several until you find one that you like. Try to find one who seems to be in touch with his or her own feelings and relates to you in a real and honest way.

Whether you seek professional help or not, make a practice of asking yourself frequently throughout the day how you are feeling. Try to learn to distinguish between what you are *thinking* and how you are *feeling* (many people have difficulty with this). As much as possible accept and enjoy your feelings, and you will find that they open the door to a rich, full, and passionate life.

Exercise

When you wake up in the morning, close your eyes and put your attention in the middle of your body — your heart, your solar plexus, and your abdomen. Ask yourself how you are feeling emotionally right now. Try to distinguish the feelings from the thoughts you are having in your head. Are you feeling peaceful, excited, anxious, sad, angry, joyful, frustrated, guilty, loving, lonely, fulfilled, serious, playful?

If there seems to be an unhappy or upset feeling inside of you, go into that feeling and give it a voice. Ask it to talk to you and tell you what it's feeling. Really try to hear it and listen to its point of view. Be sympathetic, loving, and supportive toward your feelings. Ask if there is anything you can do to take better care of yourself.

Repeat this exercise before you go to sleep at night, and at any other time during the day that feels appropriate.

12

TYRANT AND REBEL

The tyrant and the rebel are two parts of the personality I've identified in many people I work with. The tyrant is the inner voice that tells us what we should and shouldn't do. It's all our rules and rigid expectations. It is a controlling and demanding voice. The rebel is the part of us that refuses to do anything it's told to do. It reacts in total rebellion to any controlling influence and trusts no one. When the tyrant says, "You will do this," the rebel says, "No way."

The rebel was developed in early childhood in response to pressures and demands from outside authorities (parents, teachers, the church, and so on). The rebel originally tried to protect our feelings by refusing to believe anything our intuition knew was untrue. For example, if you didn't agree with your parents' plans for you, your rebel would refuse to cooperate (either by open rebellion or passive resistance). The rebel was concerned with supporting your wants. It kept your personality alive.

For some the rebel is dominant. Children who dealt with very demanding, controlling parents and authorities, and were forced to succumb to the will of others, either lost themselves or were forced to defend their wants and needs constantly, and came to be labeled rebellious and uncooperative. For example, a child who had a domineering parent that wanted to control his every action (the outside tyrant) was forced to develop a strong rebel to ensure the survival of his individuality. Or a child who grew up in an alcoholic household built an inner rebel to protect her from the inconsistencies in her environment. Because there was no one she could rely on for consistent truth, she learned to trust no one.

The overdeveloped rebel becomes a problem if the person starts rebelling against everything and everyone. The rebel learns to distrust anything remotely controlling, including your internal demands (the inner tyrant). For example, a boss on the job could make a reasonable request and you would become angry and resist doing what he asks; you might tell yourself not to eat any chocolate cake and yet eat three pieces; or you may decide to exercise every morning and end up sleeping in.

Our inner tyrant is developed by listening to the demanding voices of those around us. If we're surrounded by parents, teachers, and other authorities who have set ideas about how we should and shouldn't do things, we learn to treat ourselves in a similar manner. We begin to internalize these voices, making demands upon ourselves. We've found that the inner tyrant can bring effective results by driving us toward external achievement. For example, a child who has demanding parents may get straight As. He then learns to internalize their expectations, which results in high achievements in the world.

People develop their inner tyrant not only to gain outside approval, but to protect themselves from external tyrants. If you tell yourself you are lazy, and therefore drive yourself into action, you avoid hearing it from others. In a sense, you are fending off external criticism with your own inner tyrant.

The tyrant wants to be heard and it wants cooperation. If you try to ignore or reject this voice it will become frustrated. It will grow louder and more demanding until it's heard.

What you have, then, is the tyrant and the rebel doing battle within you. One part of you says get a job, the other part says no; one part says you better do something with your life and the other part grows lethargic. Neither the tyrant nor the rebel are listening to or protecting you anymore. They have taken on their own personalities and are working in reaction to each other. When this happens, people feel stuck. Energy cannot move in a situation where two parts of yourself are doing battle and you are not dropping into your intuition for guidance.

The most valuable thing you can do to get the energy moving again is to see what you are doing. Acknowledge that you are stuck and then observe your internal conflict. Shining light on the tyrant and the rebel, seeing them as they really are, will lessen their power. You will realize that neither one of them is your intuitive voice talking to you. They are old reactionary voices that continue to run your life. The sooner you see this, the quicker you can let go of what they are saying to you. When you are able to do this, the next step is to drop inside and see what your inner female wants, and then act on that. This is what will unblock the energy. The true source of energy movement and power is always in going to your inner voice, receiving guidance, and acting on it.

A client of mine was frustrated with her career and saw that she was bringing about her firing. She was working in an office, doing administrative work for a salesman. Although she had great organizational abilities, she found herself forgetting to do things. Her boss would come to her and remind her of what hadn't been done and she would fume with anger. She realized she was getting angry any time her boss told her to do something, however reasonable. She felt she could not afford to lose the job, but she did not want to stay there either. She felt trapped. As we talked, she started to identify the rebel side of herself. She saw she was fighting with the tyrant, who said she had to stay at that job, and against her boss, who was in a "controlling" position. She went back to her childhood and examined when she first developed a rebel inside. She saw that she'd had trouble with authorities on other jobs and in school. She realized she was being triggered by old patterns.

When she saw this, she immediately wanted to change these parts of herself. I told her she could not attack her emotions this way. If she tried to change or fix her rebel, she'd be activating the tyrant and the rebel would continue to fight. She needed to become willing to watch herself react, to accept that this was the pattern she was acting out. Once she had really grasped what I was saying to her, I asked her to close her eyes and drop into a deeper place inside herself. She needed to ask her intuition what she really wanted.

It turned out that she wanted to be a saleswoman, but was afraid to try. She was growing angry at herself for sitting behind a desk when she knew there was something else she was meant to do.

After realizing what she wanted to do, she was able to come up with several steps she could take to support her goal. She decided to keep her job for an interim period and enlist her boss's help in her goal. She decided to conduct several informational interviews at sales companies to get ideas of places she might want to work. Having seen clearly what she wanted and discussed the action she could take to help herself, she felt much better.

A week later she called me and said that although her tyrant and rebel continued to fight it out, they seemed to have less power. She had continued to support her goal to do sales work and her boss was willing to help her with any leads he had.

Neither the tyrant nor the rebel are truly you. By learning to trust and follow your intuition both the tyrant and the rebel dissolve and you emerge into who you really are.

Exercise

Identify some of your rules and behaviors that feel demanding and controlling (tyrannical) to you. Use the categories below, in addition to any of your own. Enclosed in parentheses are some examples.

Work — (I must work forty to sixty hours per week, I must work hard to get anywhere, I can't make money doing what I want).

Money — (I'm never going to have enough money, I must save money in case something happens, I must not be frivolous with money).

Relationships — (I have to find a mate, I must please my mate, I have to be monogamous, I'd better be satisfied with what I've got).

Sex — (I have to have an orgasm every time I have sex, I have to be in love with someone to have sex, I have to be the greatest, most sensual lover).

Now write down any corresponding rebel thoughts you may have. For example, "Who needs work, I'm going to quit my job," or "Who cares about money anyway, I don't need it," or "I'll just do what I want behind my mate's back."

After you've written out the tyrant and rebel dialogues, drop into a deeper place and ask yourself what you most want; discover what is true for you. Write down any thoughts or feelings that come to you.

13

VICTIM AND RESCUER

Victim consciousness is the belief that we are helpless; that the world, people, and the economy do things to us and we have no choice but to accept what is dished out to us. It's the feeling that we can be violated from the outside without our approval.

As victims, people enlist rescuers to save them. Rescuers do not know how to take care of themselves, so they focus on helping others, unconsciously trying to fulfill their own needs in an indirect way. They need victims to care for. A rescuer believes that others are weak or powerless and need his help.

I believe that many people are dealing with both sides of this process. Most victims spend time and energy trying to rescue others instead of learning to take care of themselves. You can't be a rescuer, though, unless you believe in and have a victim inside you. It may appear, however, that some people are strictly rescuers or victims. On the extreme side, there are people who are always in a mess and desperately need the help of others or there are martyrs whose meaning in life depends on saving others. Usually, we bounce back and forth between these roles in less extreme ways.

Transforming Rescuer Consciousness

We all see the pain in the world. It's everywhere, in all of us, in the people around us, in the newspapers, and on TV. Transformation of this pain begins with denying nothing. See it, feel it, and then know that the pain is not separate from ourselves. We could not be seeing starvation, murder, and disease unless there were a part of us that believed in and supported this process. (See the chapter on Transforming the World, page 178.)

To transform the rescuing, we need to take responsibility for our own pain and get in touch with the power of the universe within us to help with our own healing. When you see someone in pain or feeling helpless, know that the pain and helplessness are in you, too. You would not be drawn to help someone unless you identified with and felt a similar helplessness. Whether you're a victim or a rescuer, the energy is stuck.

The energy stays stuck as long as people are focusing on others as the problem or the solution. To move the energy and enlist the universe's help, both rescuers and victims need to go inside themselves and ask for guidance.

Rescuers do not see how much they need help. They are so busy helping others, they can not see their own pain. When they start to feel their own feelings, they cover them up by finding someone else to take care of. Rescuing is generally a deep-seated pattern from childhood. In my own case, I know I began taking care of others at an early age. My parents were divorced when I was a baby, and very early I felt the need to behave as a mature adult. I took on this responsibility, but in the process, I neglected my own feelings.

I have been an extreme rescuer. I've wanted to save the world. I was always trying to help people. I did workshops because I wanted people to hear the great knowledge I had to offer them. I thought it was so important that people needed this and needed me. In personal relationships I've done the same thing. I attracted many lovers and friends who seemingly needed my help.

As I've become more conscious, I've begun to see that in rescuing people, I've been conveying to them telepathically, "I don't trust you and I don't think you're in charge of your life. I think that you're some unfortunate being who doesn't know as much as I do and I think you need help."

The person you're rescuing picks this up telepathically, so you're undermining their power instead of helping them. More importantly, you're not taking care of yourself, which is the only thing that will move energy and transform the situation. You need to admit that you habitually rescue because you fear that others will abandon you. The fear is, "If I don't take care of others' needs, they'll leave me and I'll be alone." If you start to go inside to do your own healing, you'll begin to see that someone is there for you — yourself. Amazingly enough, when you support yourself emotionally, others mirror this by giving you lots of love and support.

I realize it's difficult to change old patterns of caretaking. Fear and guilt surface in the process. Thoughts surface, such as, "Do I really deserve to spend time on myself? What will happen to the people that need my help?" The voices of guilt and fear will only quiet when you begin to see results. The people you wanted to rescue will start taking care of themselves and you'll feel better.

I'm not trying to discourage people from helping others. I'm only suggesting that before you do this, admit that you're doing it for yourself. Admit that their pain is yours as well. Then go inside and ask the universe for help: "Universe, help me to transform this situation. Help me to heal myself so I can be a channel for your light." By doing this, you're taking the focus off the other person, admitting your own feeling of helplessness, and asking for guidance and assistance.

The only way to truly help others is to do exactly what you really want to do. If you're saying, "Oh, I *should* do something about this," that's not the universe; it's your "shoulds" and your guilt. Or it may be your mental computer trying to figure out a rational solution. If you trust your gut feeling and do only what you feel moment by moment, then the universe is free to move through you in spontaneous and unpredictable ways.

For example, it might seem harsh or cruel to you not to help a friend who wants something from you. Yet if you find yourself reluctant to give in this situation (and you know you are normally a giving person), you must trust that feeling and take the risk to say "no" to your friend. Chances are that in this situation, you might have been supporting some form of powerlessness in this person by giving to him. By trusting your gut feeling and not "helping," you will actually support your friend in finding more of his own power.

In another case, it might feel totally wonderful to you to give to someone. Trust that feeling and give freely. When the giving comes from your heart and doesn't require sacrifice on your part, you know that it is the universe coming through your channel.

The universe doesn't follow our good ideas about the ways things are supposed to be and our careful plans and rescue operations. It guides us in ways that allow the light to shine through.

Transforming Victim Consciousness

People stop being victims when there's no one left to rescue them, or when blaming others for their life becomes so painful that they are willing to change. This usually happens simultaneously. Others get tired of rescuing you at the same time you are becoming tired of being a victim.

In transforming victim consciousness, people change a lifetime of beliefs. We're told from birth that what matters is on the outside, so we look for the healing, power, love, and wealth to come from there. Then, when it doesn't, we start blaming. To look inside, instead, is to go against everything we've learned. We're discarding a long-standing habit of blame and looking to the universe for enlightenment. If you feel victimized, the key is to go inside immediately. Ask, "Universe, show me what I need to heal this. Help me know that you are my source of power." Then, stay open to the answers coming through. They may come in different ways: a message from within, a phone call, an offering of help from someone. When I say, "go within for the answers," this does not exclude receiving help from the outside, it only means making sure that you realize the power of the universe is within *you* and you can attract what you need. Know that you are completely responsible for the situation you're in and turn to the universe within you, *before* seeking help on the outside.

By doing this, you're honoring your power. Your inner female will feel this and respond by channeling more wisdom and power through to you.

The main healing in this process occurs when people refuse to see themselves and others as helpless. Even events that seem "accidental"' are drawn in by people to heal themselves of their old beliefs and patterns.

When people in my workshops find themselves in seemingly "impossible" or "hopeless" situations, I encourage them to discover their power in the situation; to observe the choices they have made and how they may have needed to create this situation to learn more about themselves.

In not knowing how to be gentle with ourselves, we have chosen some rough lessons. Our inner voices want to be heard and if we're constantly ignoring them we'll become increasingly uncomfortable. Accidents, disease, and pain can be avoided if we're willing to hear ourselves and act on our inner guidance. Consider the following stories, all of which illustrate various aspects of victim/rescuer consciousness:

A woman in one of my workshops shared that she'd been awoken from her sleep and raped. At first it was impossible for her to see her power in this situation or see how she could have chosen such a painful, frightening way to heal herself. Her rape left her feeling powerless, afraid that this could happen to her again.

To remove some of her fear, I felt it was important for her

to see why she might have created this situation. In this way, she could begin to see the potential healing it entailed. If she saw herself as having a choice, she could also release any fear of ever being victimized again.

She began to look more deeply into the cause of her rape. For years she had feared being abused by a man and deeply believed that this could happen to her. She also saw that her life had been devoted to being a victim. In general, she saw others as having power over her, while she herself had little choice but to submit to the powers that be. I believe she created an external situation that mirrored and intensified what she felt inside. By bringing her beliefs to consciousness, she could now heal them. They could no longer control her on an unconscious level.

Along with seeing some of the reasons for what had happened to her, it was also important for her to fully *feel* all her feelings about the rape. She had a lot of anger toward the rapist and toward others in her life which needed to be expressed. When we realize how we may have drawn negative things to us, it is important not to turn our anger or fear inward, on ourselves. Even though our intellect may see the higher wisdom in the situation, the feelings still need to be expressed. The woman who was raped needed to let herself totally feel her feelings so they could be cleared out and she could regain her personal power. She was ready to do this. A couple of weeks after the workshop she called me to say she'd been able to go to bed at night without leaving a light on for fear of attack.

Another client had been working as a therapist in a local hospital's drug and alcohol unit. She began to feel drained, but felt there was no way for her to take time off from work without jeopardizing her job. She also had lost herself in helping others and could not see how to help herself. She kept showing up at work, rescuing others while neglecting the inner feelings that were screaming for her attention. She grew more tired, started resenting her clients, and was generally angry. Her car broke down three times in three months, further diminishing her hope of leaving her job as car repair expenses mounted. She saw no way out.

Because she did nothing about her anger and frustration, she began to feel frightened of everything. She was frightened of going to work, frightened of her clients, and frightened by her situation. She was locked in the rescue process and felt victimized by her financial situation. She began to feel hopeless.

One day she showed up for work and was unable to see any clients. She started crying about her situation. Her coworkers encouraged her to take a few days off. Because she was also suffering some physical side effects from this stress, she saw her doctor, who put her on disability for stress reaction.

She left the city for a month and started to rest. She began to listen to her inner needs, act on them, and heal herself.

By breaking the pattern of rescue and victim, she unleashed an abundance of creative energy that had been blocked by her job. She discovered her creativity could be channeled in other ways. She started conducting playful workshops and began to express herself through writing again. She chose not to return to work at the hospital.

Another woman in one of my workshops had been having a series of small accidents around the house. She had intuitively felt she needed to stop pushing herself to complete certain work projects, but also felt she could not risk slowing down. She continued to push herself until she had a car accident and found herself in the hospital. At this point, she could no longer push herself and had to accept her need to slow down. During her stay in the hospital, she decided to sell her home and retire from her business. She started traveling, allowing herself to do what she'd always wanted. She had no further accidents and is now feeling happy and excited about her life.

Exercise
Victim/Rescue Process
Part I

1. List any ways in which you are feeling powerless or victimized.

2. Starting with the first situation on your list, close your eyes and see yourself in this powerless place. Experience your feelings of frustration, helplessness, and despair. Take a few minutes to do this.

3. Now imagine yourself feeling angry and filled with rage about how you've made yourself powerless in your life. Let your anger be the energy that helps you resolve not to do this to yourself anymore.

4. Then, see yourself filled with a sense of power, strength, creativity, magnificence, and spirit. See yourself as having choices. Once you've begun to see and feel this, explore how you would deal with the powerless situation in which you find yourself. Accept any images or ideas that come to you.

5. Repeat the steps above for each item on your list.

Part II

1. Make a list of any ways in which you are rescuing others.

2. For each situation, close your eyes and see the person or persons you are rescuing as powerful. Release them to their own strength, to their own connection with the universe.

3. Then, see what you need to do to take care of yourself in each situation. What can you do for yourself in order to feel fulfilled?

14

BECOMING BALANCED

As channels for the universe, we must have available a full range of expression and emotion. If the higher power tells us to leap, we must be able to leap without stopping to ask questions. If it tells us to wait, we must be able to relax and enjoy a space of nonactivity until the next message comes. We will always be pushed to explore aspects of ourselves that are less developed, to express and experience ourselves in new ways. If we ignore these inner impulses, we will be forced by external life circumstances to explore our inner being anyway. One way or another, our higher self makes sure that we get the message of what we have to do. We may have to go from one extreme to the other until we come into balance.

You can expect that your intuition will lead you in directions that are new and different for you. If you are comfortable in one type of personality or pattern, you will probably be asked to start expressing the opposite. It's good to know this, especially when you're in the process of learning to hear your inner voice. A good rule might be to "expect the unexpected."

I've found that there seem to be two basic personality types. It may be helpful to recognize which one is your strongest tendency. Some people are a combination of the two; usually, they follow one pattern in some areas of their life and the other pattern in other areas.

The two types could be called the "doers" and the "be-ers." They roughly correspond to type A and type B personalities in common psychological terminology.

The doers are people who are primarily action-oriented. They know how to get things done, and they usually aren't afraid to put themselves out there and take risks in expressing themselves or trying new things. Basically, they are good at expressing their outgoing energy. They have trouble receiving. They don't like feeling vulnerable. The most difficult thing of all for them is doing nothing — to not be engaged in some type of constructive activity. Unstructured time makes them uncomfortable and they usually fill it up with lots of activity. They tend to be driven and have a hard time really relaxing. They are more developed in their male, active energy, and somewhat uncomfortable with their female, receptive side.

Be-ers are mainly oriented toward inner attunement. They know how to relax and take it easy. They enjoy the subtle pleasures of life and often know how to nurture themselves and others, how to play. They are usually flexible, and are happy to "hang out" with unstructured time. They have trouble with action. They fear putting themselves out in new or unusual ways and tend to hold back a lot. They aren't very assertive and sometimes have trouble expressing feelings or opinions. They worry about what others will think of them. They may be uncomfortable in the world and lack the confidence to deal with people, business, money, and so on. They are more developed in their female receptive energy and uncomfortable or distrustful of their male outgoing side.

If you are primarily a doer, your intuition will almost surely lead you in the direction of doing less. Your feelings will tell you to stop, to relax and take a day off (or a week, or six months!), to spend more time alone with yourself, to spend time in nature, to spend time with no plan and no list, and just practice following the energy as you feel it. The hardest thing for a doer is getting no message at all, having to hang out and wait and "do nothing" until something happens. I am primarily a doer, a list-maker, a compulsively active person, and one of the hardest things for me has been when the universe has forced me to do nothing! Yet, I find that those times are the most powerful and inspirational of all because that's when I can really stop long enough to feel my spirit. In fact, I finally realized and had to admit that *I kept so busy all my life in order to avoid feeling that power.* I was afraid of "empty" time and space because it was actually so full of the universal force.

If you are more comfortable with "being," you will undoubtedly be pushed by your inner self into more action, more expression, more risk-taking in the world. The key for you is to follow your impulses and to try doing things you wouldn't normally do on impulse. You don't have to know why you're doing something or see any particular result from it at first. It's important to simply practice acting spontaneously on your feelings, especially when it comes to dealing with people, expressing your creative energy in the world, making money, or anything else you might normally avoid. *Don't push yourself harder or farther than you are ready to go.* It's very important to respect your own boundaries and rhythms for growing. Make sure the voice isn't coming from your inner tyrant, saying, "You *should* put yourself out in this way." (If it's a "should," it's never the voice of the universe.) Rather, follow the feelings you have that guide you to practice expressing yourself and building your confidence in a supportive way.

Meditation

Get comfortable and close your eyes. Take a few deep breaths and each time you exhale, relax your body and mind into a deep, quiet level of consciousness. Imagine yourself as a very balanced person. You are able to relax, play, and nurture yourself frequently, and you enjoy having time and space in your life when there is nothing special you have to do. Yet you act on your feelings and impulses spontaneously, express yourself strongly and directly, and risk trying new things whenever you are inspired to do so. You live in the full range of being and doing, so you can follow your inner guidance in whatever direction it leads you.

Exercise

If you are primarily a "doer," spend one entire day consciously doing as little as possible. Take note of how you feel and what happens.

If you are better at "being" than "doing," take a day to practice acting on any impulse or inspiration you have, without expecting any particular results. Try several new and unusual things, especially things that involve making contact with people or putting yourself out in the world in new ways. Notice how you are feeling before, during, and after you do this.

15

RELATIONSHIPS

Relationships in the old world have an external focus — we try to make ourselves whole and happy by getting something from outside ourselves. Inevitably, this expectation results in disappointment, resentment, and frustration. Either these feelings build up constantly and cause continual strife, or they are suppressed and lead to emotional numbness. Still, we cling to relationships out of emotional insecurity, or go from one to another searching for that missing piece that we haven't yet found.

We've been in this tragic predicament for at least a few thousand years; now we seem to be approaching a crisis point. Relationships and families as we've known them seem to be falling apart at a rapid rate. Many people are panicky about this; some try to re-establish the old traditions and value systems in order to cling to a feeling of order and stability in their lives.

It's useless to try to go backward, however, because our consciousness has already evolved beyond the level where we were willing to make the sacrifices necessary to live that way. In the past, most people were willing to hang onto an essentially dead relationship for an entire lifetime because it gave them physical and emotional stability.

Now, more and more of us are realizing that it is possible to have deeper intimacy, and ongoing aliveness and passion, in a relationship. We're willing to let go of old forms to search for these ideals, but we don't know where to find them. Most of us are still looking outside ourselves — sure that if we just find the right man or woman to be with we'll be blissfully happy, or thinking that if only our kids or our parents would behave the right way, then we'd be fine. We're confused and frustrated, our relationships seem to be in chaos, and we don't have the old traditions to lean on or anything new to take their place. Yet we can't go back, we must move forward into the unknown to create a whole new level of relationship.

But relationships are not outside — they are inside of us; this is the simple truth that we must recognize and accept. My true relationship is my relationship with myself — all others are simply mirrors of it. As I learn to love myself, I automatically receive the love and appreciation from others that I desire. If I am committed to myself and to the truth, I will attract others with equal commitment. My willingness to be intimate with my own deep feelings creates the space for intimacy with another. Enjoying my own company allows me to have fun with whomever I'm with. And feeling the aliveness and power of the universe flowing through me creates a life of passionate feeling and fulfillment that I share with anyone with whom I'm involved.

Taking Care of Ourselves

Because many of us have never really learned how to take good care of ourselves, our relationships have been based on trying to get someone else to take care of us.

As babies we are very aware and intuitive. From the time we are born we perceive our parents' emotional pain and neediness, and we immediately begin to develop the habit of trying to please them and fulfill their needs so that they will continue to take care of us.

Later on, our relationships continue along the same lines. There is an unconscious telepathic agreement: "I'll try to do what you want me to do and be the person you want me to be if you will be there for me, give me what I need, and not leave me."

This system doesn't work very well. Other people are seldom able to fulfill our needs consistently or successfully, so we get disappointed and frustrated. Then we either try to change the other people to better suit our needs (which never works), or we resign ourselves to accept less than we really want. Furthermore, when we're trying to give other people what *they* want, we almost invariably do things we don't really want to do and end up resenting them, either consciously or unconsciously.

At this point, we may realize that it doesn't work to try to take care of ourselves by taking care of others. I'm the only one who can actually take good care of me, so I might as well do it directly and allow others to do the same thing for themselves.

What does it mean to take care of yourself? For me, it means trusting and following my intuition. It means taking time to listen to all my feelings — including the feelings of the child within me that is sometimes hurt or scared — and responding with caring, love, and appropriate action. It means putting my inner needs first and trusting that as I do this, everyone else's needs will get taken care of and everything that needs to be done will get handled.

For example, if I'm feeling sad, I might crawl into bed and cry, taking time to be very loving and nurturing to myself. Or I might find someone caring to talk to until some of the feelings are released and I feel lighter.

If I've been working too hard, I'm learning to put the work aside no matter how important it seems, and take some time to play, or just to take a hot bath and read a novel.

If someone I love wants something from me that I don't want to give, I'm learning to say no and trust that he or she will actually be better off than if I did it when I didn't want to. This way, when I say "yes," I really mean it.

There is a very important point I want to make here; it

concerns something I was confused about for a long time and finally understood. *Taking care of yourself does not mean ''doing it all alone.''* Creating a good relationship with yourself is not done in a vacuum, without relationship to other people. Otherwise we could all become hermits for a few years until we had a perfect relationship with ourselves and then just emerge and suddenly have perfect relationships with others.

Of course, it is important that we are able to be alone, and often people *do* withdraw from outside relationships until they feel really comfortable with themselves. Sooner or later, though, you need to use the mirrors. You need to build and strengthen your relationship with yourself in the world of form through interaction with other people.

The difference is on the *focus.* In the old world of relationships the focus was *on the other person and on the relationship itself.* You communicated for the purpose of trying to get the other person to understand you and give you more of what you needed. In new-world relationships, the focus is on building your relationship with yourself and the universe. You communicate to keep your channel clear and to give yourself more of what you need. The words may even be the same, but the energy is different, and so is the result.

For example, suppose I'm feeling lonely and want my lover to spend the evening with me although I know that he has other plans. Previously, I would probably have been afraid to ask for what I wanted directly. I probably would have stayed home alone and focused on learning to enjoy being alone. Later when I talked to him, I would feel some resentment, though I wouldn't admit it, either to myself or to him. Nevertheless, he would feel this resentment and become guilty and resentful toward me. None of this would come out in the open until later when we were having an argument and I might say, "Well you don't care about my feelings anyway; you never want to be with me." At this point I'm communicating to him telepathically my underlying feeling that he is responsible for my happiness.

Now (hopefully), I would be more direct from the

beginning. I'd say, "I know you have other plans, but I'm feeling lonely right now and I really want you to spend the evening with me." I'm taking the responsibility to ask for what I want and in doing so I'm actually taking care of myself even though I'm asking for something from him. The key here is that my focus is really on myself — this is what I'm feeling and this is what I want. I have to be willing to make myself very vulnerable to do this. But I have found that it is the willingness to say what I feel and want that makes me feel whole. In a sense, I'm already feeling more fulfilled because I was willing to back myself up.

Everything is out in the open, and he's free to respond honestly. If he agrees to my request, that's icing on the cake! If he doesn't, I may feel sad or hurt. I'll communicate my feelings (again I'm doing it for my own sake, to keep myself clear) and then let go. I'll use that evening as a time to go deeper within myself and my connection with the universe.

I've found a very interesting thing. When I communicate truthfully and directly, and say everything I really want to say, it doesn't seem to matter too much how the other person responds. They may not do exactly what I want, but I feel so clear and empowered from taking care of myself that it's easier to let go of the result. If I keep being honest and vulnerable with my feelings to my lover, family, and friends, I won't end up with hidden needs or resentment.

When you take care of yourself this way, more often than not you do get what you ask for. If not, the next step is to let go. Go inside of yourself and tune in to what your inner being is telling you to do next. Always let it take you to a deeper connection with the universe.

Thus, an important part of creating a loving relationship with yourself is to acknowledge your needs and to learn to ask for what you want. We're afraid to do this because we're afraid to appear too needy. However, it's the hidden, unacknowledged needs that cause us to seem needy. They aren't coming out directly so they come out indirectly or telepathically. People feel them and back away from us because they intuitively know they can't help us if we aren't acknowledging our need for help!

It's paradoxical that as we recognize and acknowledge our own needs and ask for help directly, we are actually becoming stronger. It's the male within supporting the female. People find it easy to give to us, and we feel more and more whole.

Following Energy

I have found that when I'm willing to trust and follow my energy, it leads me into relationships with the people from whom I have the most to learn. The stronger the attraction, the stronger the mirror. So the energy will always lead me to the most intense learning situation.

It can be frightening at first to try to live this way. We have always been terrified to trust our own feelings, especially in the realm of relationships and sexuality. Because this energy is so intense, so changeable and unpredictable, we fear that utter chaos will reign. We're terrified of being hurt or hurting someone else. We don't trust that the universe knows what it's doing, or else we don't trust ourselves to be able to accurately follow our inner guidance. And there's good reason for this. In the area of relationships, we have so many old patterns and addictions that it is sometimes hard to accurately hear our true inner voice.

I don't think there is any easy way to resolve our fears about trusting our energy. You either avoid the issue, or move through it by being willing to follow your energy as best you can, learn from your "mistakes," and, in the process, heal your fears and build a clearer channel.

Until now, most of us have avoided dealing with our fears by constructing stringent rule structures for all our relationships. Every relationship is fitted into a certain category, and each category has a list of rules and appropriate behavior attached to it. This person is a friend, therefore I behave this way; this person is my husband, therefore he is supposed to do these things; this person is in my family, so this is how we act with each other; and so on. There's very little space left to discover the truth of each relationship.

Some people rebel against these rule systems and purposely create relationships that go counter to the established norms — such as multiple relationships, homosexual and bisexual relationships, and so on. If motivated by rebellion, these relationships may be largely reactions *against* the rules and still may not involve a true attunement to the energy.

Just as every being is a unique entity, unlike anyone else, every connection between two or more beings is also unique. No relationship is exactly like any other. Furthermore, the nature of the universe is constant change. People change all the time and so do relationships.

So when we try to label and control our relationships, we kill them. Then we spend a lot of time and energy fruitlessly trying to bring them to life again.

We must be willing to *let our relationships reveal themselves to us.* If we tune into ourselves, trust ourselves, and express ourselves fully and honestly with each other, the relationship will unfold in its own unique and fascinating way. Each relationship is an amazing adventure; you never know exactly where it will lead. It keeps changing its mood, flavor, and form from minute to minute, day to day, year to year. At times it may take you closer to one another. At other times it may take you farther apart.

There is one thing you can count on though. Relationships lived in this way will always take you into deeper levels of yourself and a stronger trust of the universe. This in turn will be reflected by deeper intimacy and closeness with others.

Commitment and Intimacy

When we discuss the idea of trusting and following our energy, people often ask where the concept of commitment fits into this picture.

Because we have been so focused on externals, most of us have attempted to make a commitment to an external relationship. What we are really committing to is a certain set of rules — "I agree to behave in such and such a manner so that we can feel secure about this relationship." Usually these rules are not spelled out clearly, they are assumed. People say they are in a committed relationship but seldom clarify to themselves or each other what exactly they are committed to doing or not doing.

Generally, one assumption is that they are agreeing not to have sex with anyone else. Even that is rather vague, though, as no one defines what "having sex" is. Often the implied agreement is not to feel sexual attraction toward anyone else. Yet how can you make an agreement not to feel something? Feelings aren't under our conscious control.

The real problem with commitment to an external form is that it doesn't allow room for the inevitable changes and growth of people and relationships. If you promise to feel or behave by a certain set of rules, eventually you are going to have to choose between being true to yourself and being true to those rules. When you stop being honest and real, there's not much left of you to be in the relationship. You end up with an empty shell — a nice commitment but no real people in it!

Because this type of commitment attempts to keep the *form* of the relationship from changing, more often than not it simply doesn't last. The fact is that relationships *do* change form and no commitment can guarantee that they won't. No external form can give us the security that we seek. You could be married for fifty years and the fifty-first year your spouse could decide to leave you!

If we only realize this it can save us so much pain. People who divorce almost inevitably feel that they have failed, because they assume all marriages should last forever. In most such cases, however, the marriage has actually been a total success — it's helped each person to grow to the point where they no longer need its old form.

What causes the pain in many cases is that we don't know how to allow the form to change *while still honoring the underlying love and connection.* When you are deeply involved with another being, that connection lasts forever. However, the intensity of energy in the relationship increases or decreases in accordance with how much there is to be learned from it at any given time. When you've learned a great deal from being with someone, the energy between you may eventually diminish to the point where you no longer need to interact on a personality level as much, or at all. Yet the connection between the two spirits remains strong. Sometimes the energy renews itself again later on another level.

We don't understand this, so we feel guilty, disappointed, and hurt when our relationships change form. We don't know how to share our feelings effectively with each other; thus, we often respond to these feelings by cutting off our connection with the other person. This causes us real pain, because we are actually cutting off our own deep feelings. I have found that changes in relationships can be relatively painless and even beautiful when we can communicate honestly and trust ourselves in the process.

Most people believe that sacrifice and compromise are necessary in order to preserve a relationship. The need to sacrifice and compromise is based on a misunderstanding of the nature of the universe. We fear that there is not enough love for us and that the truth may be hurtful. In fact, the universe is always loving and the truth, when we can see it, is always positive. Our limitations and fears make it appear negative.

When I'm willing to be honest and ask for what I want, to continue sharing my feelings openly, I *always* find that the underlying truth in any situation is the same for all concerned. At first it may seem that I want one thing and the other person wants something else. If we both keep telling the truth as we feel it, sooner or later it works out so that we both see that we can have what we truly want.

For example, a couple who are clients of mine were experiencing a great deal of conflict about their work. They were partners in a very successful business. She was tired of the business and wanted to do something else. He loved the work and wanted to continue but did not want to do it without her. They fought constantly about whether to sell the business (her desire) or continue and expand it (his desire).

Once they began to communicate on a deeper level, they uncovered their fears. She yearned to express herself creatively in new ways, but was terrified that she would not be able to successfully step out on her own without his constant support. She was also afraid that she would not be able to make as much money, and he would feel resentful about her diminished contribution to the family income. He was afraid that he would be unable to handle the business successfully without her; he depended heavily on her creative input and did not trust his own intuitive capacity. Also, he feared that his working life would be dull and drab without her warmth and humor.

Having expressed their feelings fully, they were able to see that they were both at the point of making a leap into a new level of independence and creativity. They were ready to let go of some of their dependency on one another and develop more trust in themselves. She gradually withdrew from the business and started a new and very different career which she ultimately found very exciting and rewarding. He continued to run the business and developed it in new and interesting directions. Their relationship was enhanced by their increased independence and self-confidence.

For me, the commitment I make is to myself — to love, honor, obey, and cherish my own being. My commitment in a relationship is to truth and honesty. To anyone I love I promise to do the best I can to tell the truth, to share my feelings, to take responsibility for myself, to honor the connection I feel with that person, and to maintain that connection, no matter how the form may change.

Real commitment makes no guarantees about a relationship's form; real commitment allows for the fact that form is constantly changing and that we can trust that process of change. It opens the door to the true intimacy that is created when people share deeply and honestly with one another. If two people stay together on this basis, it's because they really want to be together. They continue to find an intensity of love and learning with each other as they change and grow.

Monogamous and Nonmonogamous Relationships

When people first hear my views on relationships, they may find them rather radical, and perhaps they are. Often, however, I find in talking to them further that they have misunderstood certain things that I'm saying. For example, sometimes people think that I am "against monogamy" — that I am advocating nonmonogamous relationships. This is definitely not the case. What I am advocating is truth — being honest with your feelings and responses, being true to yourself.

Some people I know are truly involved in a monogamous relationship. They have one powerful, primary sexual/romantic connection and no desire for any others. A few seem to be strongly nonmonogamous and have little trouble handling more than one sexual/romantic relationship. Most people experience some degree of mixed feelings and conflict on this issue. They want depth, closeness, and security with one person; they feel guilty about being attracted to others; and they feel threatened by their partner being attracted to anyone else. On the other hand, they feel somewhat restricted and sometimes wish they could be free to explore other connections. Those who are involved in many relationships may also have a deep longing to find one person they want to be with exclusively.

These feelings are an important part of our human conditioning and need to be felt and acknowledged, at least to ourselves, and preferably to our loved ones as well. The conflicts are automatically dissolved as we learn to simply accept and trust ourselves. The real issue is not the external form of our relationships — that is resolved easily and effortlessly as we learn to trust and follow our own inner truth.

Each person will create the relationships that are exactly right for him- or herself and for everyone else concerned.

Romance

When we meet someone who is a particularly strong mirror for us, we feel an intense attraction (or we may experience it initially as a repulsion or dislike; either way, there's a strong feeling). If that person is of the right sex and has certain characteristics, we may experience the feeling as a sexual attraction. When the energy is particularly strong we have an experience we call "falling in love."

Falling in love is actually a powerful experience of feeling the universe move through you. The other person has become a channel for you, a catalyst that triggers you to open up to the love, beauty, and passion within you. Your own channel opens wide, the universal energy comes pouring through, and you have a blissful moment of "enlightenment" very similar to the experiences some people have after long periods of meditation.

This is the most thrilling and passionate experience in the world and of course we want to hold onto it. Unfortunately, we don't realize that we are truly experiencing the universe within ourselves. We recognize that the other person has triggered this experience and we think it is him or her that is so wonderful! Of course, at the moment of falling in love we are accurately perceiving the beauty of that person's spirit, but we don't recognize that it is a mirror of our own. We just know that we feel this great feeling when we're with them, so we immediately start to give our power away to them, start to put our source of happiness outside of ourselves.

The other person immediately becomes an object — something we want to possess and hold onto. The relationship becomes an addiction: as with a drug, we want more and more of the thing that gets us high. The problem is that we get addicted to the person's *form,* not recognizing that it's the *energy* we want. We focus on the personality and the body, and try to grab onto it, to keep it. The minute we do this, the energy gets blocked. By grabbing hold of the channel so tightly we are actually strangling it and closing off the very energy we seek.

True passion brings us together but neediness inevitably takes over shortly thereafter. The relationship starts to die almost as soon as it blooms. Then we really panic and usually hold on even tighter. The initial experience of falling in love was so powerful that we sometimes spend years trying to recreate it, but the more we try, the more it eludes us. It's only when we give up and let go that the energy starts to flow again and we can touch that same feeling.

Such is the tragic nature of romance in the old world. We've spent thousands of years trying to work this one out. Our favorite songs, stories, and dramas reflect and reinforce the externally addicted nature of our relationships and the resulting pain and frustration.

In the new world we are discovering something simple and beautiful that can heal all our pain: true romance is living in the light.

A Love Affair

I am finding that being alive is a love affair with the universe. I also think of it as a love affair between my inner male and female, and between my form and my spirit.

As I build and open my channel, more and more energy flows through. I feel greater intensity of feeling and passion. Being in love is a state of being not dependent on any one person. However, certain people attract me and seem to intensify or deepen my experience of the life force within me. I know that those people are mirrors to me and also that they are channels for special energy in my life.

I move toward them because I want the intensification that I experience with them. I feel the universe moving through me to them, and moving through them to me. This could happen through any form of exchange — talking, touching, making love. The energy itself lets me know what is needed and appropriate. It's a mutually satisfying and fulfilling exchange because the universe is giving each of us what we need. It may be a brief, one-time experience, a glance or a short conversation with a stranger. Or it may be an ongoing contact, a profound relationship that lasts for many years. I see it more and more as the universe coming to me constantly, through many different channels.

What I have just written is an ideal scene. I certainly am not living it fully at every moment. Many times I am caught up in my fears and relationship addictions. However, I *am* experiencing it more and more frequently, and when I do, it feels wonderful!

Exercises

1. Take yourself on a romantic date. Do everything as if you were going out with the most loving and exciting partner you can imagine. Take a luxurious hot bath, dress in your best clothes, buy yourself flowers, go to a lovely restaurant, take a moonlight stroll, do anything else that strikes your fancy. Spend the evening telling yourself how wonderful you are, how much you love yourself, and anything else that you would like to hear from a lover. Imagine that the universe is your lover and is giving you everything that you want.

2. The next time that you feel a romantic or sexual "charge" with someone, remember that it's the universe you are feeling. Whatever you do, just remember that it's all part of your true love affair with life.

16

OUR CHILDREN

Living as a channel for the universe applies to parenting as much as to every other area of our lives. While I don't yet have children myself, I have been closely involved for several years with a number of friends who are using these principles in relating to their children. It certainly isn't easy to transform our old concepts and patterns of raising children, but the results are wonderful to see: bright light radiating from these children, satisfaction and fulfillment for their parents, and the depth of closeness and sharing between them.

Our old ideas of parenting usually involved feeling totally responsible for the welfare of our children and trying to follow some behavior standard to be a "good parent." As you learn to trust yourself and be yourself spontaneously, you may find yourself violating most of your old rules about what a good parent does. Yet the energy and aliveness that is coming through you, your increasing sense of satisfaction in your life, and your trust in yourself and the universe, will do far more to help your children than anything else possibly could.

In a sense, you don't have to "raise" your children at all! The universe is the true parent to your children; you are simply the channel. The more you are able to follow your energy and do what is best for you, the more the universe will come through you to everyone around you. As you thrive, your children will, too.

When babies are born, they are powerful, intuitive beings. Newly arrived in the physical world, they spend their first few years learning to live in a body. Their *forms* are younger and less experienced than ours, but their *spirits* are just as developed as ours. In fact, I believe that we often have children who are spiritually more developed than we are, so that we can learn from them.

Our children come into the world as clear beings. They know who they are and what they are here to do. I believe that on some level of consciousness, parents and child have made an agreement. The parents have agreed to support and assist the child in developing his form (body, mind, and personality) and learning how to operate it in the world. The child has agreed to help the parents be more in touch with their intuitive selves. Because children have not yet lost their conscious connection to their spirit, they provide us with considerable support in reconnecting with our own higher selves.

Our children essentially need two things from us:

1. They need to be recognized for who they really are. If we see and know that they are powerful and sophisticated spiritual beings and relate to them that way from the beginning, they will not need to hide their power and lose touch with their spirit, as most of us have. Their being will receive the support and acknowledgement they need to remain clear and strong.

2. They need us to create an example for them of how to live effectively in the world of form. As we do this, they watch how we live and imitate us. Being very perceptive and pragmatic, they copy what we actually *do,* and not what we *say.*

In return for taking responsibility for these two things, we receive from our children endless amounts of vibrant, alive energy. Unless they are shut down at a very early age through lack of support, children are very clear and powerful channels. Because they have not yet developed much rational censorship, they are almost totally intuitive, completely spontaneous, and absolutely honest. From watching them, we can learn a great deal about how to follow energy and live creatively.

Most parents have not been able to fulfill their responsibilities as successfully as they would have wished. In general, parents have been confused about their roles and responsibilities. They haven't had any clear models or guidelines. Until very recently in human history, no one did much research on parenting, and there are still very few resources for educating oneself about how to be a parent. Most people parent in a rather hit-or-miss fashion. So everyone has made plenty of mistakes.

I've met a lot of parents who, now that they have become more conscious, feel tremendous guilt and sadness in looking back on how they've raised their children. It's helpful to remember that children are powerful, spiritual beings who are responsible for their own lives — they chose you as a parent so that they could learn the things they needed to work out in this lifetime.

Also, it helps tremendously to know that as you grow and evolve, they will be positively affected and supported by your transformation. They will change as you change, even if they are grown and live far away from you. All relationships are telepathic, so no matter what the physical distance, they will continue to reflect you.

Because we have not been sufficiently attuned to our own being, it's been hard to recognize and trust the spirit within our children. Because they were physically undeveloped and rationally unsophisticated, we thought they were less aware and less responsible than they really were.

I've observed in many people the underlying attitude that children are somewhat helpless or untrustworthy and that parents are responsible for controlling and molding them into responsible beings. Children, of course, pick up this attitude and reflect it in their behavior. If you recognize them as powerful, spiritually mature, responsible beings, they will respond accordingly.

Children as Mirrors

Because young children are relatively unspoiled, they are our clearest mirrors. As intuitive beings, they are tuned in on a feeling level and respond honestly to the energy as they feel it. They haven't learned to cover up yet. When adults do not speak or behave according to what they are actually feeling, children pick up the discrepancy immediately and react to it. Watching their reactions can help us become more aware of our own suppressed feelings.

For example, if you are trying to appear calm and collected when inside you are feeling upset and angry, your children may mirror this to you by becoming wild and disruptive. You are trying to maintain control, but they pick up the chaotic energy inside of you and reflect it in their behavior. Oddly enough, if you express directly what you are truly feeling without trying to cover it up ("I'm feeling really upset and frustrated because I've had a rotten day. I'm mad at the world and at myself and at you! I want you to be quiet so I can have some peace and quiet to try to sort out my feelings. Will you all please go outside for a few minutes?!"), they will usually calm down. They feel comfortable with the truth, the congruity between your feelings and your words.

Many parents think they have to protect their children from their (the parents') confusion or so-called negative feelings. They think that being a good parent means maintaining a certain role — always being patient, loving, wise, and strong. In fact, children need honesty — they need to see a model of a human being going through all the different feelings and moods that a human being goes through and being honest about it. This gives them permission and support to love themselves and allow themselves to be real and truthful.

Sharing your feelings with your children does not mean

dumping your anger on them or blaming them for your troubles. It also does not mean you can expect them to be your therapist and help you with your problems. The more you practice expressing your feelings honestly as you go along, the less likely you are to do either of these things. However, being human, you probably will dump your anger or frustration on them from time to time. Once you see that you've done it, tell them you realize that you dumped on them and that you are sorry, and then let it go. It's all part of learning to be in close relationships.

Children also serve as our mirrors by imitating us from a very young age. We are their model for behavior, so they pattern themselves after us. Thus, we can watch them to see what we are doing!

When your child does something you don't like, tell him or her how you feel about it and deal with it directly. However, also ask yourself in what way that behavior mirrors you or how you might be supporting it in your own process.

For example, if your children are being secretive and hiding things from you, ask yourself if you have been really open and honest about all your feelings with them. Is there something you are hiding from someone or from yourself? Is there some way you don't trust yourself and therefore don't trust them? If your children are being rebellious, take a look at the relationship between your own inner tyrant and rebel. If your inner tyrant has a lot of control in your life, your children may be acting out your suppressed rebellious side. Or if you've acted out the rebel a lot in your life, they may be imitating you.

Take a good look at how these problems reflect your inner process. If you learn from your experiences and grow, so will your children. Externally, a lot of these problems can be worked through by deeply and sincerely sharing your feelings and learning to back yourself up, and by encouraging your children to do the same. You may want to get support from a professional counselor or family therapist to help the whole family change its old patterns.

I have found that, for many people, parenting has been a convenient excuse not to do their own learning and growing. Frequently, parents spend most of their time focusing on the children, trying to make sure that the children learn and grow properly. In taking responsibility for their children's lives, they abandon responsibility for their own lives. This has the unfortunate result of making the children feel unconsciously that they have to take responsibility for their parents (because their parents are sacrificing for them). Children may imitate their parents' behavior by taking responsibility for other people, or they may rebel against the pressure to conform to their parents' expectations by acting out the opposite of what their parents want.

Parents need to shift the focus of their responsibility from their children back to themselves, where it belongs. Remember that children learn by example. They will tend to do what you *do,* not what you tell them to do. The more you learn to take care of yourself and live a fulfilling, happy life, the more they will too.

This doesn't mean you should abandon or ignore your children. It doesn't mean that you let them do whatever they want. You are in a deep relationship with them and like any other relationship, it takes a lot of caring and communication. It's important for all of you to express feelings, make needs known, and set clear boundaries. Furthermore, you have accepted certain responsibilities to care for them physically and financially. You have a right to require their co-responsibility and cooperation in that process.

The key is in your attitude. If you truly see your children as powerful, responsible entities and treat them as equal to you in spirit (while acknowledging that they are less experienced than you in form), they will mirror that attitude back to you.

From the time they are born, assume that they know who they are and what they want, and that they have valid feelings and opinions about everything. Even before they can talk, ask them for their feelings about things they are involved in and trust your intuition and the signals they give you to know what their answers are. For example, ask them if they'd like to be included in an outing or if they'd rather stay home with a babysitter. Trust your feelings about which choice they are making and proceed accordingly. Then pay attention to the signals they give. If you take them on an outing and they cry the whole time, next time try leaving them with the babysitter.

As they grow older, continue to include them in family decisions and responsibilities. As much as possible, allow them to make their own decisions about their personal lives. This means they may sometimes have to deal with the consequences of making certain decisions. Offer them your love, support, and advice, but let it be understood that their lives are basically their own responsibility. Be sure you set your own boundaries clearly — what is okay and what isn't. Making their own decisions does not include the right to take advantage of you. Above all, try to communicate your honest feelings to them and ask them to let you know how they are feeling. Almost all family problems arise from a lack of communication. Your children certainly aren't going to know how to communicate clearly if you yourself don't know how.

It seems to be terribly difficult for parents to give up living their children's lives for them and start living their own. In order to do this, parents have to be willing to admit how dependent they really are on their children and how frightened they feel about letting go of them. These feelings are usually masked by a reverse projection — parents will tell themselves that their children are dependent on them and won't be okay if the parents start focusing on fulfilling their *own* needs.

I have found that this is a false issue. The *real* issue is the parents' feelings of dependency on their children, which they usually aren't even conscious of! Children are so alive and exciting, parents often secretly fear that their lives will be drab and dull without their children. Or perhaps they are just afraid to face themselves. Once they recognize and acknowledge these feelings, they will begin to deal with the emptiness within themselves and their lives. They will begin to look at what they want and how they can satisfy themselves. They will begin to trust their own gut feelings about things and act on them.

At this point, the children really start to flourish. They are finally liberated from the unconscious task of trying to take care of their parents; they are freed to make their own lives worthwhile! The children start doing what they really need to do for themselves. They can now become the channels they truly are.

One couple who are close friends of mine have a four-year-old daughter. Since before she was born, her parents were aware of her as a beautiful, powerful being and felt that they were in communication with that being. I was present at her home birth — a wonderful event. A few minutes after she was born I was holding her and she looked strongly and directly into my eyes (I had previously heard that babies can't focus at such an early age). It was quite apparent to me that she was well aware of what was happening.

She has been raised much as I have described. She has always been afforded the respect that she deserves and treated as a highly conscious entity. As a result, she is a truly remarkable child. Wherever she goes, people remark on her strong presence. It's easy to see that she is an open channel for the universe.

Meditation

Get comfortable, relax, and close your eyes. Take a few deep breaths and move your awareness into a deep, quiet place within you.

Picture or imagine your child in front of you. Look into his or her eyes and sense the powerful being within. Take a little time just to be with this experience and receive any feelings, ideas, or impressions about who your child really is. Communicate to him or her in your own words your respect and appreciation. Imagine that your child is communicating to you his or her respect and appreciation.

If you have more than one child, do this with each one of them. This meditation is effective in opening the love and communication between you and your children, whether they are infants or adults.

Exercise

Practice telling the truth to your children and expressing your feelings honestly with them even if you feel vulnerable and uncomfortable about not being in control. Ask them how they feel about things and try to really listen to what they have to say. If you are tempted to give advice, ask them if they want to hear it first. If they don't, tell them your *feelings* instead.

17

SEXUALITY AND PASSION

Sexual energy is passion and aliveness. It is the life force, the creative force of the universe. The key to a passionate life is to trust and follow the energy within us. The more we trust ourselves and move spontaneously with our energy, the more freely and fully the life force can move through us. When we're not afraid to experience and express all our feelings, we come alive. We feel everything more deeply and everything we do has an ecstatic, orgasmic feeling about it.

When we trust and follow the energy of the universe within us, it leads us into the appropriate action for any given situation. It may lead us to speak or be silent, to move and dance or be still, to sing, shout, cry, or meditate. In interactions with others it may lead us to converse, to hug, to sit quietly together, and at times to physically make love. The passionate feeling of aliveness is there in all of these experiences and the fulfillment comes from following and expressing this energy naturally, as we really feel it. So looking at a flower or having a moment of eye contact with someone can be as pleasing and fulfilling as a physical sexual encounter, if that is where the energy is in the moment. Our lives are filled with the sexuality of the universe, although certain experiences may allow us to feel it more intensely than others.

Unfortunately, most of us have become masters at cutting off our sexual energy. We're afraid of ourselves and afraid of where our sexual energy will take us. We instinctively know that our sexual energy has the power to create and transform, and that there is nothing safe, stable, or sedentary about it. Our egos are afraid of this, so instead of trusting our natural instincts, we learn to suppress them. Our families, peers, society, and religious organizations only aid us in attempting to suppress, control, or exploit what is natural. Others only mirror the fear we are already feeling. As I've said in earlier chapters, the ego seeks what it knows — the familiar, the unchangeable. It needs to be re-educated to learn that trust of the intuitive will allow energy to flow through, bringing bliss and joy with it.

To some degree, we are beginning to be more supportive of our bodies and sexual energy. Many of us now talk more openly about our bodies and our feelings about sex. This is still on a somewhat superficial level, however. We have not, as yet, cleared out the centuries of abuse and negative beliefs that are stored in our cells. Even though we are affirming the beauty of our bodies and the value of sexual openness, underneath we may still believe our sexual energy is a sinful and dangerous force. We distrust ourselves.

Many people still suffer from the mistaken idea that spiritual energy and sexual energy are opposite, instead of recognizing that they are the same force. People split themselves: they try to deny their sexuality in order to be more spiritual, create a tremendous conflict within themselves, and end up blocking the very energy they are seeking.

The universe is pure sexual energy waiting to pour through us. This unlimited power has frightened us; we have responded by trying to package or control the energy. We have set up rules and guidelines for our sexual energy instead of trusting ourselves moment to moment.

No one knows what pure, unleashed sexual energy would look like because we're either rebelling or buying into the rules we've set up for ourselves. Both patterns prevent us from discovering the true nature of our sexual energy. It's impossible to set up external expectations for an energy that is so subtle and variable.

If you're setting limits on your sexual energy, it becomes distorted. If you believe it is something to be hidden, ignored, and controlled, then you learn to hold back completely or act sexually only at certain safe moments. Even when having sex, it can be dead because you're so used to blocking what's natural. The energy doesn't know how to flow through. A classic example of this is of a young girl who's been told to hold back her sexual energy until marriage, and then, when married, she's expected to unblock what she's held back for years. Because of this she has trouble letting the energy flow openly.

Many people don't want to get stuck in suppressive sexual rules so they rebel, pushing past their sexual energy, having sex whenever and as much as they can. The pushing eventually causes the energy to die, because it, too, does not come from the inside. As the energy starts to die, people seek increasingly stimulating ways to excite themselves in their need to be satisfied. Satisfaction is pushed further and further away. The more you try to grasp onto it, the more it eludes you.

As I said earlier, if we're either buying into external rules or rebelling against them, our natural energy gets ignored. To get in touch with that takes letting go of all previous ideas; it means changing everything you've been doing. To have ecstasy, we have to risk trusting ourselves, learn to put away external rules, and then discover our internal rhythm.

Trust Your Body — Discover Your Sexual Energy

Each person's sexual energy is individual. When freed of all our rules, limitations, and rebellions, we'll be able to discover our own natural flow. Some people will want to express themselves sexually more than others will. Some people will want one lover, some no lover, some many lovers.

I believe we can move to a place of innocence with our sexuality. We can feel our energy as pure, as the force of the universe moving through us. We can begin to trust and act on our sexual energy without the influence of preconceived ideas. This will free us to be in the moment.

To come to this place of innocence we first have to recognize where we've been. We have to acknowledge all the old beliefs, judgments, and attitudes that have kept us from experiencing our true sexuality.

Seeing this could be as simple as feeling attracted to someone you meet at a party and watching yourself jump ahead to the bedroom scene, or finding yourself suppressing the sexual feelings because you're with someone else. In both cases you've blocked the sexual feeling you were having, either by racing ahead or trying to ignore it. You can see yourself avoiding the power of simply feeling and enjoying your sexual energy. When you first see how difficult it is for you to stay with the energy, you may be tempted to feel overwhelmed. You may also want to change your old pattern and move with the energy right away. Trying to change all our judgments, limitations, and rebelliousness doesn't help. I've found it *does* help to accept myself the way I am. If I'm willing to accept myself with all my limitations, my body can relax instead of bracing itself against change. Then it changes in its own time.

Our bodies have developed intricate means of pacing (or, more accurately, controlling) the energy coming through us. Our judgments and limitations have served us well; they have slowed down the flow of energy to a comfortable level. People often use food and drugs to control and manipulate the natural flow of energy coming through. Even if it appears that you're heightening your energy through a stimulant, the reality is you're still cutting down on the power of the universe coming through you. The same is true for sex. People have developed ways to pace themselves sexually. They either push past their natural desires, to have more sex than they want, or they block their sexual desires. Both ways give us control to prevent the energy of the universe from flowing through.

Until we're ready to experience our sexual power, we will use such methods as judgments, negative beliefs, expectations, and old attitudes to pace ourselves. Simply acknowledging and accepting the reasons why we do this helps the energy unblock.

Knowing that I'll support my feelings in the moment gives me the freedom to explore my sexual energy without an expectation that I have to do it "right." There are fears, excitement, and uncertainty about sex and as we start to explore our energy all these feelings will surface. We need to accept all of them.

An example of this might be starting to make love with a new lover and then having a memory of an ex-lover that saddens you. At this point, you may choose to feel the sadness and share what you're feeling with your partner. Or, you may ignore what you feel and have sex. Again, whatever you choose, notice what you do and how you feel. Notice what it felt like to share your feeling and notice what it felt like to go past it. Your body will tell you what feels best from moment to moment.

The reward, to me, in following the energy is how good I feel. By staying with the energy, I stay with the universe inside me. Increasingly, I am willing to risk doing this because of the aliveness I experience when I do.

The following exercise will help you explore your sexual energy:

Pretend for a day, an hour, or however long you want, that you have no preconceived ideas about what your sexual feelings are and what you should and shouldn't do with them.

Before you get out of bed, observe your body and then drop inside and see if you can find an innocent, childlike place within yourself. From this place of innocence, imagine what your day will be like. Ask yourself what your sexual energy looks and feels like, what your body feels like. Start to explore any feelings or images that surface for you. Imagine what it's like to follow your energy from moment to moment. See it and experience it as real. If any negative thoughts should surface, acknowledge them and let them pass by for the moment.

As you get out of bed and prepare for the day, keep a feeling of newness with you. Notice how your body feels, notice how it reacts to those you encounter during the day. As you go through the day, stay aware of yourself, your body, and your sexual feelings. If you have a strong sexual pull toward someone, notice how you feel and what thoughts you're having (such as: I'm going to do something about this . . . I've got to have him or her . . . she's married . . . I'm married . . . she doesn't fit my expectations . . . he's too young. . .). Try not to attach yourself to any of these thoughts. If you can, return to this place of innocence and stay with yourself. If you choose to act on any of the feelings you're having, be aware of moving from that inside place, trusting and following the energy within.

Following the Energy in Relationships

People often want to know how to support their energy in relationships. How do you back yourself up when you want sex and the other person doesn't, when following your energy may mean taking another lover when you're in a monogamous relationship, or when following your energy may mean not having sex even when your partner wants it?

The fear is that what we want won't be what our partner or friends want. There's a fear that trusting ourselves means hurting someone else. Again, you *can* trust yourself and your sexual energy.

I don't believe the energy of the universe could ever move us to hurt ourselves or others. People may appear hurt momentarily, but if you're really trusting and following the energy, your actions will actually empower others.

If you want to have sex and your partner doesn't (or vice versa), support and express the feelings you have. Then, your partner will respond and you can each keep moving to a deeper level of communication. If your partner doesn't want to have sex, then you need to use this as a mirror of your insides. Ask yourself what's going on inside of you. Keep going inside to see what your next move is. That's trusting yourself. It may be that you and your partner need to talk, there may be some unexpressed hurt or anger, it may be that you need some alone time and haven't recognized it. Keep supporting and expressing what you feel; this allows the energy to move freely.

Be open to experiencing a different form of sexuality than usual; the energy may lead you into simply sitting together, lying together, holding each other, massaging one another, or something else that you don't ordinarily think of as sex but which can be just as satisfying. Be true to your feelings and the right actions will emerge.

People often ask me what to do when they're involved in a monogamous relationship and find themselves attracted to someone else. As I mentioned in the Relationships chapter, there is certainly no simple answer to this question. Usually we block the energy, either by shutting down and ignoring the attraction, or rebelling against our self-imposed rules and finding we are even more attracted to the "forbidden" situation. In neither case are we trusting the energy. In this situation, you need to look deeper within yourself to see what you are really feeling. Are you trying to act more monogamous than you really feel out of guilt or fear of losing your partner? Or are you backing away from closeness and intimacy with your partner by seeking distractions elsewhere? Inevitably there is a need for greater honesty and a deeper level of sharing feelings with all concerned.

While frightening because of its potential for emotional explosiveness, this situation can lead to greater depth in your ability to relate. Stay open to the possibility that if you are completely honest, things will work out so that everyone gets what they truly want and need. Again, you *may* find that an attraction to someone actually leads you not into bed with them, but into some other form of relationship that turns out to be totally satisfying.

Sustaining Passion in Relationships

A deadness occurs in relationships when people are no longer willing to tell each other how they really feel. When people first fall in love they're more willing to do this because they're still getting to know each other and dependency has not yet set in. As soon as it does, though, people often stop sharing their true feelings out of fear of loss.

Passion is not something that just disappears. It leaves us when we're no longer open to our feelings, when we're willing to lose ourselves to keep someone else. To experience passion, we must first be true to ourselves and then honest with others.

Passion in a partnership is true intimacy with each other. As you become an open channel for your feelings, you'll become an open channel for the passion and joy that can flow through you.

Meditation

Sit or lie down in a comfortable position. Close your eyes and take a few deep breaths. Each time you exhale, relax your body more. Then take a few more deep breaths and each time you exhale, relax your mind.

With each breath, relax into that core place inside. Feel the energy of the universe pulsate from that core and move throughout your body. Know that this energy is sexual and passionate in its expression.

See your expression as the fiery energy of the universe moving through you to others. Imagine yourself expressing your passion with your lover(s), with friends, in your work and creative projects, and in the fun you have.

Know that the power within you is innocent, alive, creative, and ecstatic. Know that you can trust the energy moving through you and that it is safe to express yourself.

Exercise

To clean out any old ideas, fears, prejudices, or negative beliefs about sex, I recommend that people do a writing process. By seeing what your beliefs are, you can become conscious of when you're acting on them. The more conscious you become, the less your beliefs will have any hidden power over you.

1. Write down all your negative beliefs, thoughts, and fears about sex.

2. When you've done that, close your eyes and see yourself handing any fears or negative beliefs over to the universe. Take a deep breath and let everything go.

3. Write affirmations to help you counteract your negative beliefs. Some examples of this are:

Negative Belief	**Affirmation**
I can't find the right lover.	*I am now attracting the perfect lover(s) for me. Or, I am now attracting a fun, passionate lover.*
I don't enjoy sex.	*It's safe to enjoy sex. I deserve to enjoy sex.*
There isn't enough time for sex. I'm always too tired.	*I trust my feelings and support them. I take time for myself. I communicate my true feelings to my lover.*
I can't trust myself when it comes to my sexual desires.	*I now trust myself completely. I trust and act on my sexual desires.*
I want too much sex.	*I now trust my sexual rhythm. I tune into what I want and act on it.*

18

WORK AND PLAY

Work and play are the same. When you're following your energy and doing what you want all the time, the distinction between work and play dissolves. Work is no longer what you *have* to do or play what you *want* to do. When you are doing what you love, you may work harder and produce more than ever before, but it will feel like play.

The people I work with, in groups and individually, are often wondering what they are "going to be when they grow up." What is it they're going to do, what is their true purpose? I tell them that each one of us has a true purpose and each one of us is a channel for the universe. When we follow the light, everything is fun, creative, and transformational. We make a contribution to the world just by being ourselves in every moment. There are no more rigid categories in our lives — this is work, this is play. It all blends into the flow of following the universe and money flows in as a result of the open channel that's created. You no longer work in order to make money. Work is no longer something you have to do in order to sustain life. Instead, the delight that comes from expressing yourself becomes the greatest reward. The money comes along as a natural part of being alive. Working and getting money may no longer even be directly related to each other; you may experience that you are doing whatever you have energy to do and that money is coming into your life. It's no longer a matter of, "You do this and then you get money for it." The two things are simply operating simultaneously in your life but not necessarily in a direct cause-and-effect relationship.

In the new world, it's difficult to pin your life's work and true purpose down to any one thing. In terms of looking for a career, our old-world concept told us that when we became adults, we had to decide what our career would be, and then pursue an education or other steps to achieve that career. The career would then be pursued for most or all of our life.

In the new world, many of us are channels for a number of things which may come together in fascinating combinations. Perhaps you haven't found your career because it doesn't exist yet. Your particular and unique way of expressing yourself has never existed before and will never be repeated again. As you practice following the energy in your life, it will start to lead you in many directions. You will begin to express yourself in a variety of ways, all of which will begin to synthesize in some surprising, interesting, and very new, creative way. You will no longer be able to say, "I am a writer (or a fireman or a teacher or a housewife)." You may be a combination of all of those things. You'll be doing what you love, what you're good at, what comes easily to you and has an element of challenge and excitement to it. Whatever you do will feel satisfying and fulfilling to you. It is no longer a matter of doing things now for later gratification: "I will work hard now so that I can get a better job later. I will work hard now so that I can retire and enjoy my life. I will work hard now in order to have enough money and time to have a vacation where I can have fun." It's the fulfillment of what you're doing at this very moment that counts. In being a channel, everything you do becomes a contribution; even the simplest things are significant.

It is the energy of the universe moving through us that transforms, not the particular things we do. When I write a book that has a certain amount of wisdom in it, it's the energy that impacts people. It's the energy of the universe that comes through me and connects to the reader's deeper levels of awareness. The words and ideas are the icing on the cake. They are the things that enable our minds to grasp what has already been changed. It is not so important that I wrote a book. What is important is that I expressed myself, opened up and allowed the creative energy to flow through me. That creative energy is now penetrating other people and things in this world. I had the joy of that energy moving through me and other people had the joy of receiving that energy. That's the transformational experience.

Whether you are washing the dishes, taking a walk, or building a house, if you're doing it with a sense of being right where you want to be and doing what you want to be doing, that fullness and joy in the experience will be felt by everyone around you. If you're building a house and somebody walks by and sees you doing it, they will feel the impact of the fullness of your experience. Their lives will be transformed to the degree that they are ready to allow the energy's impact. Though they may not know what hit them, they will start to experience life differently. It's the same when you're just being. If you walk into a room, feeling one with yourself, knowing who you are, knowing that you're a channel, and expressing yourself in whatever way feels right to you, then everyone in the room will be transformed. Even though they may not recognize it or know anything about it consciously, you will be able to see the direct result of your channel operating. You will see proof of it in watching the changes in people. It is an incredibly exciting and satisfying experience.

You can see that it is no longer an issue of focusing on one particular thing, although you may be led to focus and build structure in a particular area. You may choose to learn certain skills that you will use to allow your channel to function in a way that it wants to function. If you do this, you will be led to it easily and naturally. The process of learning will be just as much fun as the doing. In other words, it is no longer necessary to sacrifice in the moment so that in the future you will be able to have what you want. The learning process will be full of fun, joy, and excitement. You'll experience it as being exactly what you want to be doing at that time. Practicing, learning skills, going to school — all of this can be fun and fulfilling when you are following your intuitive guidance.

Conversely, the work you do will be a learning experience. For example, I teach workshops, not because I've mastered information and I am the teacher and you are the student, but because I love to share myself in this way. This sharing deepens my learning experience. Again, there is no difference between learning and teaching, just as there is no difference between work and play. It all begins to blend into one totally integrated and balanced experience.

Most people do have some sense, at least deep inside, of what they would love to be doing. This feeling is often so repressed, however, that it is experienced only in the form of some wildly impractical fantasy, something you could never do. I always encourage people to get in touch with these fantasies. Observe and explore thoroughly your most incredible fantasy of how you'd like to be and what you'd like to be doing. There is truth in this desire. Even if it seems impossible, there is at least a grain of truth in the image. It is telling you something about who you really are and what it is you really want to be doing.

Your fantasies can tell you how you really want to be expressing yourself. Many times, I've found that people have a strong sense of what they would like to do, yet they take up a career that is very different from their desire. Sometimes they go for the opposite because they feel it is practical or will gain the approval of their parents or the world. They figure it is impossible to do what they really want, so they might as well settle for something else that comes along. I encourage people to risk exploring the things that really turn them on. The following are examples of people I've worked with and their exploration of their true purpose:

1. A brilliant and talented woman I know had been

working with sick and dying people for many years. Although she was a great nurse and a powerful healer, it became evident to her that she needed to be where she could express herself more creatively. With encouragement, she started working fewer days as a nurse and began leading workshops and counseling people. Because she's doing this she feels more fulfilled and those around her feel her fulfillment, as well.

2. Joseph, following family tradition, went into business with his father and brothers. He was very successful in real estate and contracting. The problem was, he knew there was something else he wanted to do with his life. After lots of encouragement from the group in one of my workshops, he admitted that he wanted to work in the arts, but knew his family would frown on it. He most wanted to be a dancer. The first step was admitting to himself what he wanted to do. Eventually, he mustered the courage to take dance classes. He had a lot of talent and immediately attracted the attention of the teacher. He continued to explore this form of artistic expression. When he supported his desires, he actually found that his family was equally supportive.

3. A close friend of mine had three children, no education, and was living on welfare. Her desire was to get into business. She intuitively felt she was going to handle large amounts of money, but considering her situation, this didn't make sense. Nevertheless, she decided to explore some possibilities in the financial district of San Francisco. She was immediately hired as a receptionist in a firm and found the perfect live-in babysitter for her children. From receptionist, she went on to be an administrative assistant and continued to rise to higher levels of skill and responsibility. She is moving steadily toward her goal of being a stock broker. She loves what she's doing and her children are flourishing as well.

4. A woman who came to a recent workshop of mine shared that she'd been a talented pianist with hopes of becoming a concert pianist. Then, for several reasons, the most predominant being a lack of faith in herself, she had given

up her dream. She started working in an office and found that between work and her children she had little time for her music. After fifteen years she felt it was simply too late to ever go back to the piano. She felt the time she had lost in not playing rendered hopeless any chance of being great. Despite all her doubts, we encouraged her to at least start playing again. I assured her that if she was doing what she loved it would come back to her easily. As she opened to this idea, she started opening to herself. Her sense of hopelessness was replaced by a renewed sense of power. She called later to say she had been playing the piano and feeling great about it. A friend had asked her to play accompaniment for a choral group and she was feeling very excited about the musical possibilities opening up for her.

Meditation

Sit or lie down in a comfortable position. Close your eyes and relax. Take several slow, deep breaths, relaxing your body more deeply with each breath. Take several more breaths and relax your mind. Release and relax all the tension in your body. If you want, imagine that your body is almost sinking into the floor, bed, or chair.

From this very relaxed place inside, imagine that you are doing exactly what you want in your life. You have a fabulous career that is fun and fulfilling for you. You are now doing what you've always fantasized about and getting a tremendous sum of money for it.

You feel relaxed, energized, creative, and powerful. You are successful at what you do because it is exactly what you want to be doing.

You follow your intuition moment to moment and are richly rewarded for it.

Exercises

1. Follow any impulses you have in the direction of your true work/play desires. Even if it seems totally unrealistic, follow the impulse anyway. For example, if you're sixty-five years old and have always wanted to be a ballet dancer, go to

a ballet class and observe, or if you want, take the class. Watch some ballet and imagine that you're a dancer. While alone at home, put on some music and dance. This will get you in touch with that part of yourself that wants to be expressed that way. You may end up dancing much more than you thought possible, and you may be led to other forms of expression that will feel as good.

2. List any fantasies you've had around work, career, or creativity, and beside that list the action you plan to take to explore this.

3. Write an "ideal scene" — a description of your perfect job or career exactly as you would like it to be. Write it in the present tense, as if it were already true. Put in enough description and details to make it seem very real. Put it away somewhere, and look at it again in a few months or even a year or two. Unless your fantasy has changed completely in that time, chances are that you will find you have made significant progress in the direction of your dream.

19

MONEY

Money is a symbol of our creative energy. We have invented a system whereby we use pieces of paper or metal to represent a certain unit of creative energy. You earn money by using your energy, then you trade that money to me in exchange for the energy I put into writing this book or leading a workshop, and so forth. Because the creative energy of the universe in all of us is limitless and readily available, so, potentially, is money. The more willing and able we are to open to the universe, the more money we will have in our lives. A lack of money merely mirrors the energy blocks within ourselves.

Your ability to earn and spend money abundantly and wisely is based on your ability to be a channel for the universe. The stronger and more open your channel is, the more will flow through it. The more you are willing to trust yourself, and take the risks to follow your inner guidance, the more money you will have. The universe will pay you to be yourself and do what you really love!

Money in the Old World

The old world is based on our attachment to the external, physical world. We look for satisfaction from external things. Because we believe that survival depends on getting things, we may think that fulfillment can be found in material wealth.

In the old world you can build a strong financial structure and earn lots of money by learning how to act effectively in the world (the old male). However, because your actions are not based on the guidance of the universe that comes from the inner female, building your financial structure will involve fear and struggle, and you will pay a high price for the money. You can earn money, but find that you are ruled by it. You think the money itself is important: "If I have enough money, I can do these things and then I'll be happy," or "If I have enough money, then I'll feel good about myself and I'll be happy," or "Other people will like me if I have enough money and that will make me happy." From this point of view money is seen to be the important thing, but as long as it is valued in this way, money is always a problem.

If you have too little money, you're always struggling to get more money and always afraid there won't be enough. There's always that terrible pain inside that you don't have enough of what you need. On the other hand, if you have a lot of money, it's painful because you're always afraid you're going to lose it. You can never have enough money to insure that you won't be afraid.

People with little money seldom realize that people who have a lot of money are also frightened. They are basically insecure because they never know if they might lose their money. Circumstances out of their control might arise — they might make a foolish investment or somebody might steal their money. If security is based on having money, it doesn't matter whether you have a little or a lot, you're going to be afraid.

If we don't realize that money is a symbol of infinite energy, and we think there is only a limited amount of it in the world, we're stuck with two options: we can choose to have a lot of money and feel guilty, or we can choose to do without and resent those that have more. If you choose to have money, you will live with the knowledge that others have less than you. You may fear that your having more *causes* others to have less. You may choose to deal with the guilt by trying to deny or ignore the feeling, or you may choose to ease your conscience by attempting to help those who are less fortunate.

On the other hand, you can choose to say "I won't carry that guilt. I won't take more than my share. I don't care about money anyway. Therefore, I will keep what I have to a minimum. I'll make sure that I am not taking from somebody else." The problem with this attitude is that you end up feeling deprived. You see all the beautiful, wonderful things in the world that you would like to have and enjoy, but you can't. You see other people who have more than their share of money and you resent them. Basically, in this old-world framework we must choose either guilt or resentment.

The old-world structure demands we do things out of our ego strength, instead of allowing the universe to do it. We think we have to work really hard to get what we want — the work ethic that says "Work hard. Sacrifice and struggle." Most of us have that embedded so deeply in us that we don't allow ourselves to succeed financially or in any other way, except through hard work, struggle, and sacrifice. If you are succeeding and making money, you are also paying a price emotionally, and often physically. People frequently drive themselves to the point of sickness or death. They struggle and sacrifice emotionally, and in the end, even though they have achieved worldly success, they still feel deprived and empty.

Or people refuse to go after it at all. "Look what it leads to: struggle, sacrifice, pain, and deprivation of oneself, so I simply won't deal with it. I'll get by on the absolute minimum amount of money in my own life." Often, more sensitive, spiritually inclined people choose this route so they can focus on more "meaningful" things. The problem with this is you're actually depriving yourself of dealing with one of the most exciting and beautiful things in life. If you're denying money, you're also denying a big part of the energy of the universe and the way the world works. People who choose the denial route usually don't know how to handle money and refuse to learn anything about it.

Money in the New World

The new world is based on trust of the universe within us. We recognize that the creative intelligence and energy of the universe is the fundamental source of everything. Once we connect with this and surrender to it, everything is ours. Emptiness is filled from the inside.

We realize that money is a reflection of the energy moving through our channel. *The more we learn to operate in the world based on trust in our intuition, the stronger our channel will be and the more money we will have.* The money in our life is based on our ability to listen to our inner guidance and risk acting on it. When your ego stops trying to control and you learn how to listen to the universe and act on it, then money increasingly comes into life. It flows in an easy, effortless, and joyful way because there is no sacrifice involved. You're no longer attached to it. Instead you can experience the joy of learning how to follow the energy of the universe. Money is just an extra bonus in the process.

You know that the money is not really yours — it belongs to the universe. You are like a caretaker or steward for the money. You use it only as you are directed by the universe through your own intuition. There is no fear of loss because you know you are always taken care of. The money may come or go, but you can't lose the joy and fulfillment in your life. When you feel this secure and free, you attract more and more money, so that you are continually pushed to deepen your trust at more intense levels with higher stakes. Ultimately, as channels, many of us will be called upon to handle large amounts of money from this place of total surrender and commitment to the higher power. This is one of the ways that the power of the universe can be wielded effectively to transform the world.

Active and Receptive

There are active and receptive aspects to the process of channeling money, as in every other creative process. The masculine or active way of making money is to go out after something. You see something you want and go for it. The feminine or receptive way of making money is to attract that which you want to you.

We have to be able to do both. We need to release the outgoing energy that wants to move toward a certain goal and risk fearlessly acting on it. We also need to practice nurturing ourselves, appreciating ourselves, and becoming attuned to our inner selves so that we can attract and receive what we want. Many people are developed on one side or the other. They either know how to go out after things, but have a hard time attracting things to them, or they know how to attract things but are afraid to go out after them. Often a balancing process is necessary. You may need to learn to receive the gifts, appreciation, love, and energy coming to you. Or you may need to practice outflowing your energy into the world, which keeps it flowing through your channel. This way, the energy doesn't get blocked on either end.

This means, on a practical level, you have to be willing to take some risks in the area of work and money. If you do only what you think you *should* in order to make money and be secure, then you won't listen to the intuitive voice that tells you what you really *need* to do.

This can be very scary when it entails your job and your money. People often want to know, "What do I do if my intuition tells me not to go to work one day? What do I do then? Will I lose my job?" If taking off a day from work seems too risky, it may not be the best choice for you, yet. You may need to build your structure by following your impulses in smaller ways at first. You may call in and take half a day off or you may plan for a three-day weekend. One day though, you may wake up and know, "I just don't want to go to work," and you will follow through with this and feel good about it. Usually, when my insides tell me to do this, I need some nurturing, some peace and quiet, some creative time for inspiration to come through, or time to simply feel old feelings stirring up inside, feelings that need to be felt and released.

If you risk following your impulse, you'll find, maybe a few hours or days later, your energy will actually be renewed. You'll be able to go back and do what needs to be done in a fourth of the time. You'll do it in a much more inspired and creative way. Anything can happen if you risk and trust yourself. While home, you may receive a phone call from a person offering you a better job that pays much more money (that happened to a friend of mine). You may get a creative inspiration that will open up a fun, prosperous opportunity for you or you may get an inspiration to go visit someone who will give you a lead to a great adventure. If you hate your job, though, your energy for it won't come back. Also, because your true creative energy is blocked, you'll continue to feel blocked financially. Eventually you will leave your job because you cannot stay stuck in such a place for long.

Basically, the whole issue of money is doing what you really want to do all the time. The universe will reward you for taking risks on its behalf. It's important, though, that the risks you take are proportionate to the level of structure you're building. In other words, if you're just beginning to learn how to trust and follow your intuition, you probably don't want to make a million-dollar deal on a gut feeling. You probably don't want to leap off a building and hope that you can fly. It is important that you build small things first. Practice following your intuition in everyday things. Say no, even though you're feeling pressured to say yes. Do the thing you want to do even though you don't know why. Do it on an impulse. Make that call. Take that day off from work. Think of things you love to do, and do them. This will build you to the point where you can make the big leaps.

Balance

Once you understand the basic process of learning how to follow your intuition and act on it, you have your groundwork for channeling money. There are, though, some aspects of relating more specifically to money that are important to know.

Balance is an important quality to use in building the structure of your channel. If you have been extreme in one direction, you may have to go to the extreme in the other direction in order to integrate and balance both aspects of everything. For example, if you have been very careless and casual about money, or if you have been a person who has denied the existence or importance of money in your life, you may need to build structures specifically related to money. These include: learning to balance your checkbook, budgeting money, and gaining an understanding of the rules that govern how money works in the world. You will find these practices are fascinating and interesting. They are no longer something that will block you from the spirit, they will open the way for you to have more spirit flowing through you.

People who have little understanding of money have usually chosen to avoid structure on one level or another because they feel rules, regulations, and details will keep them from experiencing the magic of life. They're afraid they'll spend all their time in their rational mind, instead of following their flow. If you have this fear, tune in and ask the universe for guidance. You'll want to do this in a way that makes you feel good. Perhaps it would help to hire someone to show you how to organize your finances. It does not have to be a painful process. You'll find it to be energizing and supportive in your life, as opposed to painful and boring.

Those who have already applied a great deal of structure to working with money in the world may need to let go and relax that structure. It's time to stop following your rules and allow the inspired aspect of the spirit of money to work in your life. Trust your intuition to guide you, and take more risks to do things differently than usual.

Similarly, if you've been a person who has saved your money and been very careful about spending it, you need to learn to spend more impulsively based on your intuition. Spend on the basis of a gut feeling of wanting something. Learn to follow these impulses and you'll find you won't end up broke. In fact, it actually creates more flow of money in your life. You're able to release and give it out, based on your intuition.

If you have been a spendthrift and always spend more than you actually have, you will probably need to plan more and budget. Again, do it in accordance with an inner feeling. If you're open to it, your intuition will tell you, "Hey, learn something about planning. Learn something about budgeting." It will support and help you. It won't make you feel restricted. If you follow your intuition about that you will be led to people who can show you how to do that and it will be an interesting process. Again, it will support your channel.

Focus

Another important thing to know about how money works is that it will always flow into whatever you've created in your life to receive it. Because it's energy, it will be attracted to what you need or want or envision. If you have always operated on a survival level with money, having only enough money to take care of your basic needs, that's where your money will go. If you start to attract more money into your life, you may have a tendency to increase your basic needs and still only make enough for what you need.

That's what happened to me for a long time. I had an underlying program that said, "I can only have as much money as I need. It's not OK to have more than I need." I created more needs, and ones that weren't particularly rewarding. My car would break down and I'd have expensive repair bills, or my cat would get sick and I'd have an expensive vet bill. Any extra money that came in would go toward something that was an emergency or a basic need. There was still nothing extra for fun and creative play or greater luxury.

I found that I needed to create a budget that included what I wanted as well as what I needed. I started at a reasonable level: "I'd like to buy at least one item of clothing each month that's fun or more luxurious. I'd also like to do some activity that would be fun." I would include these in my budget and the money for them would then flow in. That's the power of budgeting. A budget is like a blueprint. If you create a list, a picture in your mind of what you want to have in your life, you will create the necessary money. You can just keep expanding step by step.

My Money History

For most of my adult life I had very little money. I never focused much on money; I wasn't particularly interested in it. Essentially, I did whatever I had to do to pay my rent and bills, but I put most of my time and attention into my education and my pursuit of higher consciousness and creative expansion.

I always did whatever I needed to get the money — creative projects, housework, other odd jobs, even my own business. Only one time in my entire life did I have a nine-to-five job — for six months!

I was used to living on the edge without much sense of where my money was coming from. In those years I learned to trust that somehow the money would be there. Sometimes I would get down to my last dollar and then, somehow or other, more money would come. I was always cared for.

Then, gradually, as I began to use this process more and more, learning to trust my intuition and act on it, learning to listen to my inner guidance and risk putting myself out in the world, I began to get more money. I began to lead a more abundant lifestyle. It continued to the point where I was actually making very good money and living in a very beautiful apartment, doing most of the things that I wanted to do. I came to count on that amount of money, although it was never a secure thing. I was still living from month to month, but money always seemed to keep flowing. I constantly affirmed my trust in the universe to take care of me, and I tried to follow its guidance.

But the time came, all of a sudden, when I had no money. Some unexpected things happened and I was caught short. I paid my rent and my bills, and I looked in my checkbook and there was nothing left. I didn't have any savings or other resources to fall back on. That was a very startling experience because by that time I was used to having a certain amount of money.

What amazes me about this experience is that I had only five minutes of fear. I thought, "Oh my god, what am I going to do?" Then I felt totally calm. I had to have that last five minutes of fear, and then it was as if there was no more fear about money left after that. I knew I was going to be OK.

A key point in all this is that I knew I would be willing to do whatever the universe asked me to do. I remember thinking, "Well, I love my apartment, but I could give it up. I love all these things I have, but I could give them up. If the universe wants me to go live in a tent in someone's backyard, I'll do that. It will probably be wonderful."

There was an incredible feeling of trusting and knowing that none of my things were that important and that I was not going to really lose. Whatever I did next, even though it might be totally different, would be wonderful, too. I would be taken care of. It wasn't just an intellectual knowingness, because I had already known that intellectually for a long time. Living through those five minutes of fear left me with a feeling of fearlessness. Emotionally I knew that I was OK. It was a very profound experience.

I ended up cutting back a little bit on my expenses and lifestyle. That felt fine and I didn't feel deprived at all. In fact, it was a nice discipline for a while. Everything was provided for. Money came in to cover my expenses and I had a feeling of relief. I knew I had come totally to the level where my form was. I wasn't ahead of myself in any way and from then on, it was like I came to Earth and I was building from a solid foundation. At that moment I knew I was standing on a strong base of complete trust in the universe. From then on I knew the flow of money in my life would keep expanding, and I would never go back to not having.

Since that happened, about two years ago, there has been increasing money and abundance in my life. Now I am learning how to really enjoy it and allow my inner guidance to tell me at all times what I'm supposed to be doing. I've moved to a new level of business and finances which I had never dealt with before. I began to recognize a need to handle these things from a place of *total* guidance from the universe. I had gotten really good at learning how to follow the universe on one level of existence, but the new challenge was learning to trust at a more expanded level where the stakes were higher.

In confronting this new level of prosperity, at first I felt rather ignorant and helpless. I knew I needed help, so I asked the universe to send me the right channels to teach and guide me in this area. After interviewing a number of different financial advisors, I was led to both an accountant and a business manager who were just right for me and who helped me learn what I needed to know.

When I was in Hawaii doing some workshops I had the opportunity to buy some land and, at the same time, learn to trust my intuition on a larger scale. I had thought for a long time that it would be wonderful to buy some land and create a retreat center. Hawaii seemed like a great place to do that, but I wasn't actively looking for anything. In fact, I saw this as a future project. Then, a beautiful piece of land literally fell in my lap. Somebody told me about it, I saw it, and fell in love with it. It was for sale at a very good price.

I knew intellectually that it was not the right time to do this, but intuitively I felt it was the right move. With this, I said to my higher power, "OK, I'm going to go after this because I feel energy in it. If you don't want me to do this and this isn't the right time, then block it and sabotage it."

I kept expecting the purchase of it to get blocked because I really thought the timing wasn't right. However, it just kept unfolding. In fact, everything kept happening miraculously to move me in that direction. When it got close to the time to make the final decision, I was still asking, "Am I really supposed to do this?" My business manager warned me that it was not a practical step for me to take at that time. Although he is normally very supportive, he was mirroring the part of me that doubted the validity of this impulse. Even while I was thinking this wasn't a good idea, my insides kept saying, "Do it."

I knew it wasn't logical, but I went with my intuition. I bought the land and everything went very smoothly. Afterward I had a very exhilarating feeling. I knew I had made a leap into a whole new level of trusting myself and being willing to be a channel and go with the energy.

Meditation

Sit or lie down in a position that is comfortable for you. Close your eyes and begin breathing in an easy, natural way. With each breath you are becoming more deeply relaxed.

Begin to notice how you're feeling. How do you feel emotionally? How does your body feel? Notice the energy in your body. What does it feel like? See yourself taking in more energy with each breath. You are energized and alive.

Start to imagine this energy as money. See money flowing through your body. As you open to your own energy, you open to abundance. There is a limitless supply of money available to you.

Imagine all the money you could possibly desire. See it in front of you, touch it, and play with it. Take some time to be with the money in your life. See money coming to you. Know that you attract money and it flows to you easily.

See yourself surrounded by all that money can buy. See the beauty and creativity in your life. See the beautiful clothes, homes, cars, and lifestyle you have. See the creative, fun ways you spend your money. Know that money flows freely to you and you outflow it as easily.

Feel yourself open to the energy in your body and the limitless supply of money available to you.

Exercise

Lack of money only mirrors the energy blocks within you. Write down all the ways in which you limit your desires and creativity. How are you not doing what you want?

Some examples of this are:

1. I'm doing administrative work in an office when I'd rather be working with children.

2. I want to meditate, but there's never time.

3. I'd like to explore my art more, but I have no time; I have to earn a living.

4. I want to tell my mother (friend, lover) how I'm feeling, but am afraid I'll hurt her.

Now imagine yourself doing exactly what you want to do in each of these areas.

20

HEALTH

Our body is our primary creation, the vehicle we have chosen to express us in the physical world. It's like a semi-formed piece of clay that molds itself to express the patterns of energy moving through it. By looking at our bodies, listening to them, and feeling them, we can read a great deal about our spiritual, mental, and emotional energy patterns. The body is our primary feedback mechanism that can show us what is and isn't working about our ways of thinking, expressing, and living.

Any normal child, who has had a reasonably positive environment, has a beautiful, alive body filled with vitality. That beauty, aliveness, and vitality are simply the natural life energy of the universe flowing freely through, unimpeded by negative habits. Small children in a supportive environment are totally spontaneous beings. They eat when they are hungry, fall asleep when they are tired, and express exactly what they feel. Therefore, their energy doesn't get blocked, and they are constantly renewed and revitalized by their own natural energy.

But because none of us have had even a close-to-perfect upbringing, very early we begin to develop habits that run counter to our natural energy. These habits are designed to help us survive in the neurotic world in which we find ourselves. We pick these patterns up from our families, friends, teachers, and the community in general.

As we follow the behavior we have observed in others, or as we attempt to follow the rules and regulations laid down by others, we move in ways that are counter to our own natural flow. We stop acting on what we know physically and emotionally; we no longer say and do what we really feel. We stop listening to the signals our body gives us about the food, rest, exercise, and nurturing it needs. It becomes too risky to follow our own energy, so we block that flow and gradually begin to experience less and less energy and vitality. As the energy flow diminishes, the body is not physically revitalized as quickly; thus, it begins to age and deteriorate. As we repeat chronic negative behaviors, our bodies begin to reflect these patterns, such as hunching over to express the inner pattern of making oneself small and powerless.

If you are willing to allow the energy of the universe to move through you by trusting and following your intuition, you will increase your sense of aliveness and your body will reflect this with increasing health, beauty, and vitality. Every time you don't trust yourself and don't follow your inner truth, you decrease your aliveness and your body will reflect this with a loss of vitality, numbness, pain, and eventually, physical disease.

Dis-ease is a message from our bodies, telling us that somewhere we are not following our true energy or supporting our feelings. The body gives us many such signals, starting with relatively subtle feelings of tiredness and discomfort. If we don't pay attention to these cues and make the appropriate changes, our bodies will give us stronger signals, including aches, pains, and minor illnesses. If we still don't change, a serious or fatal illness or accident may eventually occur. The stronger messages can always be avoided by paying attention to the subtler ones. But once a strong message has come, it is never too late to be healed, if that is what we truly desire. However, at this point, many beings do not choose the healing. They decide to leave their bodies and start over with a new one rather than trying to work their way through all the old patterns in this one.

If you are suffering from dis-ease, rest. Your body always wants rest and ease if it's sick. Then, when you've become quiet, ask your body what the message in your illness is. Your body will always tell you what you need in order to heal yourself.

One of my friends had been having severe pain on the right side of her face. Intuitively, she felt the pain would ease if she'd open her mouth and state more of what she wanted and more of what she knew. She did this and the pain eased some, but it still wasn't gone. One night, in a mood of surrender, she told the universe she was sick of the whole thing and she asked for an answer. Then, she let go of thinking about the problem and went to sleep. In her dreams that night her intuition told her to stop taking brewer's yeast. She immediately discounted the entire message as bizarre and continued to take yeast. Then a few days later, after continued prodding from her insides she stopped taking yeast. Two days later her face pain cleared up.

When you ask for a healing, you never know what your body is going to tell you. It may tell you to stop or start eating something, express some feelings to a friend, quit your job, or go see a doctor. The key is to ask and then listen for a response.

A client came to me who had been suffering from severe back pain for a year and a half. During the session I asked him to contact the pain and ask his body what it was trying to tell him. In doing this, he realized he had not yet grieved his mother's death or expressed the anger he felt toward his father. He was holding both anger and sadness in his back. Recognizing this relieved some of the pain. With more talking he was able to cry about his mother's death. Shortly after this he became willing to express his anger toward his father. He started by talking to me about it, as well as writing out all his feelings. His back pain went away. His back pain has continued to be a barometer of suppressed feelings: he knows now that if he's in pain he needs to "back himself up" by expressing some feelings.

Once we've developed a symptom, it can recur if the behavior recurs. Our bodies serve us by accurately informing us of any blocked energy. Below I've listed some common causes of pain or illness in the body. Each is accompanied with a healing affirmation.

Headache — two conflicting forces and feelings within; allow both sides to have a voice.

I am now willing to hear all my feelings.

Cold — the body needs a rest, a clearing out of the old; the body needs to get back into balance.

My body is in perfect harmony. I am now willing to have rest and ease in my life. I am now willing to let go of the old.

Complexion problems — held back male energy; a need to take action and/or express yourself more directly.

I go all out for what I feel and what I want. I express my feelings clearly and directly.

Skin rashes — wanting to break out and take action; ask yourself, "What am I itching to do?"

I act on what my intuitive tells me. I am willing to try new things. I do what I want.

Allergies — a lack of trust in the intuitive, repressed feelings; allergies related to watery eyes are indicative of suppressed sadness.

I trust and express my feelings. It's safe to feel and express my sadness and anger.

Back pain — a feeling that you have to support others, the world. A need to express and support your feelings; lower back pain is often suppressed sadness; upper back pain is often suppressed anger.

I support all my feelings. I take care of myself. I express and trust my feelings. I trust others to take proper care of themselves.

Menstrual cramps — not fully listening to and honoring

your female; a need to be quiet and go within.

I honor my female completely and act on what she tells me to do.

I relax, rest, and nurture myself regularly.

Vision problems — not wanting to look at certain things within yourself or in the world. Often there is a decision early in life not to look at what you are "seeing" intuitively because it is too painful; when the inner vision is shut down the external vision is impaired as well.

I am now willing to see everything in my life clearly.

Hearing problems — needing to shut out external voices and influences; needing to listen more to your inner voice.

I don't have to listen to anyone else. I listen to and trust my own inner voice.

Addiction

The more uncomfortable we are about trusting our natural energy, the more likely we are to use drugs such as coffee, cigarettes, alcohol, unwholesome food or too much food, marijuana, speed, cocaine, or whatever, to attempt to manipulate our energy and thereby deplete and degenerate the body further.

Most people are afraid of their energy and power. They're either afraid of being too much or too little; they're afraid of having too much energy or not enough. The truth is, if people would be willing to let go of using addictive substances they'd find their own energy. By doing this they'd tap their true source of power and creativity.

I see addiction as a means people use to pace (control) this power. Many powerful and creative people become addicts because they do not have an internal strength to support their energy. Without a trust in the universe, one's power and creativity can seem overwhelming. With substances, you can force your natural energy or you can dampen it, but either way, you're stopping the natural flow of the universe coming through.

You don't have to be a full-blown addict to realize you're using a substance to manipulate your energy. You may realize you're drinking three cups of coffee to energize yourself and then discover you're depleted later. (We are a nation addicted to coffee, which I consider a strong drug because it seriously impairs your ability to trust and follow your energy.)

If it's a physical or emotional problem, but you find you can't stop, the key is to notice what you're doing. Become aware of when and why you use coffee. Notice how it changes your energy. Eventually, you will find that you don't need to pay that price anymore.

Realize we all use some form of addiction to pace ourselves. The cure for this is to build a trust in ourselves and the universe. Become increasingly willing to experience your own power and strength. This is the true healing.

For those who have a drug or alcohol addiction, noticing that you're pacing yourself is not enough. It may make you more aware of your problem and how shut down you are, but generally the physical craving takes over any awareness. Because of this I encourage people to get help and support through a professional substance-abuse counselor, or a group such as Alcoholics Anonymous or Narcotics Anonymous, to abstain from their drug use. This gives the body a chance to heal and the spirit a chance to be heard. In drug addiction, the body and the drug are blocking any voice of the spirit.

Meditation

Sit or lie down, close your eyes, and take a few deep breaths. With each breath, feel your body letting go into a deeply relaxed place. Relax your mind and let your thoughts drift. Try not to attach yourself to any thoughts you're having. Feel yourself relax into a quiet place inside yourself.

This deep place is a source of nourishment and healing for you. Know that you can go here and find anything you need to know to heal yourself. If you've been having a problem with your health or you have a question you want to ask your intuitive about your body, take the opportunity to do this now.

Ask, "What do I need to do to heal myself now? What does my body need?" When you've asked, stay open to any answers that will come to you. An answer or an intuitive feeling may come right away, or it may come in the next couple of days. It may come to you in a direct solution or you may be guided to a person or place that will give you the answers you need.

Know that you can heal yourself and that limitless wisdom lies within you.

Say these affirmations silently or aloud, *"I am now healing myself. I am energized, alive, and filled with radiant health."*

Alternative Meditation

If there is a particular part of your body that is sick or in pain, try this meditation. Get comfortable, take a few deep breaths, completely relax your body and mind. Now put your consciousness into that place and ask it what it is feeling and what it is trying to tell you. Then be receptive to feeling and hearing what its message is to you. Ask that part of your body what you need to do to heal yourself. Pay attention to and follow whatever it tells you.

21

YOUR PERFECT BODY

Having a beautiful body starts with following the natural flow of your energy. Trust yourself. Sleep as much as you want. Stay in bed if you need more rest. Express yourself physically in ways that feel good. Eat what your body desires and follow your heart. If you're willing to trust your body, you'll learn what's best for you.

It sounds simple enough. The problem is that we've been taught to distrust our bodies and see them as needing to be controlled. Some religions even say that the spirit is good and the body is a weak, sinful tool of the devil. Although we have evolved to the point where these beliefs are not generally expressed openly, we still respond to our bodies with mistrust. As a culture, we're accustomed to ignoring our bodies and their needs. Our minds tell our bodies what to do. We decide that a nine-to-five workday, with three meals a day, is a "reasonable" way to live, then we expect our bodies to cooperate, even if this doesn't feel good. We've also developed, intellectually, theories for what's good for us and what isn't; what foods we should and shouldn't eat.

As children, we adopt parental and societal rules and habits about eating. Even if you want to eat something else for dinner or want to eat at a different time, you're most likely expected to conform to the norms of the system. The body can tell you one thing and society another. We learn to distrust ourselves at an early age. This distrust causes conflict and an imbalance in our system. It also sets up a process of rebellion in our bodies. We rebel, craving all kinds of things we would not normally desire if left to our natural flow. If we can't have what we really want, we react by going for the quickest available high. Our bodies react to this imbalance by gaining weight, becoming hyperkinetic, losing weight, developing food addictions and allergies. Then, to solve the above problems, we set up rigid expectations of our bodies, special diets and foods, specific eating schedules, restrictions on what we can eat. Our head starts to tell our body what to eat and when, depending on the particular diet we're on at the moment.

It's not just dieting. People have set ideas about exercise. Some people believe the only way they can keep their bodies at a perfect weight is to diet and exercise in a boring and driven way. Our society fosters this and makes money with this. We are constantly shown what a beautiful body should look like, and are sold ways of getting there. We are sold diets, miracle weight loss, health cures, and spa memberships. We are constantly beating our bodies into some new ideas we have for their health. The problem with the external pictures and "shoulds" we adapt from our society is that we are constantly dissatisfied with either the way we look or the way we feel.

The way to a beautiful, strong, healthy body is to start trusting yourself right now. Let go of the struggle and surrender to your body's needs. Your intuition will tell you what to eat. It may direct you to exercise vigorously (in which case you'll enjoy it), or it may tell you to slow down and rest. It may tell you to stay in bed all day, or it may tell you to get up early. There are no rules. Your body knows perfectly well what's good for it.

People generally react with fear when I suggest that they trust themselves and follow their body's needs. They're afraid they'll stay in bed all day, eat chocolates, and get fat.

These fears are based on distortions that have been caused by so many externally imposed rules. In reaction to these rules, you may run wild with old addictions and cravings for a few days, or even a few weeks, but if you'll be patient with your body you will find its natural flow. As your body learns that it can eat what it wants, when it wants, it will relax and begin to desire the foods that are good for it. Because of distortions, there may be a period where your intuition may tell you to stay away from certain foods, knowing that your body reacts in an allergic or addictive way. Trust yourself. You'll start to look and feel as your spirit is: alive and energized, beautiful and young. Your body will find its natural weight.

Assertion

The most important key to creating your perfect body is learning to assert yourself consistently in your life. I have found that overweight people usually have a pattern of doubting themselves, of being afraid to trust their feelings and act on them. They especially need to learn how to say "no" to others when they don't want to do something. Many overweight people I've worked with don't have strong personal boundaries; they try to please and take care of others and allow others to intrude on them and take advantage of them. Thus, they need to use extra weight as a buffer, a way of creating some distance from others.

Women, in particular, fear that by becoming slim, they will be too sexually attractive. They are afraid of attracting unwanted attention or energy, and don't trust themselves to know how to deal with it. Some people are afraid of feeling too sensitive and vulnerable and not knowing how to protect themselves. Others are afraid of being too "spaced out;" they use their weight to ground them. If you have these fears, you can diet forever and you will not lose weight or keep it off because you are unconsciously needing it.

That is why the process of assertion is so vital. When you learn to back your feelings with action, you create an internal strength and protection. You feel safe to move into new situations and attract attention and energy, knowing that you will be able to say "no" to anything that doesn't feel good to you. You know that you will be true to yourself and take good care of yourself. Your female aspect feels safe and supported, knowing that your inner male will back her up.

My experience has been that once people learn assertion, they are able to lose weight easily and naturally without any type of deprivation. The increased energy circulation in their bodies dissolves the blocked energy and the extra weight gradually melts away. They no longer need it for strength or protection, so they release it effortlessly. If any particular diet is needed, they feel intuitively what they need to be eating, and find it appropriate and enjoyable to do so.

Waiting = Excess Weight

If you're always waiting to be, do, or have what you want, your energy gets blocked and your body will reflect this in excess weight. By expressing yourself directly and doing what you want when you want (essentially backing yourself up), energy will move freely through your body and this circulation will dissolve your excess weight. The more you're willing to be yourself, the less you'll need to use food as a substitute nurturer; you'll be receiving the natural nurturing of the universe.

The key to backing yourself up is to take action on your feelings and intuition. I've seen people lose ten to fifteen pounds in a weekend workshop simply by doing something they've been afraid to do or by expressing some feeling they've suppressed. By continuing to do this you dissolve blocks and your weight balances out.

At first, the prospect of backing yourself up moment to moment can be frightening. We're not used to stating what we need and taking action to give it to ourselves. It takes a conscious effort for us to tune into how we feel and risk doing it. Once you start doing this though, it feels so good that you'll want to keep doing it. You'll lose weight, have more energy, and look more alive and beautiful. There really is no turning back. The alternative is numbness and death. Every time I follow my inner voice, I feel more life and energy. Every time I go against it I can feel a struggle in my body, a heaviness and tiredness occurs. If I continue to push myself past what my body wants, I become increasingly tired and lifeless. The choice is simple — life or death.

You may want to find a support group that can encourage you in your efforts to back yourself up. I have been working weekly with a group, exploring what it means to follow our energy and how to take action in support of our intuition. We have been learning how to express our feelings in the moment, as well as clear out emotional blocks that have been holding us back. Physically, the people in the group have changed. Several people in the group have lost weight. Our bodies cannot sustain excess weight when a great deal of energy is flowing through them.

One of my clients was about eighty pounds overweight when she started working with me. She had tried every conceivable weight-loss program in an effort to lose weight but had not successfully solved her problem. Then, as she learned how to trust and take care of herself, she began to heal herself by expressing her suppressed feelings. At the weekly group she got support for expressing herself directly, saying what she felt and what she wanted. She began to trust her body and started eating only what she really wanted. She grew physically and spiritually lighter, and after a few months she had lost about forty pounds.

At this point, she thought she'd gotten all she needed from the group and wanted to drop out, even though she was still carrying a lot of excess weight. However, I felt that she was still holding back a lot of feelings (as evidenced by her weight), so I encouraged her to express what she was still "waiting" to say. She shared that three members in the group had started to bother her and she didn't feel safe in sharing her feelings with them. They reminded her of people and painful events from her past. In them, she saw her husband, her son, and herself mirrored. They reminded her of things she had not said or done. They reminded her of self-betrayal. Because of this she felt angry every time she looked at them.

I encouraged her to work with me privately, and if she was willing, to come back to the group and express her feelings with group members. She needed to say what she had not said in the past. She did do this. Because of this she has begun to heal her old emotional wounds and forgive herself for the past. Her energy is no longer tied to the past, so it can move more freely through her body. She has continued to lose weight without dieting.

I've seen this happen over and over again. People can lose weight without depriving themselves. In fact, the opposite is true: they are feeding their inner needs and becoming more alive in the moment.

There is no secret to having a beautiful body. Simply trust yourself and learn to follow your natural needs. Tune in and honor your intuition. Keep the energy moving by backing yourself up moment by moment. Most importantly, love and nurture yourself now. You are beautiful.

Pacing with Food

People use food to pace their natural energy level. If you're a person who has too much nervous energy, you may use it to slow yourself down, or if you feel a need for a pick-up, you may use it for that. Both ultimately lead to a partial suppression of your true energy.

People are generally frightened of their power and energy, so they feel the need to pace the degree to which it flows through them. Some people use food to do this. Others use drugs, alcohol, relationships, work, or various other addictions. As people become more willing to experience and express their natural energy, the need to use food in this way will lessen.

Clearing Out Negative Beliefs

Most of us have negative beliefs about our bodies and the foods we eat. It's important to examine these beliefs and become more conscious of what we tell ourselves. When you find you are telling yourself something negative and untrue, you can take the opportunity to turn these thoughts into affirmations. (For affirmations, see number five of the following core belief exercise.) Some common negative beliefs are:

Everything that tastes good is bad for me.

If I smell delicious food I'll gain weight.

I can only eat a little bit, or I'll gain weight.

My body cannot be trusted.

My body needs to be controlled.

If I did what my body wanted I'd get fat and/or sick.

My body won't cooperate with me.

My body doesn't look the way it should.

I'll never weigh what I want.

I have to starve and struggle to have a perfect body.

Negative thoughts that you're consciously aware of do not cause the real problems, because they are already on the way to being cleared up. You simply need to become aware of them and turn them into affirmations to help combat the negativity that is going into your body. The negative beliefs we unconsciously hold onto cause the most negative experiences in our lives and prevent us from creating what we consciously want. For example, people can consciously be affirming thinness and still be holding onto the need to be fat. Underneath the desire to be thin is a negative belief that unconsciously motivates the body. The key is to discover this belief. Once a belief has been brought to light, it loses its power.

Some core negative beliefs and reasons that people hang

onto weight are: self-hate and self-punishment; psychic protection — feeling too vulnerable and using the weight to give you a layer of protection; fear of being too sexy and attractive to the opposite sex and having to deal with your own sexual feelings and those of others toward you; fear of being too beautiful, attracting too much attention, or being too powerful; feeling that weight equals strength; deep need for love; fear of expressing your creativity, literally holding energy in that creates weight on your body; fear of confronting space and emptiness — the void; fear of having your life and relationships succeed; fear of giving up your problems.

Some of these beliefs may fit for you and some of them may not. The key is to find what your core negative beliefs are. Below is a process I found to be valuable in doing this.

1. Take out a pen and paper. Make three columns on your paper, and in the first one write down all your beliefs about food and your body: any and all beliefs. Write down anything that comes to you even if it doesn't make sense or seem connected. Keep writing — the more the better. This gives your conscious, as well as your unconscious, thoughts a chance to be seen. A short example of this is: I'll never be my perfect weight. I hate my body. I wish I could change the way I look. I'm not sexy anymore. I'm destined to be fat like my mother. She ate ice cream all the time like I do. Ice cream is fattening. Food makes me fat. Every time I'm near food, I gain weight. I have no will power or strength. The only way to lose weight is to diet.

2. Examine these beliefs. In the second column, see if you can remember where you first got some of them. Did you pick them up from a parent, a sibling, a teacher, or a friend? You don't need to struggle to establish the origin of all your beliefs. Simply look at the ones that affect you most deeply and observe the connections and memories that surface. If additional memories surface later, you can also write them in the second column. An example of this might be relating the statement, "I'll never be my perfect weight" back to my mother. In column two next to this statement, I'd write, "I saw my mother was never able to lose weight," or

next to the statement "I'm not sexy anymore," I'd write, "I've heard everyone say, 'thin is beautiful'. " I've heard this from peers, my parents, and the media.

3. Look over your beliefs. Identify the ones that are not serving you now. Ask yourself what is keeping you from letting go of these beliefs. For example, a payoff for keeping the belief, "I'll never be my perfect weight" is safety. Perhaps it's too frightening to be fully seen.

4. When you've identified your negative beliefs, the next step is to let go of them. Realize they've served you for years. If you want, thank them for the service they've provided and let them know you are now willing to let go of them. An affirmation I've found helpful in letting go is: *I am now willing to let go.*

5. In the third column create an affirmation to counteract and correct each negative belief. Here are some guidelines:

a) The affirmation should be short, as simple as possible, and meaningful for you.

b) It should be in the present tense, as if it were already happening.

c) It should use your name. Example: I, Shakti, have a beautiful body.

d) The affirmation should directly relate to your negative belief and turn it into a positive, expansive one.

e) Your affirmation should feel exactly right for you. It may cause a strong emotional feeling. If it's not right, try changing it until it is. Then:

f) Say your affirmation silently to yourself in meditation, picturing everything working out perfectly as you want it.

g) If you have a partner, have your partner say your affirmation to you using your name and looking deeply into your eyes.

h) After he or she says it, you say...Yes, that's true.

i) Write your affirmation ten or twenty times a day. If negative thoughts arise, write them on the back of the paper, then keep writing the affirmation on the front until it feels clear. Examples: *I am now my perfect weight. I love and accept my body. My body is perfect the way it is. I am beautiful and sexy. I am a beautiful, powerful woman (or man). I have now let go of the past. I am free to be myself. It is safe for me to eat food. Food nourishes and energizes me. Every calorie I eat is burned into pure energy. I love food. Food loves me. I eat whatever I want, whenever I want, and always stay my perfect weight. As I trust and act on my feelings, it's safe to be slim and beautiful.*

This process will help you examine your beliefs and bring to consciousness hidden beliefs. You can use this process any time to clear away negatives that stand in the way of your having a beautiful, strong, healthy body. Once you clear away these negatives, you will begin to see your body as beautiful, and any food you eat as nourishing.

Appreciating Your Body

Appreciate the beauty in your body and in yourself, today. Focus on what you do like about yourself. The more willing you are to do this, the easier it will become. Your body will respond to this appreciation and grow increasingly beautiful.

It's become a habit to see what needs to be changed about ourselves. We're waiting for perfection before we'll love ourselves completely. You can change these self-critical tapes by looking at what you like about yourself and giving yourself positive feedback.

If you have trouble appreciating yourself, start by looking at others who have the same qualities you have and admire them.

A friend of mine who was twenty pounds overweight was continually putting herself down for the way she looked. She felt the only way she could possibly like herself would be if she were thin. Because she could not see her own beauty, she thought she'd start by looking at women who were overweight, like herself, and learn to appreciate them. She started to see how beautiful other "overweight" women were and noticed how sensual and alive they looked. She started complimenting others on their looks. By doing this, she could look at her own body in a new way. She began to accept and appreciate herself. Her body responded to this approval with more life and energy. She gradually lost the extra pounds and has continued to appreciate her body as it is.

Ritual for Loving Your Body

Stand naked in front of a full-length mirror. Send positive thoughts to every part of your body. Even if you don't like your body or don't approve of certain parts of your body, look for something of beauty in every part of yourself. Realize that your body has been serving you for years. Thank your body for its service. Realize it has only been following your directions.

For example, you might say to yourself, "You have beautiful, thick, shiny hair." Then look in the mirror at your hair and see its beauty, its shine and glow. Even if it isn't shining and glowing as much as you like — continue to see it and appreciate yourself as you are, saying, "I love the way you look. You have beautiful hands. You have strong healthy legs. You have clear skin. You have shining eyes."

Run through each part of your body in this way and really send it love and appreciation. Find a way to appreciate every part of yourself. And thank your body for being with you for however many years, following your desires and serving you. It has been doing for you what you have asked of it. If you like, you can play music that you love, and use candles or flowers while performing this ritual. Do this ritual once or twice a day for at least a week. This ritual shows your body how much you appreciate and respect it. Your body has been criticized, judged, and rejected by you for years. It will respond quickly to love and energy. You will feel lighter and more energized. You will start looking more beautiful. The lines in your face will relax. You will start to glow with strength and health. You will be amazed at the results of loving your body.

Visualization Exercises

In *Creative Visualization* I recommended visualization techniques to beautify our bodies. I find these tools very helpful; my clients and readers have achieved wonderful results with them. Because of this, I want to describe two techniques you can use.

1. Whenever you think of your body, see it the way you want it to be. Know that your body is perfect and affirm this. Take a few minutes during the day to close your eyes and visualize your body at the weight, size, and strength you desire. See your body as energized and powerful. See and feel energy moving through you.

2. Use a picture from a magazine to help you visualize your perfect body. Choose a picture of a body that looks the way you would look in great shape, cut it out, and paste it on the wall. Place it where you'll look at it daily. See the picture as your body. You can even paste a picture of your face on the picture so it's your face with your perfect body.

Meditation

Sit or lie down in a comfortable position. Take a few deep breaths and relax your body. With each exhalation let go of what you don't want or need; see any tension, frustration, or tiredness leave your body. As you inhale, take in everything you want or desire: relaxation, serenity, strength, prosperity, and joy.

From this relaxed, rejuvenated place see your body before you. Imagine your body looking exactly the way you want it to be. Observe it in as much detail as possible. You are now your perfect weight, size, and shape. Your body is energized, strong, and powerful. When you look at your face and body, you see your beauty. You look exactly the way you want to look. You feel the way you want to feel.

You can feel what it is like to have a body that supports your spirit. Your spirit says "do this" and your body, in all its perfection, is there to match your inner wisdom.

You are beauty, strength, and energy.

Exercise

1. List all the ways you see yourself waiting (weighting). What are you waiting to say, do, have, or become?

2. Next to each item on your list, write how you can take action. What can you do to change the waiting into saying, doing, or having what you want now?

22

LIFE AND DEATH

Life is the choice to follow the flow of energy within us. Death is the choice to block or go against this life energy. We are faced with this life-or-death choice every moment of our lives.

Each time that we choose to trust and follow our intuition, our channel opens more, and more of the life force flows through. The cells of our body actually receive more energy and are renewed and revitalized faster. Physically, emotionally, and mentally we feel more alive, and more of our spiritual light can shine through. Our body stays young, healthy, and beautiful, and radiates vitality.

When we choose not to follow our intuitive promptings, we close off our channel and our cells receive less energy. The body begins to deteriorate faster. When we aren't following the flow of energy, life becomes a struggle. Stress and strain take their toll on the physical form and we can see the struggle in our faces and bodies. Lines of worry form and the body begins to bend with the effort it is making. If we continue to choose to close off the energy moment after moment, day after day, year after year, eventually the body will age, deteriorate, and die. If we change our pattern and begin to trust ourselves more, the body will begin to be renewed.

A part of all of us wants life, wants to make the commitment to live, and is willing to trust our intuition and follow it from moment to moment. There's also a part of us that doesn't trust ourselves: "I can't do this, it's too much, too intense, I don't want to surrender." When we go against ourselves we experience only effort and struggle; when we surrender to life we feel passion, aliveness, and flow.

Any time somebody dies they are unconsciously choosing to leave this physical body. It may appear that they're victims of a disaster or a deadly disease, but they are in charge of their own journey. Their spirit knows what it's doing, even if the body denies this. When you start to believe this, you will also begin to feel it telepathically. If you're close to someone who dies you can get a sense of them making a choice.

Either people come in to accomplish a specific purpose and having accomplished it, they leave, or, failing to accomplish it, they decide to take it on again in this realm or the next. Some beings feel they've gotten stuck and it's not working. They feel like they're not learning fast enough. "This life started with too many negative odds against me. I don't want to deal with this anymore. I'd rather start over."

By consciously making a choice for life, you influence the choice of those around you. Moment by moment, if you choose to trust your intuition and act on it, you're choosing aliveness rather than death and you're increasing the aliveness that radiates from you. Anybody who is connected with you will feel this and it will strengthen the choice they make to live.

The more we choose to live in the light, the healthier and more vital our bodies will become. By living as channels for the universe, I believe that we will retard or perhaps even stop the aging process as we know it. I think it's possible to become more energetic, alive, and beautiful as we get older, rather than less so. We will no longer leave our bodies unconsciously, through accident or illness. We will stay in the physical body as long as we desire, and will make the conscious choice to leave at whatever time we desire to do something else. Death, if and when we choose it, will not be a tragedy but a conscious transition into another realm.

Meditation

Sit or lie down in a comfortable position. Close your eyes. Take several deep breaths and relax your body. With each breath, let go of everything in the way of your being with yourself. Slowly relax into that core place within.

Recall a recent situation where you chose not to follow your energy; where you did not do what you wanted to do. Replay this scene in your mind. See yourself going against what you know is true for you. Then, notice how you felt. Look at your body and notice how you looked and felt physically, emotionally, and spiritually.

Now, go back to that same situation and see yourself doing exactly what you want; see yourself choosing to follow the energy. Then, notice how your body feels, notice how you look and feel about yourself. Spend a few minutes feeling what it's like to trust yourself and act on what you want.

Exercise

This exercise will help you become conscious of when you choose life or death.

Keep a journal of some of the decisions you made during the day. Notice when you did what you wanted and when you chose not to. (For example, notice if you chose to go to a party when you really wanted to stay home.) Then, write how you felt about the choices you made. Notice how you felt physically and emotionally.

As you become more aware of when you follow your energy, when you go against it, and the results of this, you'll increasingly choose life and aliveness in each moment.

23

TRANSFORMING OUR WORLD

Transformation begins on an individual level and moves out into the world. The more I'm learning to trust my intuition and act on it, and the more I'm willing to experience and accept all my feelings, the more the energy of the universe can move through me. As it comes through, it heals and transforms me and everyone and everything around me.

This is true for each one of us. The more you are willing to trust and be yourself, the more you will live in the light. Everyone around you will benefit from your energy and begin to trust and be more themselves. In turn, they become powerful channels for everyone in their sphere of influence. And so transformation spreads rapidly throughout the world.

You may have heard of the hundredth-monkey syndrome. In Japan, in 1952, scientists were studying the behavior of wild monkeys. The principle food of these monkeys was sweet potatoes. One day they noticed one monkey do something they had never seen before — she washed her potato before she ate it. She repeated this behavior on subsequent days, and soon they noticed several other monkeys were washing their potatoes before eating them. More and more monkeys began to do this. Then, in 1958, after all the monkeys on the island were exhibiting this new behavior, scientists on nearby islands began to report that monkeys on their islands were *also* beginning to wash their potatoes. There was no physical connection between the islands, and no one had transported any monkeys from one island to another.

This study illustrates something of overwhelmingly powerful importance for the human race and for our planet. Washing potatoes was a new level of consciousness for these monkeys, and when enough of them had accepted it, it was apparently transferred to the monkeys on surrounding islands without any physical contact or direct communication.

I believe that this is how evolution of consciousness takes place. Every individual's consciousness is connected to, and is a part of, the mass consciousness. When a small but significant number of individuals have moved into a new level of awareness and significantly changed their behavior, that change is felt in the entire mass consciousness. Every other individual is then moved in the direction of that change. And the whole thing may have started with one individual who first made the leap.

So often we look at the world around us and feel terribly helpless to effect any significant positive change. The world seems so big, and in such a mess, and we feel so small and powerless. The hundredth-monkey story helps us to see how powerful one individual or a few individuals can be in transforming the world.

Because the world truly is our mirror, as we change, it must change. You can see this easily in your personal life. As you develop the habit of trusting and taking care of yourself, you will gradually release your old patterns. Soon, you notice that your friends, family, and business associates all seem to be feeling and acting differently as well. People you encounter seem to be dealing with less serious problems (or if their problems are serious, they are more quickly healed) and more creative issues. Things that previously frightened and upset you seem to have lost their emotional "charge." Even the serious problems of the world, while they still concern you, may not seem quite as scary as before.

The reason for this shift is that you are beginning to *feel* the power of the universe inside of you. *To the degree that you experience the presence of the universe in your own body, you don't feel afraid.* Of course, every time you open up to more power, more of the old fear gets flushed to the surface and released, so in the healing process you will experience alternating states of power and fear. Gradually, however, a solid base of trust will be established within you. Others will feel this and in it will find the support to open up to more of their own power and truth. The people and things around you reflect you in increasingly positive ways. The more light you allow within you, the brighter the world you live in will be.

Creating the Change

One idea I frequently encounter, especially in groups of spiritually oriented people, is that all we have to do to change the world is think more positively about it and visualize the change we desire. Visualization and affirmation are powerful tools. I use them often and strongly recommend them as part of this process (after all, I wrote *Creative Visualization* and I deeply believe in the effectiveness of the techniques it describes). However, there is another part of the process which is frequently ignored, yet it is just as important.

If the world is our mirror, then whatever we see out there in some way reflects what is in us. We must take responsibility for it and be willing to transform it *within ourselves* if we want to see it change on the outside. So when we look at the world and see poverty, pain, violence, and chaos we must be willing to say to ourselves, "What is the poverty, pain, violence, and chaos within me that this is reflecting? I know that my world is my mirror and, in a sense, my creation. If the things I see weren't in me, they couldn't exist in my world."

The trick here is not to take on *blame* or *guilt* for the

world's problems. None of us is truly responsible for other people's lives; we are all co-creating this world together. And we are all doing the best we know how. We are here to learn, and we must learn from what is not perfect rather than blame ourselves for it. We need to adopt a positive attitude of responsibility, saying "I am willing to learn to trust and follow my own inner truth, knowing that as I do, I will release the pain and fear within me and thus heal the pain and fear in the world."

Such a vow is very powerful and to follow through on it is no easy task. To do so, we must be willing to move through the deepest layers of our consciousness and recognize not only our own personal fears, but also the centuries-old negative beliefs of humanity which exist in our bodies. To move through these layers we need to be willing to recognize and experience all the fears, knowing that the light is healing and dissolving them.

When people ask me what they can do about the problems of the world, I usually suggest that they start by recognizing and affirming that as they sincerely do their own inner work, the world is being transformed. I tell them to look at the social problems that frighten or disturb them and determine what fear or pain it touches within them and how it reflects their personal situation.

For example, if they are disturbed by reports of violence, I ask them to look at how violence has played a part in their lives. Has someone been violent toward them in their early life? Have they had violent thoughts and feelings? Have they repressed or disassociated from their own violent feelings? In what way have they done violence to themselves internally (harshly criticizing themselves, and so on)?

It has been my experience, incidentally, that many of us need help, in the form of supportive therapy or counseling, to deal with deep levels of emotional healing. For some people there's a certain reluctance to seek such help, perhaps because they fear it's an indication of sickness or craziness. Personally, I have sought therapy of various types at many times in my life and it has helped me greatly, as long as I trusted my own intuition about who to work with, when to stop, and so on.

If you are deeply touched by the poverty in which much of the world's population is currently living, you may feel moved to make some external gesture to help alleviate someone's pain (i.e., contribute some money, do some social or political work). At the same time, look within yourself to see in what way you believe in or support poverty or scarcity in your own life. This may not be a question of money — you may be living in some form of emotional or spiritual poverty while surrounded by material luxury. Or you may be at peace spiritually and emotionally but holding onto a belief that money is evil; thus, keeping yourself in a state of financial poverty.

Poverty on both a personal and worldwide level is supported by our mass consciousness belief in scarcity. We deeply fear that there is *not enough to go around* of whatever we need — money, food, love, energy, appreciation. So we create a world that supports that belief. There have been studies which show that there is plenty of food produced in this world to amply feed everyone. Yet, because of our underlying belief in poverty, we allow food to be thrown away in one place while millions are starving to death elsewhere.

If you are concerned by environmental issues, consider this point of view. Mother nature is symbolic of the nurturing, feminine aspect of ourselves. Disrespect and lack of harmony with nature are only possible in a society of individuals who disrespect and disregard their own feminine, intuitive nature. If you are attuned to your inner guidance, there is no way you can become severely out of balance with your natural environment.

Just as our bodies are the manifestation of our consciousness in physical form, the Earth is the manifestation of our mass consciousness. In a sense, Earth is our collective "body." The way we treat her mirrors the way we treat our own bodies.

The lack of respect and attunement to our bodies is demonstrated on a global level by the way we treat our Earth. As we learn to love and trust our bodies; to listen to their signals; to give them the food, rest, and nurturing they need; to stop polluting them with drugs and unwholesome food; and to stop trying to control them with our ideas of what's right, I don't believe we will be able to continue to mistreat our "Earth body."

We must be willing to recognize and heal any form of violence, poverty, and imbalance within ourselves as individuals if we hope to eradicate these problems from our world. Healing does not take place on a personal or planetary level as long as we hide or deny our feelings. All feelings, beliefs, and emotional patterns must be brought to the light of consciousness in order to be dissolved. When the light shines into the darkness, the darkness disappears.

World Healing

People frequently talk about what terrible shape the world is in. In many ways, things seem to be going from bad to worse, and this can be very frightening.

It has helped me considerably to recognize that the world is currently going through a major healing crisis, very similar in form to what individuals are experiencing.

When we as individuals begin to wake up to the light, we also begin to become aware of the darkness in which we have been living. The patterns of living which formerly seemed "normal" begin to look crazier and crazier from the perspective of our newly acquired sanity. Fears and distortions which have been denied and ignored because they were too painful to look at begin to come into our consciousness in order to be released. Problems that were "swept under the rug" come forth to be solved.

This is what I see happening on a worldwide level today. If we recognize the seeming chaos and pain in the world as a giant manifestation of our individual healing process, we can see that it's a very positive step. Rather than feeling like victims, we can recognize the power of the universe at work. We appreciate ourselves as the channels through which the world's healing is being manifested. For the time being, the more light we are living in, the more darkness we are seeing. The more we accept both these polarities within ourselves, the faster the world can be healed.

Social and Political Action

Some who have heard these ideas become angry because they believe I am endorsing a narcissistic self-absorption that denies the problems of the world and negates the necessity of social and political action. Upon further discussion I am usually (though not always!) able to make them understand that this is not the case. Being willing to deal internally and individually with the original source of the problem is simply the most practical and powerful way to effect real change. It does not deny the necessity for external action on a large scale.

The issue for me is the source and motivation for that action. I find that people are frequently moved by their own "good ideas" more than by the universe within them. Often they are motivated by their feelings of pain, fear, and guilt into wanting to "do something to make it better." This is the ego, coming from a position of helplessness and fear, struggling vainly to do something to eradicate these feelings. Unfortunately, this approach only perpetuates the problems it is trying to solve.

The underlying cause of world problems is the pain, fear, and ignorance we experience from being disconnected from the power of the universe. If we continue to project our problems outside of ourselves and fail to recognize the inner power we actually have, I believe we will support the very evils we are fighting.

On the other hand, if we are willing to take responsibility for our fears and deal with them, we will clear the way for being able to hear the voice of the universe within us. If it tells us to take action, we can be sure the action will be powerful and truly effective.

For example, a woman friend of mine became very active in the nuclear disarmament movement. When she talked about the issue and her work, it was obvious that she was feeling absolutely terrified of the possibility of nuclear war. This is actually a reasonable reaction, given the insanity of the nuclear race. The problem as I saw it was that she was not recognizing her own terror and the issues of powerlessness and death that she was struggling with internally. So her actions and words had a frantic quality — almost like a drowning person clutching vainly for something to hold onto.

Gradually, over several years, I saw her work through this phase of her process. I believe that she reached a deeper level of trust in the universe. She continued her anti-nuclear activity because it was something she deeply believed in and found great satisfaction in doing, but the energy was quite different. There was power and strength in her involvement which I'm certain has made her more effective in her work.

The same principles hold true in the social and political arena as in every other area of life: if you are doing what you think you "should" do, if you are motivated primarily by fear and guilt, then no matter how good your actions, you are probably not being as effective as you'd like to be, and you may even be hindering more than you are helping.

On the other hand, if you *are* trusting your intuition and following your heart — going where your energy takes you and doing what you really want to do — you will see that *everything* you do has a positive effect in changing the world. You will be able to recognize the transformational nature of your actions. For many, this will include direct social and political action, and you'll be doing it because you love it! People around you will also be affected by your energy and vitality even more than they are affected by your words and actions.

For now, my inner guidance has told me that living my life as I am doing — writing books, leading workshops, exploring my creativity, being myself — is what I personally need to be doing to effect maximum change in my life and the world. I've also gotten a strong feeling that I may someday be actively involved in politics (as I was earlier in my life) — perhaps even occupying a political office of some sort! I know that if that's what I'm meant to do, I'll find it an exciting adventure. I'm curious to see what the universe has in store for me.

The Media

I was once informed by my inner guidance that television would be the savior of the world! I resisted this idea because I am not a TV buff. However, I did recognize that, as mindless and idiotic as much television programming may appear at this time, television is obviously an extraordinarily powerful tool for reaching millions of people instantaneously. I think it is no accident that it has been developed at this time and will probably soon be found in almost every home in the world.

Although currently controlled mainly by people whose consciousness is thoroughly embedded in the old world, there are even now occasional flashes of the light. It is only a matter of time until new-world consciousness begins to penetrate television programming in a regular and significant way.

Television is undoubtedly a major educational tool. With the universe in charge, it can literally become a "channel." It provides a "network" for instantaneously reaching a majority of the world population with positive new ideas.

Can you imagine housewives watching a soap opera in which people go through all the usual human dramas, but instead of the typical doom and despair, there is an attitude of learning and growing through life's changes? It could be highly entertaining, with all the usual sex and romance, birth and death, drugs and disease, marriage and divorce, but the characters could be seen to use their trials and tribulations in a positive way to evolve in consciousness, just as we are learning to do. Once the housewives get it, it's certain that children and husbands will get it in short order!

It's obvious that the power of the media — radio, newspapers, magazines, and books, as well as television — is unmatched in its potential for fast positive change once our mass consciousness is ready for that shift.

A Five-step Process for Personal and Planetary Healing

1. Affirm to yourself: *The power of the universe is healing and transforming me. As I am healed and transformed, the whole world is healed and transformed.*

2. Notice the social, political, and environmental issues around you. Pay particular attention to those that trigger the most emotional reaction in you. Ask to see how they may reflect your personal issues, fears, beliefs, and patterns. You may not immediately see any connection, but stay open to receiving this information through your intuitive channel.

3. Ask for the light of the universe to release and heal all the darkness of ignorance, fear, and limitation within you and in the world. Be open to any inner guidance you may receive to seek support in your healing process through a counselor or therapist, friends, a workshop or group, or any other form.

4. Regularly visualize your life and the world as you would like them to be (see the meditation at the end of this chapter).

5. Ask your inner guidance to let you know clearly if there is any specific action you need to take toward your own or the world's healing. Then continue to trust and follow your intuition, knowing that you will be led to do whatever is necessary.

Basic Negative Belief Process

This process looks at the underlying negative belief(s) in any given situation in your life. Once you're willing to look at them, you can begin to dissolve and transform them with affirmations.

You can do this process either alone or with a partner. If doing it alone, write the answers to the questions. If you're doing it with a partner, you'll state your answers to your partner. One person will answer all the questions while the other listens and then you'll switch.

1. Begin by closing your eyes. Take a deep breath, and as you exhale, relax your body. Take another deep breath, and as you exhale, relax your mind. Take another deep breath, and as you exhale, move into a very deep, quiet place inside of you. Become aware that you are the co-creator with the universe. You can choose what you believe, what you create, and what you experience in your life. You can choose to become conscious and aware of the old beliefs and attitudes that are limiting you. Then, you can release them and adopt beliefs and attitudes that will support you in expressing more of your true self.

2. Pick a particular issue or area of your life that you want to work on. This could be a problem you're having or something you feel might be holding you back in terms of your own beliefs and fears. Open your eyes and take about two minutes to describe to your partner (or write down) what the particular issue is that you want to work on.

3. Describe the different thoughts in your mind about this issue. What tapes play in your mind? For example, what are all the pros and cons of this particular situation? What are the worries, fears, and programming you have about it? What goes through your mind?

4. When you think about this issue of your life, what do you feel emotionally? For example: I feel sad, angry, excited, frustrated, or happy.

5. When you become aware of the emotional feelings you have about this issue, what kind of feelings do you notice in your body? Do you notice any place that's tight or tense? Do you notice any place where there's jittery energy, butterflies, or nervousness? What do you feel in your physical body in relation to these emotional feelings?

6. Describe the worst thing that could happen if your greatest fear came true. What would that be? Then, if your worst fear came true, what would be the worst thing that

could happen after that? And then, what would be the worst that could happen after that, the worst of all worsts?

Close your eyes and be with your worst fear. Give yourself a chance to experience what that is, and be in the same space with your worst fear; rather than running away from it, feel it. Does it have a lot of power over you? Is it something that you can almost laugh at or does it hold some real fear for you?

Now, ask the universe for help. Take this fear and give it over to the universe, give it over to your higher self. Ask for help, resolution, strength, wisdom, or whatever you need in order to release it. Take a deep breath. As you exhale, feel yourself letting go. When you feel ready, open your eyes and describe what you just experienced.

7. Now, going in the opposite direction: what is the best that could possibly happen? What is it that you really want? What would be your ideal scene in this situation? Describe it exactly the way you want it. Then, close your eyes and relax. Picture and imagine having it just the way you want. Picture it, feel it, experience it as if it were already the way you want it to be. What does it feel like? Try it on for size. Then, put your ideal scene in a beautiful pink bubble. Once you've done that see yourself tossing it in the air. You're now releasing your pink bubble with your ideal scene in it over to the universe. It is now free to attract to it what it needs for its manifestation.

8. When you open your eyes, ask yourself what negative belief or fear has kept you from creating what you want. What's your most negative thought or greatest fear about this particular area of your life? For example, "I can't have what I want," "I'm worthless," or "Nobody loves me." Once you've determined what your negative beliefs are, write them down.

9. You can now turn your negative beliefs into affirmations. See page 170 of the Perfect Body chapter for directions on writing affirmations. Write or say your affirmation to yourself regularly until it becomes real for you.

Meditation

Sit or lie down in a comfortable position. Take a few deep breaths and relax your body. Feel yourself dropping into a deep, quiet place within. Feel yourself contacting that place of power and creativity, your source of strength.

From this source of strength, project yourself into the future, a month, six months, a few years or more, and in this projection see yourself exactly the way you want to be. You are the creator of your universe and your life is as you've designed it.

Start by noticing how you feel spiritually and emotionally. Feel the strength and power within you. You trust your intuition and act on your inner guidance. Because of this miracles unfold around you.

See your body. How do you look and feel physically? You now have a body that matches your spirit — strong, courageous, beautiful, filled with life and energy. Experience what that feels like.

How do you take care of your body? What do you eat and how do you nurture yourself?

Notice how you dress. See yourself dressed exactly the way you want to be dressed. You wear your clothes beautifully. When you open your closets and drawers, you have just the clothes you want there.

What is your home like? See yourself living exactly where you want to be. You have created your environment as you want it. See yourself there. Feel what it's like to live in a way that suits you perfectly. Perhaps you have several homes in different parts of the country or throughout the world. Be in all of them.

You have found the perfect job and creative outlet. You receive an abundance of money for doing what you most love. See yourself expressing yourself in a way that brings you joy.

Next, look at the people in your life. You now have relationships that are alive, passionate, and creative. People love and nurture you. If you have a special lover or lovers in your life, experience the joy and intimacy this brings you.

Then, from this place of creativity and joy look out into the world. Picture the world as a mirror of the transformation that has taken place within you. Sense the healing of the planet. Imagine the world transformed to be exactly the way you would like it to be.

When you've done this, affirm: *"This, or something better, is now manifesting for the highest good of all concerned."*

24

A VISION

From the window of my apartment I look across the San Francisco Bay at the beautiful city of San Francisco. The light on the water and on the city skyline is constantly changing. Sometimes it is cloudy and misty, sometimes bright and shining, but it always looks mystical. Perhaps this view inspired an image that I frequently have:

I see an ancient city, gray and decaying. It is literally disintegrating, the old structures crumbling into piles of rubble. But it is being pushed aside, because in its place a beautiful new city is arising. This new city is magical — it seems to shimmer delicately with every color in the universe. I know that it is being built inside of us. It is created from the light.

SHAKTI CENTER

For many years now my dream has been to create a center/school for those making the transition from the old world into the new world to have a totally supportive environment in which to learn, grow, and create. This dream is becoming a reality now. I have created Shakti Center, a workshop facility in Marin County, California (near San Francisco).

Shakti Center offers classes, workshops, ongoing support groups, a teacher training program, and a creative arts program. We also sponsor special retreats and intensives in Hawaii and other locations, as well as weekend workshops all over the country led by myself and/or Laurel King.

For information write or call:

Shakti Center
P.O. Box 377
Mill Valley, California 94942
(415) 927-2277

OTHER BOOKS AND TAPES FROM WHATEVER PUBLISHING

Books

Creative Visualization by Shakti Gawain. This clear and practical guide contains easy-to-use techniques to: feel more relaxed and peaceful, increase your vitality and improve your health, develop your creative talents, create more fulfillment in relationships, reach your career goals, dissolve negative habit patterns, increase your prosperity, and much, much more.

The Creative Visualization Workbook by Shakti Gawain. This companion volume to *Creative Visualization* provides a convenient format in which to write down and practice many creative visualization techniques. The Workbook is designed to be fun; in addition to the exercises, there are pages on which to record your dreams, creative ideas, inspiring quotes, and more.

Friends and Lovers—How to Create the Relationships You Want by Marc Allen. An upbeat, knowledgeable, and contemporary guide to living and working with people. Contains a six-step process that is *guaranteed to settle arguments* at home or at work.

Work With Passion—How To Do What You Love For A Living by Nancy Anderson. This highly effective guide will help you master the secrets of finding your niche in life — doing what you love to do and getting paid well for it. *Work With Passion* is filled with inspiring stories of ordinary people who have achieved extraordinary results by following the nine-step program of the author, developed during her years as a highly successful career consultant. This is *the* career book of the 1980's!

Tantra for the West—A Guide to Personal Freedom by Marc Allen. Practical and informative, *Tantra for the West* presents proven principles and techniques to improve the quality of your life in all areas: relationships, sex, work, money, being alone, creativity, food and drink, meditation and yoga, aging and healing, politics, enlightenment and freedom. "A clear and timely book..."—Marilyn Ferguson.

Cassettes

Living in the Light. In this exciting hour-long interview, Shakti Gawain reveals the main principles and techniques from her book of the same title, showing us how to connect with our intuition and become a creative channel for personal and planetary transformation.

Creative Visualization. Shakti Gawain guides you through some of the most powerful and effective meditations and techniques from her book. An inspirational cassette.

The Creative Visualization Workshop. This three-hour, four-cassette series is taped from one of Shakti Gawain's most dynamic day-long seminars. She alternates her clear insights with a number of exercises and meditations on topics which include creative visualization, trusting yourself, moving through fear, male and female energy, and more.

Anybody Can Write—A Playful Approach. Jean Bryant, writing teacher extraordinaire, guides you in her inspiring yet humorous manner to discover the writer within you. Use the powers of your right brain to create your work, and your left brain to critique it. Learn to trust yourself and your unique fund of experience, as you express your ideas naturally and authentically.

Stress Reduction and Creative Meditations. Marc Allen guides you through a deeply relaxing, stress-reducing experience on the first side. Side Two contains effective, creative meditations for health, abundance, and fulfilling relationships. Soothing background music by Jon Bernoff.

ORDERING INFORMATION

We invite you to send for a free copy of our full-color catalogue so that you can see our complete selection of books and cassettes.

Whatever Publishing, Inc.
P.O. Box 13257, Northgate Station
San Rafael, CA 94913
(415) 472-2100

ORDER TOLL FREE WITH YOUR VISA/MC
(800) 227-3900
(800) 632-2122 in California

"A clear and practical guide."

— Irving Oyle, M.D.
Author of *The New American Medicine Show*

"Inspiring and uplifting."

— Bay Area Lifestyle

"An open mind and heart, plus the desire to greatly enrich one's life, are all you need to bring to this book — then prepare yourself for some rather startling and truly marvelous results."

— New Age Magazine

"Shakti Gawain provides us with the means to be our own instruments in dramatically and positively changing our lives."

— Kay Kaiser Cook, Mothering

"You have helped me obtain a new lease on life."

— WF, Woodland Hills, Calif.

"I was very excited to find a source which put so much information together in such a clear fashion. I'm using many of the techniques you suggest in my own work with patients who are chronically ill."

— LD, San Anselmo, Calif.

"I have been using your book with delinquent kids and I have seen miracles!"

— JS, Ware, Mass.

"Great! Thanks for your contribution to healing ourselves and our planet."

— JB, Yellow Springs, Ohio

Creative Visualization

Shakti Gawain

Whatever Publishing, Inc.
San Rafael, California

Published by Whatever Publishing, Inc.
58 Paul Drive, San Rafael, CA 94903

Cover design by Kathleen Vande Kieft
Artwork by Rainbow Canyon
Back cover photo by Russ Fischella

87 88 89 90 20 19 18

Library of Congress Cataloging in Publication Data
Gawain, Shakti, 1948-
Creative Visualization

Bibliography: p. 154
1. Visualization 2. Success I. Title
BF367.G34 158'.1 79-13760
ISBN 0-931432-02-2

This book is dedicated
to
you

Acknowledgements

Thank you Mark Allen and Dean Campbell for your love and support in writing this book and in all other ways. Thank you Rainbow Canyon for your beautiful artwork and your beautiful friendship. And special thanks to my mother, Elizabeth, for all your love, wisdom, and encouragement.

I'd also like to thank all the incredible teachers who have contributed so much to my life and happiness, as well as to the understanding that has been channeled into this book. Some of you I have known as gurus, some as personal friends and lovers, and others of you have come to me in the form of books. To all of you I send my love and deep appreciation.

Last but not least I'd like to acknowledge and thank my own inner guide who keeps showing me the way . . . reminding me how beautiful life really is . . . and who actually is responsible for writing this book.

Contents

A Letter to my Readers

Dear Friends,

I decided to write this book because it seemed like the best way I could think of to share with others the many wonderful things I have learned which have so deepened and expanded my experience and enjoyment of life.

I do not consider myself by any means an expert on the art of creative visualization. I am a student of the subject, and the more I study and use creative visualization myself, the more I discover how vast and deep is its potential . . . truly it is as infinitely creative as your own imagination.

This book is meant as an introduction and workbook for learning and using creative visualization. Very little of the material is original to me; it is a synthesis of the most practical and useful ideas and techniques that I've learned in my personal study.

My sources are many. I've included at the end a list of books, tapes, records, and courses which have been most important to me, and which I think you will find interesting and helpful.

One note: this book contains many different techniques. You will probably find that it works best not to try to absorb them all at once, but more gradually. I suggest that you read the book slowly, trying some of the exercises as you go along, and giving yourself the chance to absorb them deeply. Or you might want to read it once through, then re-read more slowly.

Please feel free to write me with your comments and suggestions (c/o Whatever Publishing). Although I may not be able to reply personally to all your communications, I do very much value your feedback.

This book is my gift to you in love ... may it be a blessing to you ... may it help you to bring more and more joy, satisfaction, and beauty into your life ... may it nurture the light that is shining within you ...

Enjoy!

Love,

Shakti

Part One

Basics of Creative Visualization

Every moment of your life is infinitely creative
and the universe is endlessly bountiful.
Just put forth a clear enough request,
and everything your heart desires must come to you.

What is Creative Visualization?

Creative visualization is the technique of using your imagination to create what you want in your life. There is nothing at all new, strange, or unusual about creative visualization. You are already using it every day, every minute in fact. It is your natural power of imagination, the basic creative energy of the universe which you use constantly, whether or not you are aware of it.

In the past, many of us have used our power of creative visualization in a relatively unconscious way. Because of our own deep-seated negative concepts about life, we have automatically and unconsciously expected and imagined lack, limitation, difficulties, and problems to be our lot in life. To one degree or another that is what we have created for ourselves.

This book is about learning to use your natural creative imagination in a more and more conscious way, as a technique to create what you *truly* want — love, fulfillment, enjoyment, satisfying relationships, rewarding work, self-expression, health, beauty, prosperity, inner peace and harmony ... whatever your heart desires. The use of creative visualization gives us a key to tap into the natural goodness and bounty of life.

Imagination is the ability to create an idea or mental picture in your mind. In creative visualization you use your imagination to create a clear image of something you wish to manifest. Then you continue to focus on the idea or picture regularly, giving it positive energy until it becomes objective reality ... in other words, until you actually achieve what you have been visualizing.

Your goal may be on any level — physical, emotional, mental, or spiritual. You might imagine yourself with a new home, or a new job, or having a beautiful relationship, or feeling calm and serene, or perhaps with an improved memory and learning ability. Or you might picture yourself handling a difficult situation effortlessly, or simply see yourself as a radiant being, filled with light and love. You can work on any level, and all will have results ... through experience you will find the particular images and techniques which work best for you.

Let us say, for example, that you have difficulty getting along with someone and you would like to create a more harmonious relationship with that person.

After relaxing into a deep, quiet, meditative state of mind, you mentally imagine the two of you relating and communicating in an open, honest, and harmonious way. Try to get a feeling in yourself that your mental image is possible; experience it as if it is already happening.

Repeat this short, simple exercise often, perhaps two or three times a day or whenever you think about it. If you are sincere in your desire and intention, and truly open to change, you will soon find that the relationship is becoming easier and more flowing, and that the other person seems to become more agreeable and easier to communicate with. Eventually you will find that the problem will resolve itself completely, in one way or another, to the benefit of all parties concerned.

It should be noted here that this technique *cannot* be used to "control" the behavior of others or cause them to do something against their will. Its effect is to dissolve our internal barriers to natural harmony and self-realization, allowing everyone to manifest in their most positive aspect.

To use creative visualization it is not necessary to believe in any metaphysical or spiritual ideas, though you must be willing to entertain certain concepts as being possible. It is not necessary to "have faith" in any power outside yourself.

The only thing necessary is that you have the desire to enrich your knowledge and experience, and an open enough mind to try something new in a positive spirit.

Study the principles, try the techniques with an open mind and heart, and then judge for yourself whether they are useful to you.

If so, continue using and developing them, and soon the changes in yourself and your life will probably exceed anything you could have originally dreamed of . . .

Creative visualization is magic in the truest and highest meaning of the word. It involves understanding and aligning yourself with the natural principles that govern the workings of our universe, and learning to use these principles in the most conscious and creative way.

If you had never seen a gorgeous flower or a spectacular sunset before, and someone described one to you, you might consider it to be a miraculous thing (which it truly is!). Once you saw a few yourself, and began to learn something about the natural laws involved, you would begin to understand how they are formed and it would seem natural to you and not particularly mysterious.

The same is true of the process of creative visualization. What at first might seem amazing or impossible to the very limited type of education our rational minds have received, becomes perfectly understandable once we learn and practice with the underlying concepts involved.

Once you do so, it may seem that you are working miracles in your life . . .and you truly will be!

How Creative Visualization Works

In order to understand how creative visualization works, it's useful to look at several interrelated principles:

The physical universe is energy

The scientific world is beginning to discover what metaphysical and spiritual teachers have known for centuries. Our physical universe is not really composed of any "matter" at all; its basic component is a kind of force or essence which we can call *energy*.

Things appear to be solid and separate from one another on the level at which our physical senses normally perceive them. On finer levels, however, atomic and subatomic levels, seemingly solid matter is seen to be smaller and smaller particles within particles, which eventually turn out to be just pure energy.

Physically, we are all energy, and everything within and around us is made up of energy. We are all part of one great energy field. Things which we perceive to be solid and separate are in reality just various forms of our essential energy which is common to all. We are all one, even in a literal, physical sense.

The energy is vibrating at different rates of speed, and thus has different qualities, from finer to denser. Thought is a relatively fine, light form of energy and therefore very quick and easy to change. Matter is relatively dense, compact energy, and therefore slower to move and change. Within matter there is great variation as well. Living flesh is relatively fine, changes quickly, and is easily affected by many things. A rock is a much denser form, slower to change and more difficult to affect. Yet even rock is eventually changed and affected by the fine, light energy of water, for example. All forms of energy are interrelated and can affect one another.

Energy is magnetic

One law of energy is this: energy of a certain quality or vibration tends to attract energy of a similar quality and vibration.

Thought and feelings have their own magnetic energy which attracts energy of a similar nature. We can see this principle at work, for instance, when we "accidentally" run into someone we've just been thinking of, or "happen" to pick up a book which contains exactly the perfect information we need at that moment.

Form follows idea

Thought is a quick, light, mobile form of energy. It manifests instantaneously, unlike the denser forms such as matter.

When we create something, we always create it first in a thought form. A thought or idea always precedes manifestation. "I think I'll make dinner" is the idea which precedes creation of a meal. "I want a new dress," precedes going and buying one; "I need a job" precedes finding one, and so on.

An artist first has an idea or inspiration, then creates a painting. A builder first has a design, then builds a house.

The idea is like a blueprint; it creates an image of the form, which then magnetizes and guides the physical energy to flow into that form and eventually manifests it on the physical plane.

The same principle holds true even if we do not take direct physical action to manifest our ideas. Simply having an idea or thought, holding it in your mind, is an energy which will tend to attract and create that form on the material plane. If you constantly think of illness, you eventually become ill; if you believe yourself to be beautiful, you become so.

The law of radiation and attraction

This is the principle that whatever you put out into the universe will be reflected back to you. "As you sow, so shall you reap."

What this means from a practical standpoint is that we always attract into our lives whatever we think about the most, believe in most strongly, expect on the deepest levels, and/or imagine most vividly.

When we are negative and fearful, insecure or

anxious we will tend to attract the very experiences, situations, or people that we are seeking to avoid. If we are basically positive in attitude, expecting and envisioning pleasure, satisfaction and happiness, we will attract and create people, situations, and events which conform to our positive expectations. So the more positive energy we put into imaging what we want, the more it begins to manifest in our lives.

Using creative visualization

The process of change does not occur on superficial levels, through mere "positive thinking." It involves exploring, discovering, and changing our deepest, most basic attitudes toward life. That is why learning to use creative visualization can become a process of deep and meaningful growth. In the process we often discover ways in which we have been holding ourselves back, blocking ourselves from achieving satisfaction and fulfillment in life through our fears and negative concepts. Once seen clearly, these limiting attitudes can be dissolved through the creative visualization process, leaving space for us to find and live our natural state of happiness, fulfillment, and love . . .

At first you may practice creative visualization at specific times and for specific goals. As you get more in the habit of using it, and begin to trust the results it can bring you, you will find that it becomes an integral part of your thinking process. It becomes a continuous awareness, a state of consciousness in which you know that you are the constant creator of your life.

That is the ultimate point of creative visualization — to make every moment of our lives a moment of wondrous creation, in which we are just naturally choosing the best, the most beautiful, the most fulfilling lives we can imagine . . .

A Simple Exercise in Creative Visualization

Here is an exercise in the basic technique of creative visualization:

First, think of something you would like. For this exercise choose something simple, that you can *easily* imagine attaining. It might be an object you would like to have, an event which you would like to happen, a situation in which you'd like to find yourself, or some circumstance in your life which you'd like to improve.

Get in a comfortable position, either sitting or lying down, in a quiet place where you won't be disturbed. Relax your body completely. Starting from your toes and moving up to your scalp, think of relaxing each muscle in your body in turn, letting all tension flow out of your body. Breathe deeply and slowly, from your belly. Count down slowly from 10 to 1, feeling yourself getting more deeply relaxed with each count.

When you feel deeply relaxed, start to imagine the thing you want exactly as you would like it. If it is an object, imagine yourself with the object, using it, admiring it, enjoying it, showing it to friends. If it is a situation or event, imagine yourself there and everything happening just as you want it to. You may imagine what people are saying, or any details that make it more real to you.

You may take a relatively short time or quite a few minutes to imagine this — whatever feels best to you. Have fun with it. It should be a thoroughly enjoyable experience, like a child daydreaming about what he wants for his birthday.

Now keeping the idea or image still in your mind, mentally make some very positive, affirmative statements to yourself (aloud or silently, as you prefer) about it, such as

"Here I am spending a wonderful weekend in the mountains. What a beautiful vacation," or

"I now have a wonderful, happy relationship with __________. We are really learning to understand each other."

These positive statements, called affirmations, are a very important part of creative visualization, which we will discuss in more detail later.

Always end your visualization with the firm statement to yourself

"This, or something better,
now manifests for me
in totally satisfying and harmonious ways,
for the highest good of all concerned."

This leaves room for something different and even better than you had originally envisioned to happen, and serves as a reminder to you that this process only functions for the mutual benefit of all.

If doubts or contradictory thoughts arise, don't resist them or try to prevent them. This will tend to give them a power they don't otherwise have. Just let them flow through your consciousness, and return to your positive statements and images.

Do this process only as long as you find it enjoyable and interesting. It could be five minutes or half an hour. Repeat every day, or as often as you can.

As you see, the basic process is relatively simple. To use it really effectively, however, usually requires some understanding and refinement.

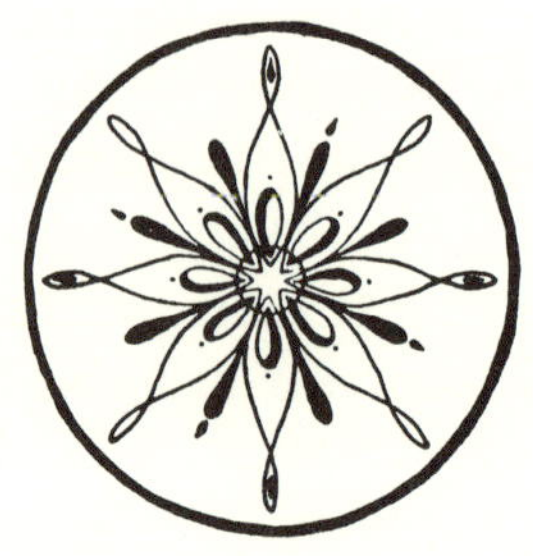

It's Important to Relax

It's important to relax deeply when you are first learning to use creative visualization. When your body and mind are deeply relaxed, your brain wave pattern actually changes and becomes slower. This deeper, slower level is commonly called alpha level (while your usual busy waking consciousness is called beta level), and much research is currently being done on its effects.

The alpha level has been found to be a very healthful state of consciousness, because of its relaxing effect on mind and body. And interestingly enough, it has been found to be far more effective than the more active beta level in creating real changes in the so-called objective world, through the use of visualization. What this means for our practical purposes is that if you learn to relax deeply and do creative visualization, you will be able to make far more effective changes in your life than you will by thinking, worrying, planning, and trying to manipulate things and people.

If you have any particular way that you are accustomed to relaxing deeply or entering a quiet, meditative state, by all means use that method. Otherwise you may wish to continue using the method I've described in the previous chapter — breathing slowly and deeply, relaxing each muscle in your body in turn, and counting down from 10 to 1 slowly. If you have any trouble physically relaxing, you might want to seek yoga or meditation instruction which will be helpful in this regard. Usually though, a little practice in relaxation will make perfect.

Of course, a side benefit of all of this is that you will find deep relaxation healthful and beneficial both mentally and physically.

It is especially good to do creative visualization at night just before sleeping, or in the morning just after awakening, because at those times the mind and body are often already deeply relaxed and receptive. You might like to do it while lying in bed, but if you tend to fall asleep, it's best to sit up on the edge of the bed or in a chair, in a comfortable position with your spine straight and balanced. Having your spine straight helps the energy to flow and makes it easier to get a deep alpha wave pattern.

A short period of meditation and creative visualization done at mid-day will relax and renew you, and cause your day to flow more smoothly.

How to Visualize

Many people wonder exactly what is meant by the term "visualize." Some worry because they don't actually "see" a mental picture or image when they close their eyes and try to visualize.

Don't get stuck on the term "visualize." *It is not at all necessary to mentally see an image.* Some people say they see very clear, sharp images when they close their eyes and imagine something. Others feel that they don't really "see" anything, they just sort of "think about" it or imagine that they are looking at it, or become aware of a feeling impression. That's perfectly fine. We all use our imaginations constantly, it's impossible not to, so whatever process you find yourself doing when you imagine, is fine.

If you still don't feel sure what it means to visualize, read through each of these exercises, then close your eyes and try it:

Close your eyes and relax deeply. Think of some familiar room such as your bedroom or living room. Remember some familiar details of it, such as the color of the carpet, the way the furniture is arranged, how bright or dark it is. Imagine yourself walking into the room and sitting or lying down on a comfortable chair, couch or bed.

Now recall some pleasant experience you have had in the last few days, especially one involving good physical sensations such as eating a delicious meal, receiving a massage, swimming in cool water, or making love. Remember the experience as vividly as possible, and enjoy the pleasurable sensations once again.

Now imagine that you are in some idyllic country setting, perhaps relaxing on soft green grass beside a cool river, or wandering through a beautiful, lush forest. It can be a place that you have been, or an ideal place where you would like to go. Think of the details, and create it any way that you would like it to be.

Whatever process you used to bring these scenes to your mind is your way of "visualizing."

There are actually two different modes involved in creative visualization. One is the receptive, the other is active. In the receptive mode we simply relax and allow images or impressions to come to us without choosing the details of them; we take what comes. In the active mode we consciously choose and create what we wish to see or imagine. Both these processes are an important part of creative visualization, and your receptive and active abilities will both be strengthened through practice.

Special Problems with Visualization

Occasionally a person has completely blocked his ability to visualize or imagine at will, and feels that he simply "can't do it." This type of block usually arises from a fear, and it can be worked through if the person desires to do so.

Usually a person blocks his ability to use creative visualization out of a fear of what he may encounter by looking inside himself — fear of his own unacknowledged feelings and emotions.

For example, a man in one of my classes was consistently unable to visualize, and kept falling asleep during the meditations. It turned out that he had once had a profoundly emotional experience during a visualization process, and he was afraid he would be embarrassed by becoming emotional in front of others.

The truth is that there is *nothing* within us that can hurt us; it is only our fear of experiencing our own feelings that can keep us trapped.

If anything unusual or unexpected arises during meditation, the best thing is simply to look at it fully, be with it and experience it as much as you can, and you will find that it loses any negative power over you. Our fears arise from things we don't confront. Once we are willing to look *fully* and *deeply* at the source of a fear, it loses its power.

Fortunately, such problems with visualization are rare. As a rule, creative visualization comes naturally, and the more you practice it, the easier it will become.*

---

* I recommend the Silva Mind Control course for those desiring special practice with visualization. See recommended reading list.

Four Basic Steps for Effective Creative Visualization

1. Set Your Goal

Decide on something you would like to have, work toward, realize, or create. It can be on any level — a job, a house, a relationship, a change in yourself, increased prosperity, a happier state of mind, improved health, beauty, or better physical condition, or whatever.

At first, choose goals that are fairly easy for you to believe in, that you feel are possible to realize in the fairly near future. That way you won't have to deal with too much negative resistance in yourself, and you can maximize your feelings of success as you are learning creative visualization. Later, when you have more practice, you can take on more difficult or challenging problems.

2. Create a Clear Idea or Picture

Create an idea or mental picture of the object or situation exactly as you want it. You should think of it in the present tense as *already* existing the way you want it to be. Picture yourself with the situation as you desire it, now. Include as many details as you can.

You may wish to make an actual physical picture of it as well, by making a treasure map (described in detail later). This is an optional step, not at all necessary, but often helpful (and fun!).

3. Focus on it Often

Bring your idea or mental picture to mind often, both in quiet meditation periods, and also casually throughout the day when you happen to think of it. In this way it becomes an integrated part of your life, it becomes more of a reality for you, and you project it more successfully.

Focus on it clearly, yet in a light, gentle way. It's important not to feel like you are striving too hard for it or putting an excessive amount of energy into it — that would tend to hinder rather than help.

4. Give it Positive Energy

As you focus on your goal, think about it in a positive, encouraging way. Make strong positive statements to yourself: that it exists, that it has come or is now coming to you. See yourself receiving or achieving it. These positive statements are called "affirmations." While you are using affirmations, try to temporarily suspend any doubts or disbelief you may have, at least for the moment, and practice getting the feeling that that which you desire is very real and possible.

Continue to work with this process until you achieve your goal, or no longer have the desire to do so. Remember that goals often change before they are realized, which is a perfectly natural part of the human process of change and growth. So don't try to prolong it any longer than you have energy for it — if you lose interest it may mean that it's time for a new look at what you want.

If you find that a goal has changed for you, be sure to acknowledge that to yourself. Get clear in your mind about the fact that you are no longer focusing on your previous goal. End cycle on the old, and begin cycle on the new. This helps you avoid getting confused, or feeling like you've "failed" when you have simply changed.

When you achieve a goal, be sure to acknowledge consciously to yourself that it has been completed. Often we achieve things which we have been desiring and visualizing, and we forget to even notice that we have succeeded! So give yourself some appreciation and a pat on the back, and be sure to thank the universe for fulfilling your requests.

Creative Visualization Works Only For Good

Don't fear that the power of creative visualization can be used for harmful ends. Creative visualization is a means of unblocking or dissolving the barriers we ourselves have created to the naturally harmonious, abundant and loving flow of the universe. It is only truly effective when it is used in alignment with our highest goals and purposes, for the highest good of all beings.

If someone should attempt to use this powerful technique for a harmful or destructively selfish end, he would only be demonstrating his ignorance of the law of karma. This is the same basic principle as the law of radiation and attraction, "as you sow, so shall you reap." Whatever you try to create for another will always boomerang back to you. That includes both loving, helpful, or healing actions and negative, destructive ones.

This means, of course, that the more you use creative visualization to love and serve others as well as your own highest ends, the more love, happiness, and success will just naturally find their way to you.

Just to make sure that you are aware of this, it's good to always add the following phrase to any creative visualization process you do:

"This, or something better,
now manifests for me
in totally satisfying and harmonious ways
for the highest good of all concerned."

As an example, if you are visualizing getting a promotion on your job, don't picture the person above you being fired, but imagine him or her moving on to other, better things or a better, more fulfilling job, so that it works out for the good of all. You don't need to understand or figure out *how* that will happen, or try to decide what is the best way it could work out; simply assume that it is working out for the best, and let universal intelligence take care of the details.

Affirmation

Affirmations are one of the most important elements of creative visualization. To affirm means to "make firm." An affirmation is a strong, positive statement that something is *already so*. It is a way of "making firm" that which you are imaging.

Most of us are aware of the fact that we have a nearly continuous inner "dialogue" going on in our minds. The mind is busy "talking" to itself, keeping up an endless commentary about life, the world, our feelings, our problems, other people, etc.

The words and ideas that run through our minds are very important. Most of the time we aren't consciously aware of this stream of thoughts, and yet what we are "telling ourselves" in our minds is the basis on which we form our experience of reality. Our mental commentary influences and colors our feelings and perceptions about what's going on in our lives, and it is these thought forms that ultimately attract and create everything that happens to us.

Anyone who has practiced meditation knows how difficult it can be to quiet this inner "mind talk," in order to connect with our deeper, wiser intuitive mind. One traditional meditation practice is to simply observe the inner dialogue as objectively as possible.

This is a very valuable experience, as it allows you to become consciously aware of the types of thoughts you habitually think. Many of these thoughts are like tape recordings of old patterns we've had all our lives. They are old "programming" we picked up long ago, which is still influencing what's happening to us today.

The practice of doing affirmations allows us to begin replacing some of our stale, worn out, or negative mind chatter with more positive ideas and concepts. It is a powerful technique, one which can in a short time completely transform our attitudes and expectations about life, and thereby totally change what we create for ourselves.

Affirmations can be done silently, spoken aloud, written down, or even sung or chanted. Even ten minutes a day of doing effective affirmations can counterbalance years of old mental habits. Naturally, the more frequently you remember to be conscious of what you're "telling yourself," and choose positive, expansive words and concepts, the more positive a reality you will create.

An affirmation can be any positive statement. It can be very general or very specific. There are an infinite number of possible affirmations; here are a few just to give you some ideas:

Every day in every way I'm getting better, better, and better.

Everything is coming to me easily and effortlessly.

I am a radiant being, filled with light and love.

I am naturally enlightened.

My life is blossoming in total perfection.

I have everything I need to enjoy my here and now.

I am the master of my life.

Everything I need is already within me.

Perfect wisdom is in my heart.

I am whole and complete in myself.

I love and appreciate myself just as I am.

I accept all my feelings as part of myself.

I love to love and be loved.

The more I love myself, the more love I have to give others.

I now give and receive love freely.

I am now attracting loving, satisfying, happy relationships into my life.

My relationship with ___________ is growing happier and more fulfilling every day.

I now have a perfect, satisfying, well paying job.

I love doing my work, and I am richly rewarded, creatively and financially.

I am an open channel of creative energy.

I am dynamically self-expressive.

I always communicate clearly and effectively.

I now have enough time, energy, wisdom and money to accomplish all my desires.

I am always in the right place at the right time, successfully engaged in the right activity.

It's okay for me to have everything I want!

This is a rich universe and there's plenty for all of us.

Abundance is my natural state of being. I accept it now!

Infinite riches are now freely flowing into my life.

Every day I am growing more financially prosperous.

The more I have, the more I have to give.

The more I give, the more I receive, and the happier I feel.

It's okay for me to have fun and enjoy myself, and I do!

I am relaxed and centered. I have plenty of time for everything.

I am now enjoying everything I do!

I feel happy and blissful just being alive.

I am vibrantly healthy and radiantly beautiful!

I am open to receiving all the blessings of this abundant universe!

______________________ *(you fill in the blank) is coming to me, easily and effortlessly.*

I have a wonderful job with wonderful pay. I do a wonderful service in a wonderful way.

The light of God within me is producing perfect results in every phase of my life now.

The light within me is creating miracles in my life here and now.

I give thanks for divine restoration in mind, body, financial affairs, and in all my relationships now.

All things are now working together for good in my life.

I am now attuned to the divine plan of my life.

I now recognize, accept, and follow the divine plan of my life as it is revealed to me step by step.

I give thanks now for my life of health, wealth, happiness, and perfect self-expression.

Here are some important things to remember about affirmations:

1. Always phrase affirmations in the present tense, not in the future. It's important to create it as if it *already exists*. Don't say, "I will get a wonderful new job," but rather "I now have a wonderful new job." This is not lying to yourself; it is acknowledging the fact that everything is created *first* on the mental plane, before it can manifest in objective reality.

2. Always phrase affirmations in the most positive way that you can. Affirm what you *do* want, not what you *don't* want. Don't say "I no longer oversleep in the morning" but rather "I now wake up on time and full of energy every morning." This insures that you are creating the most positive possible mental image.

At certain times you may find it helpful to phrase affirmations negatively, especially when you are working on clearing out specific emotional blocks or bad habits; i.e. "I don't need to get tense in order to get things accomplished." If so, you should always *follow* this type of affirmation with a positive one which describes that which you desire to create, i.e. "I now stay deeply relaxed and centered, and everything is accomplished easily and effortlessly."

3. In general, the shorter and simpler the affirmation the more effective. An affirmation should be a clear statement that conveys a strong feeling; the more feeling it conveys, the stronger impression it makes on your mind. Affirmations that are long, wordy and theoretical lose their emotional impact and become a "head trip."

4. Always choose affirmations that feel totally right for you. What works for one person may not work at all

for another. An affirmation should feel positive, expansive, freeing, and/or supportive. If it doesn't, find another one, or try changing the words until it feels right.

Of course, you may feel emotional resistance to any affirmation when you first use it, especially one which is really powerful for you and is going to make a real change in your consciousness. That is simply the ego's initial resistance to change and growth.

5. Always remember when doing affirmations that you are creating something new and fresh. *You are not trying to redo or change what already exists*. To do so would be to resist what *is*, which creates conflict and struggle.

Take the attitude that you are accepting and handling whatever already exists in your life, and at the same time every moment is a new opportunity to begin creating exactly what you desire and will make you happiest.

6. Affirmations are not meant to *contradict* or *try to change* your feelings or emotions. It is important to accept and experience *all* your feelings, including so-called "negative" ones without attempting to change them. At the same time, affirmations can help you create a new point of view about life which will enable you to have more and more satisfying experiences from now on.

7. When using affirmations, try as much as possible to create a feeling of belief, an experience that they can be true. Temporarily (at least for a few minutes) suspend your doubts and hesitations, and put your full mental and emotional energy into them.

If doubts, resistance, or negative thoughts are getting in the way of doing your affirmations, do one of the clearing processes or the writing affirmations process given in section four of this book.

Rather than saying affirmations by rote, try to get the feeling that you really have the power to create that reality (which in fact you do!). This will make a big difference in how effective they are.

Affirmations can be used alone, or in combination with visualizing or imaging. You should always include affirmations as part of your regular creative visualization meditation periods. Later in the book I'll give you ideas for many other ways to use affirmations.

Affirmations are often most powerful and inspiring when they include references to spiritual sources. Mention of God, Christ, Buddha or any great master adds spiritual energy to your affirmation, and acknowledges the universal source of all things. You may prefer to use such phrases as divine love, the light within me, or universal intelligence.

Some examples:

Divine love is working through me here and now to create this.

The Christ within me is creating miracles in my life here and now.

I am one with my higher nature and I have infinite creative power.

My higher self is guiding me in everything that I do.

God lives within me and manifests in the world through me.

The light of God surrounds me, the love of God unfolds me, the power of God flows through me.
Wherever I am, God is, and all is well!

A Spiritual "Paradox"

Sometimes people who have studied eastern philosophy or are on a consciousness growth path feel a certain hesitation about using creative visualization when they first hear of it. Their conflict comes from the *apparent* paradox they see between the idea of "being here now," letting go of attachments and desires, and the idea of setting goals and creating what you want in life. I say *apparent* paradox, because in actuality there is no contradiction between the two teachings when they are understood on a deeper level. They are both important principles which must be understood and lived in order to become a conscious person. In order to explain how they fit together, allow me to share with you my viewpoint about the process of inner growth:

Most people in our culture have become cut off from their awareness of who they really are. They have temporarily lost their conscious connection with their higher selves and thus they have lost their own sense of power and responsibility for their lives. In some inner way, they have a sense of helplessness; they feel basically powerless to make real change in their lives or in the world. This inner feeling of powerlessness causes them to overcompensate by striving and struggling very hard to have *some* degree of power or control in their world.

Thus people become very goal oriented; they become emotionally attached to things and people outside of themselves which they feel they need in order to be happier. They feel there is something "missing" inside themselves, and they become tense, anxious and stressed, continuously trying to fill up the gap, trying to manipulate the outside world in order to get what they want.

This is the state of being from which most people are setting goals and trying to create what they want in life, and unfortunately from this level of consciousness it doesn't work at all . . . either you set up so many obstacles to yourself that you *can't* succeed, or you *do* succeed in reaching your goals only to find that they don't bring you inner happiness.

It is at the point where we realize this dilemma that we begin to open up to a spiritual path. We realize that there simply has to be something more to life, and we begin to search for it.

We may go through many different experiences and processes on our search, but eventually we are gradually restored to ourselves. That is, we come back into an experience of our true selves, the God-like nature or the universal mind that is within us all. Through this experience we are eventually restored to our full spiritual power, the emptiness inside us is filled up *from within*, and we become radiant beings, sharing the light and love that comes from within us with everyone around us.

This is the process known as enlightenment, and I believe that it is an ongoing evolution for every individual, which cannot be complete until all our fellow beings are sharing in it. So we are all equally responsible for our own enlightenment and the enlightenment of all fellow beings on our planet . . .

Now to get back to our supposed paradox.

When you are coming out of the empty, grasping, manipulative condition, the first and foremost lesson to be learned is just to *let go*. You must relax, stop struggling, stop trying so hard, stop manipulating things and people to try to get what you want and need, in fact just stop *doing* so much and have an experience of just *being* for awhile.

When you do this, you suddenly discover that you're really perfectly okay, in fact you feel quite wonderful, just letting yourself be, and letting the world be, without trying to change things. This is the basic experience of *being here now* and it's what the Buddhist philosophy means by "letting go of attachment." It's a very freeing experience, and a most basic one on any path of self-awareness.

Once you have begun to have this experience more and more often, you are opening up the channel to your higher self, and sooner or later a great deal of natural creative energy will begin to flow through you. You start to see that you yourself are already creating your whole life and every experience that happens to you, and you become interested in creating more rewarding experiences for yourself and others. You begin to want to focus your energy toward the highest and most fulfilling goals that are real for you at any given moment. You realize that life is basically good, abundant, and fun, and that having what you want, without struggle and strain, is part of your natural birthright as a function of just being alive. This is the time when creative visualization can become a most important tool.

Here is a metaphor that I hope will make it even clearer:

Let us imagine that life is a river. Most people are clinging to the bank, afraid to let go and risk being carried along by the current of the river. At a certain point, each person must be willing to simply let go, and trust the river to carry him or her along safely. At this point he learns to "go with the flow" and it feels wonderful.

Once he has gotten used to being in the flow of the river, he can begin to look ahead and guide his own course onward, deciding where the course looks best, steering his way around boulders and snags, and choosing which of the many channels and branches of the river he prefers to follow, all the while still "going with the flow."

This analogy shows us how we can be enjoying our here and now, flowing with what is, and at the same time be guiding ourselves consciously toward our goals by taking responsibility for creating our own lives.

Remember, too, that creative visualization is a tool that can be used for any purpose, including one's own consciousness growth. It is often very helpful to use creative visualization in picturing yourself as a more relaxed, open person, flowing, living in the here and now, and always connected with your inner essence.

May you be blessed
with everything
your heart desires

Part Two

Using Creative Visualization

Ask, and it shall be given you;
seek, and ye shall find;
knock, and it shall be opened unto you.

For every one that asketh, receiveth;
and he that seeketh, findeth;
and to him that knocketh it shall be opened.

Matthew 7: 7,8

Making Creative Visualization Part of Your Life

As you can see from Part One, the basic technique of creative visualization is not difficult.

The important thing now is to learn to use it in a way that really works for you ...that helps you to make positive change in your life. In order to use creative visualization most effectively it's helpful to understand certain concepts and learn some further techniques.

The most important thing to remember is to use creative visualization often, to make it a regular part of your life. Most people seem to find that it works best to practice it at least a little every day, especially when you are first learning.

I suggest that you have a regular creative visualization meditation period for fifteen minutes or so each morning when you wake up, and each evening before sleeping (these are the times when it is most effective), as well as the middle of the day if you can manage that. Always start your meditation periods with deep relaxation, then follow with any visualizations or affirmations you wish.

There are many different ways that creative visualization can be used, and it's up to you to remember to try them at appropriate times. Creative visualization may be a new way of thinking, a new way of living, and as such it will take some practice.

Try it out in different situations and different circumstances, and use it as often as you can for any type of problem solving. If you find yourself worrying or puzzling about anything, or feeling discouraged or frustrated about a problem, ask yourself whether there is a way you could use creative visualization to help you. Form a creative habit of using it at every appropriate moment.

Don't feel discouraged if you don't *immediately* feel totally successful with your creative visualization. Remember that most of us have years of negative thought patterns to overcome. It takes time to change some of these life-long habits. And many of us have some underlying feelings and attitudes which can slow us down in our efforts to live more consciously.

Fortunately creative visualization is such an innately powerful process that even five minutes of conscious, positive meditation can balance out hours, days, even years of negative patterns.

So be patient. It has taken a lifetime to create your world the way it is now. It may not necessarily change instantly (although it often does). With perseverance and a proper understanding of the process, you will succeed in creating what seem like many miracles in your life.

Two things I have found most important in my growth process with creative visualization are:

1. Regular reading of inspiring and uplifting books that help to keep me in touch with my highest ideals and aspirations. I usually keep a book by my bed and read a page or two each day. Many of my favorites are listed in the bibliography.

2. Having a friend or (ideally) a community of friends who are also tuned into learning to live more consciously and who will support you and help you in your efforts. Attending regular or occasional consciousness classes or workshops can be an important way of getting this type of support, and giving it to others as well.

In the following chapters I will be giving you many different techniques, ideas, exercises, and meditations. Choose the ones that feel right to you and seem to work for you. There are many different levels and approaches to the creative visualization process, and I have tried to include a wide variety of possible practices. In any given situation, one may be appropriate and another may not. Follow the flow of your own energy, and use the ones that you feel drawn to.

For example, in a certain situation, you may try to do affirmations and find that you simply can't do it, or it doesn't feel like it's accomplishing anything. In that case you might want to try a clearing process, or get in touch with your higher self or spirit guide and ask what to do.

What works at one time may not at another; what works for one person may not for another. Always trust yourself and your own inner impulses.

If it feels like you are forcing, pushing, efforting, straining, don't do it.

If it feels positive, releasing, opening, strengthening, inspiring, do it.

Being, Doing, and Having

We can think of life as containing three levels, and we can call those levels beingness, doingness, and havingness.

Beingness is the basic experience of being alive and conscious. It is the experience we have in deep meditation, the experience of being totally complete and at rest within oneself.

Doingness is movement and activity, it stems from the natural creative energy that flows through every living thing and is the source of our vitality.

Havingness is the state of being in relationship with other people and things in the universe. It is the ability to allow and accept things and people into our lives; to comfortably occupy the same space with them.

Beingness, doingness and havingness are like a triangle where each side supports the others.

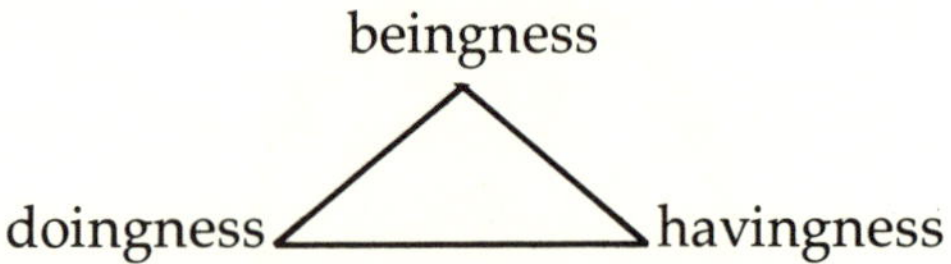

They are not in conflict with each other.

They all exist simultaneously.

Often people attempt to live their lives backwards: They try to *have* more things, or more money, in order to *do* more of what they want, so that they will *be* happier.

The way it actually works is the reverse. You must first *be* who you really are, then *do* what you need to do, in order to *have* what you want.

The purpose of creative visualization is:

To connect us with our beingness

To help us focus and facilitate our doingness

To increase and expand our havingness

Three Necessary Elements

There are three elements within you which determine how successfully creative visualization will work for you in any given situation:

1. *Desire.* You must have a true desire to have or create that which you have chosen to visualize. By desire I don't mean addictive, grasping desire, but a clear, strong feeling of purpose. Ask yourself "Do I truly, in my heart, desire this goal to be realized?"

2. *Belief.* The more you believe in your chosen goal and the possibility of attaining it, the more certain you will be to do so. Ask yourself "Do I believe that this goal can exist?" and "Do I believe that it is possible for me to realize or attain it?"

3. *Acceptance.* You must be willing to *accept* and *have* that which you are seeking. Sometimes we pursue goals without actually wanting to attain them; we are more comfortable with the process of pursuing. Ask yourself "Am I really willing to *have* this completely?"

The sum total of these three elements is what I call your *intention*. When you have total intention to create something — that is you deeply desire it, you completely believe that you can do it, and you are totally willing to have it — it simply cannot fail to manifest, and usually within a very short time.

The clearer and stronger your intention, the more quickly and easily your creative visualization will work. In any given situation, ask yourself about the condition of your intention. If it is weak or uncertain, it can often be strengthened by affirming:

I now have total intention to create this
here and now!

Contacting Your Higher Self

One of the most important steps in making your creative visualization work effectively and successfully is to have the experience of coming from "source."

Source means the supply of infinite love, wisdom, and energy in the universe. For you, source may mean God, or the universal mind, or the oneness of all, or your true essence. However we conceptualize it, it can be found here and now within each of us, in our inner being.

I like to think of contacting source as connecting with your higher self, the God-like being who dwells within you. Being in contact with your higher self is characterized by a deep sense of knowingness and certainty, of power, love, and wisdom. You know that you are creating your own world and that you have infinite power to create it perfectly.

We have all had experiences of being connected with our higher selves, although we may not have conceptualized it in that way. Feeling exceptionally high, clear, strong, "on top of the world," or "able to move mountains," are indications of being connected with your higher self; so is the experience of "falling in love" . . . when you feel wonderful about yourself and the world because your love for another human being is causing you to manifest as your highest self.

When you first become consciously aware of the experience of your higher self, you will find that it seems to come and go rather sporadically. At one moment you may be feeling strong, clear and creative, the next moment you may be thrown back into confusion and insecurity. This seems to be a natural part of the process. Once you are aware of your higher self, you can call on it whenever you need it, and gradually you will find that it is with you more and more of the time.

The connection between your personality and your higher self is a two way channel, and it's important to develop the flow in both directions.

Receptive: When you quiet your personality during meditation, and come into a beingness space, you open the channel for higher wisdom and guidance to come to you through your intuitive mind. You can ask questions and wait for answers to come to you through words, mental images, or feeling impressions.

Active: When you are experiencing yourself as the creator of your universe, you make choices about what you desire to create, and channel the infinite energy, power, and wisdom of your higher self into manifesting your choices, through active visualization and affirmation.

When the channel is flowing freely in both directions, you are constantly being guided by your higher wisdom, and based on that guidance, you are making choices and creating your world in the highest, most beautiful way.

Almost any form of meditation will eventually take you to an experience of yourself as source, or your higher self. If you are not sure of what this experience is, don't worry about it. Just continue to practice relaxation, visualization, and affirmation. Eventually you will start experiencing certain moments during your meditation when there is a sort of "click" in your consciousness and you feel like things are really working; you may even experience a lot of energy flowing through you or a warm radiant glow in your body. These are signs that you are beginning to channel the energy of your higher self.

Here's an exercise in creative visualization that will help you tune into the feeling. You might wish to do this exercise regularly at the beginning of your meditation periods:

Sit or lie in a comfortable position. Relax completely . . . let all tension drain out of your body and mind . . . breathe deeply and slowly . . . relax more and more deeply.

Visualize a light within your heart – glowing radiant and warm. Feel it spreading and growing – shining out from you farther and farther until you are like a golden sun, radiating loving energy on everything and everyone around you.

Say to yourself silently and with conviction,

"Divine light and divine love are flowing through me and radiating from me to everything around me."

Repeat this over and over to yourself until you have a strong sense of your own spiritual energy. If you wish, use any other affirmations of your own power, light, creative ability, such as:

God is working through me now,

or

I am filled with divine light and creative energy

or

The light within me is creating miracles in my life here and now,

or whatever phrase has meaning and power for you.

Going With The Flow

The only effective way to use creative visualization is in the spirit of the way of the Tao — "going with the flow." That means that you don't have to "effort" to get where you want to go; you simply put it out clearly to the universe where you would like to go, and then patiently and harmoniously follow the flow of the river of life until it takes you there. The river of life sometimes takes a winding course toward your goal. It may even seem temporarily to be going in a different direction entirely, yet in the long run it is a more effortless and harmonious way to get there than through struggling and striving.

Going with the flow means holding onto your goals lightly (even though they may seem very important) and being willing to change them if something more appropriate and satisfying comes along. It is that balance between keeping your destination clearly in mind, and yet also enjoying all the beautiful scenes you encounter along the way, and even being willing to change your destination if life starts taking you in a different direction. In short, it means being firm, yet flexible.

If you have a lot of heavy emotions riding on whether you attain your goal (that is, if you will be upset if you don't get it) you will tend to work against yourself. In your fear of *not* getting what you want, you may actually be energizing the idea of not getting it as much or more as you are energizing the goal itself.

If you do find yourself very emotionally attached to a goal, it may be most effective and appropriate to work first on your feelings about the matter. You may have to take a good look at what you fear about *not* achieving the goal, and do affirmations to help you feel more confident and secure, or to help you face your fears.

For example:

The universe is unfolding perfectly
I don't have to hang on
I can relax and let go
I can go with the flow
I always have everything I need to enjoy my here and now
I have all the love I need within my own heart
I am a lovable and loving person
I am whole in myself
Divine love is guiding me and I am always taken care of
The universe always provides

You may find some of the clearing processes given later helpful. And once again I refer you to my recommended reading list for books that may offer help and insight.*

Of course it's perfectly okay to creatively visualize something to which you have a lot of attachment — and it will often work quite well. But if it doesn't, realize that your own inner conflict is sending out conflicting messages. In this case, it's important to relax and accept your feelings, accept the idea that you may not immediately realize your goal, and understand that resolving the conflict is probably an important area of growth for you and a wonderful opportunity to look more closely at your own attitudes about life.

If you get a feeling at any time while doing creative visualization that you are trying to *force* or *push* something that doesn't want to happen, back off a little and ask your higher self whether this is really the best thing for you or whether you truly desire it. The universe may be trying to show you something better that you haven't even considered.

---

* See especially *Handbook to Higher Consciousness* by Ken Keyes, Jr. and *Mystic Path to Cosmic Power* by Vernon Howard.

Prosperity Programming

A very important part of the whole creative visualization process is prosperity programming. This means having the understanding, or consciously taking the point of view, that the universe is totally abundant . . . it is a cornucopia of everything that your heart could ever desire, both on the material plane and on emotional, mental, and spiritual planes as well. Everything you need or want is here for the asking; you only need to *believe* that it is so, to truly *desire* it, and to be willing to *accept* it, in order to have whatever you wish.

One of the most common causes of failure to get what you want is "scarcity programming." This is an attitude or set of beliefs about life that goes something like this:

There isn't enough to go around . . .

Life is suffering . . .

It is immoral or selfish to have plenty when others don't have enough . . .

Life is hard, difficult, a vale of tears . . .

You must work hard and sacrifice for everything you gain . . .

It's more noble and spiritual to be poor . . .

and so forth.

These are all false beliefs. They are based on a lack of understanding of how the universe works, or a misunderstanding of some important spiritual principles. These beliefs are not of service to you or anyone else; they simply limit *all of us* from realizing our natural state of prosperity and plenty on all levels.

At the present time there is a reality in this world of starvation and poverty for many people, *but we do not need to keep creating and perpetuating that reality any longer.*

The fact is that there is more than enough to go around for every being on earth, if we are willing to open our minds to that possibility.* The universe *is* a place of great abundance and we are all naturally prosperous, both in material and spiritual wealth. Those who are not experiencing their world as rich and abundant, are on some level believing in scarcity programming rather than abundance. They have, through ignorance, bought into the popular belief in the inevitability of poverty and lack, and do not realize yet that the ultimate power of creation rests in the hands (or rather, minds) of each of us.

---

*I refer you to the Hunger Project source book, listed in the recommended reading.

The truth about this earth is that it is an infinitely good, beautiful, nourishing place to be. The only "evil" comes from lack of understanding of this truth. Evil (ignorance) is like a shadow — it has no real substance of its own, it is simply a lack of light. You cannot cause a shadow to disappear by trying to fight it, stamp on it, by railing against it, or any other form of emotional or physical resistance. In order to cause a shadow to disappear, you must shine light on it.

Take a look at your belief system and see if you are holding yourself back by not believing sufficiently in the universal good. Can you actually realistically imagine yourself as a successful, satisfied, prosperous, fulfilled person? Can you really open your eyes to the goodness and beauty and abundance that are all around you? Can you imagine this world transformed into a happy, prosperous and enlightened environment in which everyone can flourish?

Unless you can create a context that the world is a good place to be that can potentially work for everyone, you will experience difficulty in creating what you want in your personal life.

This is because human nature is basically loving, and so most of us will not allow ourselves to have what we want as long as we believe that we might be depriving others in order to do so.

We have to understand in a deep way that having what we want in life contributes to the general state of human happiness and supports others in creating more happiness for themselves.

In a spirit of fun, try this exercise to stimulate your imagination and expand your ability to "have it all":

Cornucopia meditation

Relax completely in a comfortable position:

Picture yourself in any lovely natural environment – perhaps a green, open meadow with a lovely brook, or on white sand by the ocean. Take some time to imagine all the beautiful details, and see yourself fully enjoying and appreciating it. Now begin to walk, and soon find yourself in some totally different surrounding, perhaps a waving field of golden grain, or swimming in a lake. Continue to wander and explore, finding more and more exquisitely beautiful environments of great variety – mountains, forests, deserts, whatever suits your fantasy. Take a little time to appreciate each one . . .

Imagine yourself taking a boat to a lush tropical paradise, with incredible fruit on each tree. Picture yourself coming to a huge castle, where you are welcomed with an enormous feast, music, and dancing, then taken to the vast treasure room where you are presented with incredible jewels, precious metals, gorgeous clothes, more than you could ever use. Use your imagination, and see yourself wandering around the world, finding or being given everything you could ever want, in much greater quantity than you could even wish for.

Imagine the world as a magnificent paradise in which everyone you meet is experiencing the same fullness and abundance that you are.

Enjoy it thoroughly. Go to other planets, if you wish, and find miraculous things there too. There are infinite possibilities! Eventually come home, happy and contented, and think about the fact that the Universe is truly a place of incredible wonder and abundance.

Affirmations:

This is a rich universe and there is plenty for all of us.

Abundance is my true state of being. I am now ready to accept it fully and joyously.

God is the unfailing, unlimited source of all my supply.

I deserve to be prosperous and happy. I am now prosperous and happy!

The more I prosper, the more I have to share with everyone else.

The universe is total abundance!

I'm ready now to accept all the joy and prosperity life has to offer me.

I now take responsibility for creating the world as a happy, abundant place for everyone.

Financial success is coming to me easily and effortlessly.

I am now enjoying great financial prosperity!

Life is meant to be fun and I'm now willing to enjoy it!

Infinite riches are now flowing freely into my life.

I am rich in consciousness and manifestation.

I now have more than enough money for my own personal use.

I now have a satisfying income of $__________ per month.

Every day I'm growing more financially prosperous.

I am rich, well, and happy.

Accepting Your Good

In order to use creative visualization to create what you want in life, you must be willing and able to *accept* the best that life has to offer you — your "good."

Strange as it may seem, many of us have difficulty accepting the possibility of having what we want in life. This usually stems from some basic feelings of unworthiness which we took on at a very early age. The basic belief goes something like this: "I'm really not a very good (lovable, worthwhile) person so I don't deserve to have the best."

This belief is usually mixed with other, sometimes contradictory feelings that you really are perfectly good and deserving. But if you find that you have any difficulty imagining yourself in the most wonderful possible circumstances, or that you have thoughts like "I could never have that" or "That couldn't possibly happen to *me,*" it might be well to take a good look at your self-image.

Your self-image is the way you see yourself, how you feel about yourself. It is often complex and multi-faceted. To get in touch with different aspects of your self-image, begin to ask yourself "How do I feel about myself right now?" at various times throughout the day, and in various different situations. Just begin to notice what kinds of ideas or images you hold in mind about yourself at different times.

One very interesting thing to do is to get in touch with your *physical* images of yourself by asking "How do I look to myself right now?" If you find yourself feeling awkward, ugly, fat, skinny, too big, too small, or whatever, it may be a clue to the fact that you aren't loving yourself enough to give yourself what you truly deserve — the best. It is often astounding to me to discover how many perfectly beautiful, attractive people frequently think of themselves as ugly, unworthy, undeserving.

Affirmations and creative visualization are a wonderful way of creating a more positive and loving self-image. Once you get in touch with the ways in which you are not loving yourself, begin to take every opportunity to tell yourself positive, appreciative, loving things. Notice when you are being mentally harsh or critical with yourself, and consciously begin being kinder and more appreciative. You will find this immediately helps you to be more loving towards others, as well.

Think of specific qualities that you do appreciate about yourself. In the same way that you can love a good friend while clearly seeing his or her faults and shortcomings, you can love yourself for all that you truly are, while still being aware that there are ways you need to grow and develop. It feels very good to do this for yourself, and it can really work wonders in your life.

Begin to tell yourself:

I am beautiful and lovable

I am kind and loving, and I have a great deal to share with others

I am talented, intelligent and creative

I am growing more and more attractive every day

I deserve the very best in life

I have a lot to offer and everyone recognizes it

I love the world and the world loves me

I am willing to be happy and successful

or whatever words seem appropriate and helpful to you.

It is often very effective to do this type of affirmation in the second person, using your own name:

"Susan, you are a brilliant and interesting person. I like you very much" or

"John, you are so warm and loving. People really appreciate that about you."

This way of talking directly to yourself is especially effective because much of our negative self-image comes from being convinced in various ways at an early age by other people that we are bad, stupid, or inadequate in some way.

Try to picture yourself as clearly as you can, and think of giving love to yourself, the same way you would to anyone else you care for. You might think of it as the parent in you giving love and appreciation to the child in you. Tell yourself:

"I love you. You are a very beautiful person. I appreciate

your sensitivity and honesty."

Creative visualization is a great way to work on any physical problems you may feel you have. For example, if you feel you are too fat, you need to work on two things simultaneously:

1. Through affirmations and loving energy, start learning to love and appreciate yourself more *as you already are*.

2. Through creative visualization and affirmations, start creating yourself as you *want to be* — slim, trim, healthy, and happy. These techniques are extremely effective in making real changes.

These same two techniques hold true for working on any "problem" in the way you see yourself.

Remember, you are a new person at every new moment. Every day is a new day, and each one is an opportunity to realize the wonderful, loving, and lovable person you truly are . . .

In addition to improving your self-image, it is valuable to do affirmations about opening up to and accepting the goodness of the universe.

For example:

I am open to receiving the blessings of this abundant universe

Everything good is coming to me easily and effortlessly (any word you want can be substituted for 'everything good', i.e. love, prosperity, creativity, a perfect relationship)

I accept my good, which is flowing to me here and now

I deserve the best and the best is coming to me now

The more I receive the more I have to give

Here is a meditation you can do to improve your self-esteem and increase your capacity to handle the love and energy that the universe is ready and eager to flow in your direction:

Self-appreciation meditation

Imagine yourself in some everyday situation, and picture someone (maybe someone you know, or a stranger) looking at you with great love and admiration and telling you something they really like about you. Now picture a few more people coming up and agreeing that you are a very wonderful person. (If this embarrasses you, stick with it.) Imagine more and more people arriving and gazing at you with tremendous love and respect in their eyes. Picture yourself in a parade or on a stage, with throngs of cheering, applauding people, all loving and appreciating you. Hear their applause ringing in your ears. Stand up and take a bow, and thank them for their support and appreciation.

Some affirmations for self-appreciation:

I love and accept myself completely as I am.

I don't have to try to please anyone else. I like myself and that's what counts.

I am highly pleasing to myself in the presence of other people.

I express myself freely, fully and easily.

I am a powerful, loving, and creative being.

Outflowing

Another key principle is that of giving, or "outflowing." The universe is made up of pure energy, the nature of which is to move and flow. The nature of life is constant change, constant flux. When we understand this, we tune into its rhythm and we are able to give and receive freely, knowing that we never really lose anything, but constantly gain.

Once we begin to learn to *accept* the goodness of the universe, we naturally want to *share* it as well, realizing that as we give out of our energy, we make space for more to flow into us.

When, through insecurity (fear) and a feeling that there "isn't enough," we try to hold onto or cling to what we have, we begin to cut off this wonderful flow of energy. In hanging onto what we have, we fail to keep the energy moving and we don't make space for new energy to come to us.

Energy takes many forms, such as love, affection, appreciation and recognition, material possessions, money, friendship, etc. and the principles apply equally to all these forms.

If you look around you at those who are most unhappy, you'll find they are often people who have a "starved" feeling in some way, and are therefore in a very grasping posture toward life. They feel that life in general and other people in particular are not giving them what they need. It is as if they have a stranglehold on life, trying desperately to wring out the love and satisfaction they crave, yet actually choking off the supply. And many of us have a little of this tendency.

When we find that place within ourselves that is giving, we begin to reverse the flow. Giving happens not from a space of sacrifice, or self-righteousness, or an idea of spirituality, but for the pure *pleasure* of it — because it's fun. It can only come from a full, loving space.

We each have an infinite supply of love and happiness within us. We have been accustomed to thinking that we have to get something from outside us in order to be happy, but in truth it works the other way: we must learn to contact our inner source of happiness and satisfaction and flow it outward to share with others — not because it is virtuous to do so, but because it feels really good! Once we tune into it we just naturally want to share it because that is the essential nature of love, and we are all loving beings.

As we outflow our loving energy, we make room for more to flow into us. We soon discover that this process feels so good in itself we just want to do it more and more. And the more you share of yourself from this space, the more you seem to get from the world, because of the outflow-inflow principle. (Nature abhors a vacuum, so as you outflow you create space into which something must inflow.) Giving becomes its own reward.

When we fully understand and live this we have manifested our innately loving nature.

So you will find in your use of creative visualization, that the more basically "giving" orientation you have to life, the easier it will be to fulfill your dreams . . . but remember always that you can't continue to give unless you are equally open to receiving . . . and that "giving" also means giving to yourself . . .

When it comes to outflowing, practice makes perfect. You must consciously practice it in order to get the experience of how good it feels. Here are some exercises in outflowing you can try if you need some expansion in this area:

1. Make a point to express more appreciation to others in as many ways as you can think of. Sit down right now and make a list of people to whom you would like to outflow love and appreciation, and think of a way you can do so to each one within the next week. Outflow can take the form of words, touching, a gift, a phone call or letter, money, or any sharing of your talents that makes another person feel good. Choose something that makes you feel especially good too, even if it's a little more difficult for you.

Practice speaking more words of thanks, appreciation and admiration to people when you feel like it. "It was kind of you to help me." "I want you to know that I appreciate that." "Your eyes were shining and beautiful as you said that, and it made me feel good to see you." (We don't need to feel embarrassed!)

2. Go through your things and find things you don't really want or use very often and give them to others who will appreciate them more.

3. If you're a person who tries to spend as little money as possible and always hunts for a bargain, try spending a little money each day unnecessarily. *Buy the product that costs a few cents more instead of less, treat yourself to a little something extra, pay for a friend's coffee, donate to a good cause, etc. Even a small action of this sort is a visible demonstration to yourself that you have faith in the abundance that you have been affirming. Actions speak as loud as words in this case.*

4. Tithe your income. Tithing is the practice of giving a percentage of your income to a church, spiritual organization, or any group that you feel is making a worthwhile contribution in the world. It is a way of supporting that energy, and at the same time acknowledging that all you receive comes from the universe (or God) and therefore you give a token back to the universal source. It doesn't matter what the percentage is – even tithing just one percent of your income will give you a continuous experience of outflowing. Just be sure to do it regularly.

5. Be creative. Think of other ways to outflow your energy into the universe for the good of yourself and others.

Healing

Healing Ourselves

Creative visualization is one of the most important tools we have for creating and maintaining good health.

One of the basic principles of holistic health is that we cannot separate our physical health from our emotional, mental, and spiritual states of being. All levels are interconnected and a state of "dis-ease" in the body is always a reflection of conflict, tension, anxiety, or disharmony on other levels of being as well. So when we have a physical disorder, it is inevitably a message for us to look deeply into our emotional and intuitive feelings, our thoughts and attitudes, to see what we can do to restore natural harmony and balance to our being. We must tune in and "listen" to the inner process.

There is constant communication between mind and body. The body perceives the physical universe, and sends messages to the mind about it; the mind interprets the perceptions according to its own individual past experience and its belief system, and signals the body to react in a way which it feels is appropriate. *If the mind's belief system (on a conscious or unconscious level) says that it is appropriate or inevitable to get sick in a certain situation, it will signal the body accordingly, and the body will obligingly manifest symptoms of illness;* it will in fact become ill. So the whole process is closely tied in with our deepest concepts and ideas about ourselves, life, and the nature of disease and health.

Creative visualization refers to the way in which we communicate from our mind to our body. It is the process of forming images and thoughts in our mind, consciously or unconsciously, and then transmitting them to the body as signals or commands.

Conscious creative visualization is the process of creating positive thoughts and images to communicate with our bodies, in place of negative, constrictive, literally "sickening" ones.

People get sick because they believe on an inner level that illness is an appropriate or inevitable response to some situation or circumstance, because it in some way seems to solve a problem for them or get them something that they need, or as a desperate solution to some unresolved and unbearable inner conflict.

Some examples of this are: the person who becomes ill because he has been "exposed" to a communicable disease (he believes it is inevitable or highly likely), the person who dies of the same disease as a parent or other member of her family (she has unconsciously programmed herself to follow the same pattern), the person who gets sick or has an accident in order to get out of work (either there's something he can't confront at work, or he won't allow himself the relaxation and quiet he needs unless he is sick), the person who gets sick in order to get love and attention (this was how she was able to get her parents' love as a child), the person who represses his feelings all his life and eventually dies of cancer (he cannot resolve the conflict between the pressure of his stored-up emotions, and his belief that it's not okay for him to express himself . . . so he eventually kills himself as a solution).

I do not mean to imply by these examples that I believe all illness is a simple problem with a pat explanation. As with all our problems, there are often many complex factors. I do intend to illustrate the fact that illness is a result of our mental concepts and beliefs, and that illness is an attempt to find a solution to a problem we are having inside ourselves. If we are willing to recognize and change our innermost beliefs, we can find more constructive solutions to our problems, and we can eliminate illness and disease altogether.

The most positive, powerful, healthy and healing consciousness can be created by taking this point of view:

We are all in essence perfect, spiritual beings. We are each a perfect expression of the universal mind or God consciousness that is within us.

As such, our natural birthright is radiant health, beauty, boundless energy, youthful vitality and joy throughout our lives.

There is in actual fact no evil or limitation. There is only ignorance or misunderstanding of the universal nature of good (or God), combined with our infinite creative abilities.

The only limitations on our health, beauty, energy, vitality, and joy come from our own self-created blocks, our own resistance to the goodness of life, based on fear and ignorance.

Our bodies are simply a physical expression of our consciousness. The concepts we hold of ourselves determine our health and beauty or the lack thereof. When we deeply change our concepts, our physical self follows suit. The body is continuously changing, replenishing, and rebuilding itself at every moment and it has no other pattern to follow in doing so except the guidance given to it by the mind.

The more we bring our consciousness into alignment with our highest spiritual realization, the more our bodies will express our own individual perfection.

The natural outgrowth of this point of view is a more constructive attitude about illness. Rather than thinking of illness as an inevitable disaster or unavoidable misfortune, we think of it as a powerful and useful message. If we are suffering physically in some way, it is a message that there is something to be looked at within our consciousness, something to be recognized, acknowledged, and changed.

Often the message of illness is to be quieter and spend some time just being in contact with our inner self. Illness often forces us to relax, let go of all our busyness and "efforting," and drop into a deep, quiet level of consciousness where we can receive the nourishing energy that we need.

The healing always comes from within. When we allow ourselves quiet and inner contact regularly, we no longer need to get sick in order for our inner self to get our attention.

Illness and "accidents" are messages that our concepts need changing or some inner problem needs to be resolved. Get as quiet as you can, listen for your inner voice, and ask what the message is, or what it is that you need to understand in this situation. You may be able to accomplish this alone, or in some cases you may need a counselor, therapist, friend, or healer to assist and support you.

Creative visualization is the perfect tool for healing because it goes straight to the source of the problem — your own mental concepts and images. Begin to picture yourself and affirm to yourself that you are in perfect radiant health; see your problem as completely healed and cured. There are many different approaches that can be taken on many different levels; you need to find the particular type of affirmations and images that work best for you. I've given some suggestions in section three of this book, and you can find others in the recommended reading.*

Of course "preventative medicine" is always the best . . . If you have no health problems, so much the better; simply affirm and visualize that you will always remain healthy and vital; that way you will never have to worry about healing yourself. If you already have health problems, it will be comforting to know that many "miraculous" cures are being accomplished every day, even for very serious illnesses, such as cancer, arthritis, heart disease, through the simple use of various forms of creative visualization.

In many cases, creative visualization is a completely effective therapy in itself. In other cases, because of the person's own belief system (i.e. it is difficult to let go of the concept that we need something outside ourselves to be healed), it is necessary to use other forms of treatment

---

* I particularly recommend the books and tapes of Joel Goldsmith and *The Nature of Personal Reality* by Jane Roberts. Also the books of Catherine Ponder and the Silva Mind Control course.

as well. *As long as you have an inner confidence in some form of therapy then by all means use it!* It will work if you desire and believe it will. But whatever type of treatment is used, from conventional medicine or surgery, to more holistic therapies such as acupuncture, yoga, massage, diet, and so on, *creative visualization is always a helpful supplement,* one that you can use in conjunction with anything else. Conscious use of creative visualization will speed and smooth the normal healing process amazingly.

Healing Others

The same principles that work in healing ourselves also work to heal others. The healing consciousness I outlined earlier is just as powerful in healing others as in healing oneself (sometimes even more so).

This is so because of the oneness nature of the universal mind. There is a part of our consciousness that is directly linked with that part in everyone else's consciousness. Since that part is also our link with divine omnipotence and omniscience, we *all* have incredible healing power which we can tap into at will.

Just as the concepts we hold about ourselves determine our health or lack of health, the concepts we hold about others can support their health or lack of health. If a friend has a concept which has caused her to become ill, and we buy into or believe that concept of her illness, we are supporting her ill health, no matter how lovingly we may desire her to become well. On the other hand, if we hold the concept of her health and perfection strongly in mind, we will truly support her healing process. It is not even necessary for her to know anything about what we are doing; in fact it is sometimes better that she not consciously know.

It is an amazing thing, but simply changing your

own concepts about another person and consciously holding and projecting an image of health and well-being can *instantly cure* someone in many cases, and speed and smooth their healing in many other cases.

I was brought up with a very scientific and rational background and education, and the ability to heal other people at a distance has been one of the hardest things for me to understand and accept. Yet I have seen it and experienced it too often to doubt it any longer.

I've found that in my experience the best way to work on healing is to picture myself as a clear channel for healing energy, the spiritual energy of the universe, to flow *through* me and to the person who needs it. I think of my higher self sending energy to the other person's higher self to support them in whatever they need to do to heal themselves. At the same time I picture them as they truly are . . . a divine being, a beautiful and perfect expression of God . . . naturally healthy and happy.

In section three I describe the healing methods that I have found work best for me. I encourage you to try them, and to discover your own.

Part Three

Meditations and Affirmations

Thou shalt decree a thing,
and it shall be established unto thee:
and the light shall shine upon thy ways.

Job 22: 28

Grounding Yourself and Running Energy

This is a very simple visualization technique, and one which is good to do at the beginning of any meditation. The purpose of it is to get your energy flowing, dissolve any blocks, and keep you firmly connected to the physical plane so that you don't "space out" during meditation.

Sit comfortably with your back straight, either in a chair or cross legged on the floor. Close your eyes, breathe slowly and deeply, counting down from 10 to 1 until you feel deeply relaxed.

Imagine that there is a long cord attached to the base of your spine and extending down through the floor and way down into the earth. If you wish, you can imagine that this is like the root of a tree, growing deep into the ground. This is called a "grounding cord."

Now imagine that the energy of the earth is flowing up through this cord (and up through the soles of your feet if you are sitting in a chair) and flowing up through all parts of your body, and out through the top of your head. Picture this until you really feel the flow well established. Now imagine that the energy of the cosmos is flowing in through the top of your head, through your body and down through your grounding cord and your feet into the earth. Feel both these flows going in different directions, and mixing harmoniously in your body.

This meditation keeps you balanced between the cosmic energy of vision, fantasy, and imagination, and the stable, earthy energy of the physical plane . . . a balance which will increase your sense of well being and your power of manifestation.

Opening the Energy Centers

This is a meditation for healing and purifying your body, and for getting your energy flowing. It is an excellent one to do in the morning when you first wake up, or at the beginning of any meditation period, or anytime you want to be relaxed and refreshed:

Lie down on your back with arms at your sides or with hands clasped on your stomach. Close your eyes, relax and breathe gently, deeply and slowly.

Imagine that there is a glowing sphere of golden light surrounding the top of your head. Breathe deeply and slowly in and out five times while you keep your attention on the sphere of light, feeling it radiate from the top of your head.

Now allow your attention to move down to your throat. Again imagine a golden sphere of light emanating from your throat area. Breathe slowly in and out five times with your attention on this light.

Allow your attention to move down to the center of your chest. Once again imagine the golden light, radiating from the center of your chest. Again take five deep breaths, as you feel the energy expanding more and more.

Next put your attention on your solar plexus; visualize the sphere of golden light all around your midsection. Breathe into it slowly, five times.

Now visualize the light glowing in and around your pelvic area. Again take five deep breaths, feeling the light energy radiating and expanding.

Finally, visualize the glowing sphere of light around your feet, and breathe into it five more times.

Now imagine all six of the spheres of light glowing at once so that your body is like a strand of jewels, radiating energy.

Breathe deeply, and as you exhale, imagine energy flowing down along the outside of the left side of your body from the top of your head to your feet. As you inhale, imagine it flowing up along the right side of your body to the top of your head. Circulate it around your body this way three times.

Then visualize the flow of energy going from the top of your head down along the front of your body to your feet as you slowly exhale. As you inhale, feel it flow up along the back of your body to the top of your head. Circulate the flow in this direction three times.

Now imagine that the energy is gathering at your feet, and let it flow slowly up through the center *of your body from your feet to your head, radiating from the top of your head like a fountain of light, then flowing back down the outside of your body to your feet. Repeat this several times, or as long as you wish.*

When you finish this meditation you will be deeply relaxed, yet energized and exhilarated.

Creating Your Sanctuary

One of the first things you should do when you start using creative visualization is to create a sanctuary within yourself where you can go anytime you want to. Your sanctuary is your ideal place of relaxation, tranquillity and safety and you can create it exactly as you want it.

Close your eyes and relax in a comfortable position. Imagine yourself in some beautiful natural environment. It can be any place that appeals to you ... in a meadow, on a mountaintop, in the forest, beside the sea. It could even be under the ocean, or on another planet. Wherever it is, it should feel comfortable, pleasant and peaceful to you. Explore your environment, noticing the visual details, the sounds and smells, any particular feelings or impressions you get about it.

Now do anything you would like to do to make the place more homelike and comfortable an environment for you. You might want to build some type of house or shelter there, or perhaps just surround the whole area with a golden light of protection and safety, create and arrange things there for your convenience and enjoyment, or do a ritual to establish it as your special place.

From now on this is your own personal inner sanctuary, to which you can return at any time just by closing your eyes and desiring to be there. You will always find it healing and relaxing to be there. It is also a place of special power for you, and you may wish to go there every time you do creative visualization.

You may find that your sanctuary spontaneously changes from time to time, or that you want to make changes and additions to it. You can be very creative in your sanctuary and have a lot of fun there ... just remember to retain the primary qualities of peacefulness, tranquillity and a feeling of absolute safety.

Meeting Your Guide

Each one of us has all the wisdom and knowledge we ever need right within us. It is available to us through our intuitive mind, which is our connection with universal intelligence. However, we often find it difficult to connect with our higher wisdom. One of the best ways to do so is by meeting and getting to know our inner guide.

The inner guide is known by many different names, such as your counselor, spirit guide, imaginary friend, or master. It is a higher part of yourself, which can come to you in many different forms, but usually comes in the form of a person or being whom you can talk to and relate to as a wise and loving friend.

Here is an exercise to help you meet your spirit guide. If you wish, you can have a friend read this to you while you do the meditation. Otherwise, read through it first, close your eyes and do it.

Close your eyes and relax deeply. Go to your inner sanctuary and spend a few minutes there, relaxing, getting oriented. Now imagine that within your sanctuary you are standing on a path which stretches off into the distance. You start to walk up the path, and as you do so, you see in the distance a form coming toward you, radiating a clear, bright light.

As you approach each other you begin to see whether the form is a man or woman, how they look, how old they are, and how they are dressed. The closer they get, the more details you can see of their face and appearance.

Greet this being, and ask him or her what their name is. Take whatever name comes to you first, and don't worry about it.

Now show your guide around your sanctuary and explore it together. Your guide may point out some things that you've never seen there before, or you may enjoy just being in each other's presence.

Ask your guide if there is anything he or she would like to say to you, or any advice to give you at the moment. If you wish, you can ask some specific questions. You may get immediate answers, but if not, don't be discouraged, the answers will come to you in some form later.

When the experience of being together feels complete for now, thank your guide and express your appreciation, and ask him or her to come to meet you in your sanctuary again.

Open your eyes and return to the outside world.

People have many different types of experience in meeting their guides, so it is difficult to generalize. Basically if you feel good about your experience, then it's fine. If not, be creative and do whatever you need to do to change it.

Don't worry if you did not perceive your guide clearly and precisely. Sometimes they remain in the form of a glow of light, or a blurry, indistinct figure. The important thing is that you sense their power, their presence, and their love.

If your guide should come to you in the form of someone you know, that is fine, *unless* you don't feel particularly good about it. In that case, repeat the exercise and request that your guide come to you in a form that is easy and pleasant for you to relate to.

Don't be surprised if your guide seems eccentric or unusual in some way . . . the form in which they show themselves to us springs from our own creative mind which is limitless. For example, your guide may have a very unusual and surprising sense of humor, or an exotic name and a flair for the dramatic. Sometimes they don't communicate in words at all, but in a direct transmission of feeling impressions or intuitive knowledge.

Also your guide *may* change form and even name from time to time. Or you may have the same one for years. You may have more than one guide at the same time.

Your guide is there for you to call on anytime you need or want extra guidance, wisdom, knowledge, support, creative inspiration, love or companionship. Many people who have established a relationship with their guide meet them every day in their meditation.

Pink Bubble Technique

This meditation is simple and wonderfully effective.

Exercise:

Sit or lie down comfortably, close your eyes and breathe deeply, slowly, and naturally. Gradually relax deeper and deeper.

Imagine something that you would like to manifest. Imagine that it has already happened. Picture it as clearly as possible in your mind.

Now in your mind's eye surround your fantasy with a pink bubble; put your goal inside the bubble. Pink is the color associated with the heart, and if this color vibration surrounds whatever you visualize, it will bring to you only that which is in perfect affinity with your being.

The third step is to let go of the bubble and imagine it floating off into the universe, still containing your vision. This symbolizes that you are emotionally "letting go" of it. Now it is free to float around in the universe, attracting and gathering energy for its manifestation.

There is nothing more you need to do.

Healing Meditations

Healing Ourselves

Sit or lie down, breathe, and relax deeply. Starting with your toes, feet, legs, pelvis and so on, put your attention on each part of your body in turn and tell it to relax and let go of any tension. Feel all tension dissolving and draining away.

If you wish to, do the meditation on opening the energy centers in order to get your energy really flowing.

Now imagine golden, healing light energy all around your body . . . feel it . . . sense it . . . enjoy it.

If there is a particular part of your body that has been ill or in pain, ask that part of you whether it has a message for you. Ask whether there is something you need to understand or to do, right at this moment or in your life in general.

If you get an answer, do your best to understand and follow it. If you don't get an answer, just continue with the process.

Now send special loving, healing energy to that part of you, and any part of you that needs it, and see or feel it being healed. You may want to have your guide, or any master or healer, there to help you do the healing.

Picture the problem dissolving and flowing energy away, or whatever image works for you.

Now imagine yourself in perfect, radiant, natural good health. Think of yourself in different situations feeling good, active and healthy. See yourself as divinely, radiantly beautiful.

Affirmations:

I have now transcended all patterns of illness. I'm free and healthy!

I am now full of radiant health and energy.

I love and accept my body completely.

I am good to my body, and my body is good to me.

I am energetic and full of vitality.

My body is balanced, in perfect harmony with the universe.

I give thanks for ever increasing health, beauty, and vitality.

I am a radiant expression of God. My mind and body now manifest divine perfection.

From now on, each time you do this meditation, picture yourself only in perfect health, with golden healing light around you. Do not give any more power or energy to the "problem" unless you feel that there's something more that you need to understand about it.

Healing Others

This meditation is to be done alone, *not* in the other person's presence. You may or may not wish to tell them that you are doing healing meditations for them, depending on how well they would accept that idea on a personality level.

Relax deeply and do whatever type of preparation you wish in order to enter a deep, quiet state of mind.

Think of yourself as a clear channel through which the healing energy of the universe is pouring. This energy does not come from you personally, it comes from a higher source, and you serve to focus and direct it.

Now picture or think of the person as clearly as you can. Ask him if there is anything in particular he would like you to do for him in your meditation. If so, do it to the best of your ability, if it feels right to you.

If you feel the impulse to work on.healing a particular part of his body, or a particular problem, do so. Just see all problems dissolved, everything being healed and functioning perfectly.

Then picture him surrounded in golden, healing light . . . looking radiantly healthy and happy. Speak to him directly (in your mind); remind him that he is actually a perfect, god-like being and that no illness or affliction need have any power over him. Tell him that you support him in being totally healthy and happy, and that you will continue to send him your loving support and energy.

When you feel complete, open your eyes and come back to the outer world feeling refreshed, renewed, healthy and invigorated.

From now on, in your meditations see the person as perfectly well. Don't give any more mental energy or power to the illness; just keep seeing him as completely healed.

Healing In Groups

Healings are very powerful when done in groups.

If the person to be healed is present in the room, have him lie down in the center or sit in a chair (whichever is most comfortable) with everyone else seated in a circle around him.

Everyone should close their eyes, be quiet, and relax deeply, then begin to imagine sending healing energy to the person in the center. Remember that it is the healing energy of the universe which is being channeled through you. See the person surrounded in golden light, feeling well, and in perfect health.

If you wish, you can have everyone raise their hands with the palms facing out toward the person in the center, and feel the energy flowing out to him through your hands.

It is especially powerful to have everyone chant "OM" together for a few minutes while doing the healing, thus adding the healing vibration of sound to the process (to chant "OM" you sing a long, deep resonant note with the syllable a-a-au-m-m, holding it as long as you can, and repeating it over and over).

If the person is not present in the room, just inform everyone of his name and the city where he is, and then proceed as if he were there. The power of healing energy is not affected at all by distance, and I have seen as many miraculous cures accomplished for people in distant cities as for those present in the room.

Healing meditation for pain

Here is a meditation technique you can do with a person who is experiencing a headache or any other specific pain:

Have the person lie down, close his eyes, and relax deeply. Have him focus on his breath for awhile, breathing deeply and slowly yet naturally. Have him count down from 10 to 1 slowly, feeling himself drift into a deeper, more relaxed state of being with each count.

When he is very deeply relaxed, have him picture or imagine a bright color, any color he wishes (have him take the first color that comes to him). Ask him to picture it as a sphere of bright light about six inches in diameter. Now ask him to picture it gradually growing bigger and bigger, until eventually it fills his whole field of mental vision. When he has experienced this, ask him to picture it shrinking, growing smaller and smaller, until it's back to its original size. Now have it grow smaller still, until it's only an inch or so in diameter, still shrinking, and finally disappearing completely.

Now go through the visualization exercise again, and this time have the person imagine that the color is his pain.

Invocation

To invoke means to "call in" or "call upon." Invocation used in meditation is a technique with which you can summon any type of energy or quality to come to you:

Close your eyes and relax deeply. Do some type of preparatory meditation such as grounding and running energy, or opening the energy centers, or simply going to your sanctuary, relaxing and breathing deeply for awhile.

When you feel relaxed and energized, say to yourself silently, yet firmly and clearly, "I now call forth the quality of love." Feel the energy of love coming to you, or coming out from someplace inside of you, filling you up, and radiating out from you. Remain for a few minutes totally experiencing the feeling. Then if you wish, direct it toward any particular goal through visualization and affirmation.

You can use the power of invocation to summon any quality or energy that you want or need . . .

strength	*warmth*
wisdom	*clarity*
serenity	*intelligence*
compassion	*creativity*
softness	*healing power . . .*

Simply make a strong, clear statement to yourself that this quality is now coming to you.

Another wonderful way to use the power of invocation is to summon the spirit or essence of a particular person who has qualities that you desire. If you invoke one of the masters, such as Buddha, Christ, or Mary, you are calling forth the universal qualities which that person symbolizes, which also lie within each of us. For example, if you call for Christ to work in you and through you, you are summoning in a very powerful way your own qualities of love, compassion, forgiveness, and healing ability.

If there is any particular master or teacher or hero with whom you resonate, call upon him or her through invocation whenever you feel the need to manifest his special qualities within yourself.

This type of meditation works beautifully when there is a special skill or talent that you wish to cultivate. For example, if you are studying music or art, call upon any great master in these fields whom you especially admire; picture him supporting and helping you, and feel his creative energy and genius flowing through you. It is not necessary to incorporate any personal problems or weaknesses he may have had; you are summoning him in his *highest aspect.* Many amazing results can be achieved through this meditation.

Ways to Use Affirmations

There are so many ways that affirmations can be used powerfully and effectively to give you a more positive, creative outlook and to help you achieve specific goals.

Remember, it's important to feel *relaxed* as you affirm. Do not be addicted to getting results. Remember that you already *are* everything you need; every improvement is just icing on the cake.

In meditation

1. Say them to yourself silently while meditating or relaxing deeply, especially right before going to sleep or right after waking up.

Spoken

1. Say them to yourself silently or aloud throughout the day, whenever you think of it, especially while driving, doing housework, or other routine tasks.

2. Say them to yourself aloud while looking at yourself in the mirror. This is especially good for affirmations to improve your self-esteem and self-love. Look yourself right in the eyes and affirm your beauty, lovableness, and worthiness. If you feel uncomfortable, stick with it until you push through those barriers and are able to fully experience looking at yourself and loving yourself. You may find that some emotion arises and is released through this process.

3. Record your affirmations on a tape recorder and play them to yourself around the house, while driving, etc. Use your name, and try doing them in the first, second, and third persons. For example, *"I, Shakti, am always deeply relaxed and centered in myself." "Shakti, you are always deeply relaxed and centered in yourself." "Shakti is always deeply relaxed and centered in herself."*

Or you can record a little speech, maybe three or four paragraphs long, describing your ideal visualization of yourself or a particular situation. This also can be done in the first, second, and/or third person.

Written

1. Take a particular affirmation and write it out 10 or 20 times in succession, *really thinking* about the words as you write them. Change the affirmation as you go along if you think of better ways to say it. This is one of the most powerful techniques I've ever found, and one of the easiest to do. I've devoted a chapter to it in Section Four.

2. Write or type out affirmations and paste them up in various places around your house or at your job as

reminders. Good places are: on the refrigerator, your phone, your mirror, your desk, over your bed, on the dining table.

With others

1. If you have a friend who wants to work on affirmations as well, you can do them very effectively in partners. Sit facing each other, look into each other's eyes, and take turns saying affirmations to each other and accepting them.

David: "Linda, you are a beautiful, loving, and creative person."

Linda: "Yes, I know!"

Repeat this 10 or 15 times the same way, then switch partners so that Linda says the affirmation to David and he agrees with it. Then try it in the first person:

David: "I, David, am a beautiful, loving, and creative person."

Linda: "Yes, you certainly are."

Repeat several times.

Be sure to say the affirmations sincerely and meaningfully, even if you feel a little silly at first. It's a wonderful opportunity to outflow love and support to another person, and to really support them in changing their negative concepts to positive ones.

It's practically guaranteed that after doing this process together you will be experiencing a deep love space together . . .

2. In a more informal way, ask your friends to say affirmations to you frequently. For example, if you want to affirm that you are learning to express yourself more easily, you might ask a good friend to say to you often, *"Jeannie, you are certainly speaking out and expressing yourself clearly these days!"*

Make a game out of doing this for each other and you will find it helpful. We automatically tend to give a lot of power to what our friends say to us, for good or bad; our minds tend to accept what others tell us about ourselves. So getting strong positive feedback from friends in the form of affirmations really works.

3. Begin to include affirmations in your conversations — making strong positive statements about things and people (including yourself) that you want to see in a more positive way. It's amazing what dramatic changes can be made in your life by just beginning to consciously speak more positively in daily conversation.

A word of caution: *do not* use this technique in such a way that you feel like you are contradicting your true feelings. Do not use it when you are feeling upset or strongly negative or it will feel like you are repressing yourself. Use it from a constructive space, to help change your unconscious negative speech patterns and underlying assumptions.

Singing and chanting

1. Make a point of learning songs that affirm the reality you would like to create for yourself; listen to them and sing them often. A large part of our present consciousness has been formed by popular music which creates a reality in which we feel hopelessly dependent on our lover, would die if he left us, wonder if life is worth living if we can't "have" a certain person, and so on.

In my recommended reading list I've mentioned a few records and music tapes which consciously come from a different point of view.

2. Make up your own songs or simple chants using the affirmations you want to work with.

More affirmations

Accepting Ourselves

I accept myself completely here and now.

I love myself completely as I am, and I'm getting better all the time.

I accept all my feelings as part of myself.

I'm beautiful and loveable however I'm feeling.

I am now willing to experience all my feelings.

It's good to express my feelings. I now give myself permission to express my feelings.

I love myself when I express my feelings.

Feeling Good

It's okay for me to have fun and enjoy myself and I do!

I like to do things that make me feel good.

I am always deeply relaxed and centered.

I now feel deep inner peace and serenity.

I'm glad I was born and I love being alive.

Relationships

I love myself and I naturally attract loving relationships into my life.

I am strong and loving in my relationships.

I deserve love and sexual pleasure.

I am now ready to accept a happy, fulfilling relationship.

I am now ready for all my relationships to work.

The more I love myself the more I love ________.

I love ________ and ________ loves me.

All difficulties between me and ________ are now being dissolved. We have a wonderful relationship.

Divine love is working through me now to create a perfect relationship with __________.

I am now attracting exactly the kind of relationship I want.

I am now divinely irresistible to my perfect mate.

Opening Creativity

I am now an open channel for creative energy.

Creative ideas and inspiration are coming to me every day.

I am the creator of my life.

I am now creating my life exactly as I want it.

Divine Love and Guidance

Divine love is doing its perfect work in this situation now for the good of all concerned.

Divine love and light are working through me now.

Divine love goes before me and prepares the way.

God is showing me the way now.

My inner wisdom is guiding me now.

I am now being guided to the perfect solution to this problem.

The light within me is creating miracles in my body, mind, and affairs, here and now.

Part Four

Special Techniques

If you would learn the secret of right relations .
look only for the divine in people and things,
and leave all the rest to God.

J. Allen Boone
in *Kinship With All Life*

A Creative Visualization Notebook

It's a very good idea to start a notebook which can serve as your creative visualization workbook. In this section I will be giving you a number of written exercises and processes which you might want to do and keep in your notebook. You may wish to write down affirmations that you hear or think of, so that you can refer to them when you need them. There are many other creative ways to use your notebook, such as recording your dreams and fantasies, keeping a journal of your progress with creative visualization, writing down inspiring thoughts and ideas, or quotes from books and songs that are meaningful to you, drawing pictures or writing your own poems and songs that express your expanding awareness.

I have a notebook in which I regularly work on my goals, affirmations, ideal scenes, and treasure maps, and I have found it a very valuable tool in the transformation of my life.

Here are a few suggestions for starting your notebook:

1. Affirmations. Write down your favorite affirmations. You can list them all on one page, or you might want to make a separate page for each, with decorative borders and designs, so that each time you read through it you have a beautiful experience as you pause and meditate on each one.

2. Outflow List. Make a list of all the ways that you can outflow your energy to the world and to others around you, both generally and specifically. Include ways that you outflow money, time, love and affection, appreciation, physical energy, friendship, touching, and your special talents and abilities. Add to this list anytime you think of new things.

3. Success List. Make a list of everything you feel you are a success at, or have been a success at, or have done successfully at some time in your life. Include things in all areas of your life, not just your work. Write down everything that has meaning for you, even if it might not to someone else. Keep adding to it as you think of more things, or accomplish new successes. The purpose of this list is to acknowledge yourself and your abilities, which gives you added energy for accomplishing more.

4. Appreciation List. Make a list of everything you can think of that you are especially thankful for, or that you especially appreciate having in your life. Making and adding to this list can really open up your heart, and your awareness of the many riches we all have in our lives that we often take for granted. It increases your realization of prosperity and abundance on every level, and thus your ability to manifest.

5. **Self-Esteem List.** Make a list of all the things you like about yourself, all your positive qualities. This is not an "ego trip" — the better you feel about yourself and the more you acknowledge your own wonderful qualities, the happier and more loving you will be, the more your creative energy will flow, and the greater contribution you will make to the world.

6. **Self-Appreciation List.** Write down all the ways you can think of to be good to yourself, nice things that you can do for yourself, things that are just for your own pleasure and satisfaction. They can be small or large, but make some of them things you can easily do every day, and then do them! This increases your sense of well-being and satisfaction in life, which in turn helps you to come from a clearer space in creating your life.

7. **Healing and Assistance List.** Write down the names of any people you know who need healing, or special support and assistance of any sort. Write down special affirmations for them. Every time you look through your notebook you will be giving them a special boost of your energy.

8. **Fantasies and Creative ideas.** Jot down any ideas, plans, or dreams for the future, or any creative ideas that come to you, even if they seem farfetched, or you're sure you'll never follow through on them. This will help to loosen you up and stimulate your imagination and your natural creative ability.

You may find it difficult to take time out of your busy schedule to work in your notebook. Yet if you take a few minutes a day, or an hour or two every week or so, you will find that so much work is accomplished on the inner plane, it is often worth a hundred times the amount of time and energy you would have spent on the outer plane.

Clearing

In learning to use creative visualization you may get in touch with blocks in yourself that hold you back from attaining your highest good.

A "block" is a place where energy is constricted — not moving, not flowing. Usually blocks are caused initially by repressed emotions of fear, guilt, and/or resentment (anger) which cause a person to tighten up and close down spiritually, emotionally, mentally and even physically.

In dealing with a block on any level, what's needed is to get energy moving and flowing in that area. The keys to this are:

1. Mental and emotional acceptance (on a physical level this manifests as relaxation and release).

2. Clear observation, which leads to understanding of the root of the problem — which is always a limiting attitude or belief.

So in dealing with an area of consciousness where we have a block, we need to first experience (as fully as possible) the emotion we have locked up in that area, in a loving, accepting way. In doing so, we get the blocked up energy moving and we have a chance to observe the underlying negative beliefs or attitudes which caused the problem to begin with. We can take a good clear look at them and let them dissolve themselves.

Amazingly enough, it seems to be the process of pinpointing the constrictive belief and accepting the feelings you have around it which works magic; the difficulty almost inevitably dissolves and disappears eventually once you've understood and accepted yourself. It's much simpler than you may think.

The trick is to simultaneously *love and accept yourself* compassionately for having this belief, and at the same time to *see clearly that you are ready to let go of it* because it is limiting, destructive, self-defeating and *untrue.*

Some common core beliefs that are most prevalent and troublesome are:

I'm not okay . . . there's something wrong with me . . . I'm unworthy and undeserving.

I've done bad things (or a bad thing) in my life and I deserve to suffer (be punished) for it.

People (including me) are basically bad – selfish, cruel, stupid, untrustworthy, foolish, etc.

The world is an unsafe place.

There's not enough _______________ *(love, money, good things, etc.) to go around, so:*

I have to struggle to get my share

or

It's hopeless, I'll never get enough

or

If I have a lot, someone else will have to do without

Life is painful, suffering, hard work . . . it's not meant to be fun.

Love is dangerous . . . I might get hurt.

Power is dangerous . . . I might hurt someone.

Money is the root of all evil. Money corrupts.

The world doesn't work and never will. In fact it's getting worse all the time.

I don't have control over what happens to me . . . I'm powerless to do anything about my life or the state of the world.

As you read through these negative ideas, see whether any of them reflect an underlying assumption of your own belief system or emotional pattern.

Depressing though they may seem when you read through them all at once, the fact is that every one of us has bought into some of these (or other) negative viewpoints about reality, at least in some degree. If we hadn't, we would all be manifesting as fully realized beings, as it is only the degree to which we accept these beliefs that separates us from realization of our God-like nature.

And it's no wonder that we have incorporated these ideas into our sense of reality — they are all extremely prevalent in our world at this time in our evolution. In fact, the world is currently being run according to these ideas, although fortunately this is rapidly changing.

The important thing to realize is that they are only *beliefs*; they have no objective truth. Although they may *seem* to be true at times when we look around us, that is only because so many human beings believe them and act accordingly.

The most powerful thing you can do (and it is very powerful) to change the world, is to change your own beliefs about the nature of life, people, reality, to something more positive . . . and begin to act accordingly.

This book will give you some tools to do so.

Clearing exercises:

If you are having trouble realizing a goal, or sense resistance in yourself to its achievement, try this exercise:

1. Take a piece of paper and write at the top, "The reason I can't have what I want is . . . ", then immediately begin to write a list of any thoughts that come into your head to complete the sentence. Don't take too much time and don't take it too seriously, just quickly write down about 20 or 30 things that come to you even if they seem silly or stupid. A sample list might start like this:

The reason I can't have what I want is . . .

I'm too lazy
I don't have enough money
It doesn't exist
I've tried before and it never worked
Mother said I couldn't
I don't want to
It's too hard
I'm afraid to
John wouldn't like it
It's too much fun.

and so on . . .

2. Try the same exercise, only this time specifically name the thing that you want, i.e. "The reason I can't have a good job is . . . " and proceed as before.

Now just sit quietly for a few minutes with your list and see whether any of the thoughts you've written down ring true for you . . . whether in some way or degree you believe them. Just get a sense of what kind of limitations you put on yourself and your world.

3. Now write a list of all the most negative attitudes you can think of about yourself, other people, relationships, the world, life.

Again, sit quietly with your list and get in touch with which of these ideas may consciously or unconsciously hold emotional power over you.

If at any point in any of these exercises you feel emotions coming up, just stay with that and allow yourself to experience it as much as possible, with total acceptance. You may get a flash of an early experience, or something your parents or teachers used to tell you which programmed your view of the world in a certain way.

4. Whenever you feel complete with this process, especially if you've gotten in touch with one or more negative beliefs that you hold, simply tear up your lists and throw them away. This symbolizes how little power they actually need to have in your life.

Then sit quietly, relax, and do some affirmations to replace your constricted, limiting beliefs with more opening, constructive, positive ones.

A few possible clearing affirmations:

I now release my entire past. It is complete and I am free!

I now dissolve all negative, limiting beliefs. They have no power over me!

I now forgive and release everyone in my life. We are all happy and free.

I don't have to try to please others. I am naturally lovable and likeable no matter what I do!

I now let go of all accumulated guilt, fears, resentment, disappointments, and grudges. I am free and clear!

All of my negative self-images and attitudes are now dissolved. I love and appreciate myself!

All barriers to my full expression and enjoyment of life are now dissolved.

The world is a beautiful place to be.

The universe always provides.

More clearing exercises:

1. Forgiveness and release. Write down on a piece of paper the names of everyone in your life whom you feel has ever mistreated you, harmed you, done you an injustice, or toward whom you feel or have felt resentment, hurt or anger. Next to each person's name write down what they did to you, or what you resent them for.

Then close your eyes, relax, and one by one visualize or imagine each person. Hold a little conversation with each one, and explain to him or her that in the past you have felt anger or hurt toward them, but that now you are going to do your best to forgive them for everything, and to dissolve and release all constricted energy between you. Give them a blessing and say, "I forgive you and release you. Go your own way and be happy."

When you have finished this process, write on your paper "I now forgive you and release you all" and throw it away, as a symbol that you are letting go of these past experiences.

Many people find that this process of forgiveness and release is miraculous in relieving them immediately of their long-standing burdens of accumulated resentment and hostility. The wonderful thing is that the other people involved, even if you never see them again, will on a psychic level pick up your forgiveness and it will help to clear up their lives as well.

It may be that the first time you do this process you will not have an experience of relief and release with certain people (especially a parent, spouse or other very significant person in your life). If not, continue to do the process from time to time, continue blessing and forgiving them as much as you can find it in your heart to do so, and eventually it will be resolved for you. (Remember it is for your *own* benefit, health and happiness that you are doing this.)*

Many people experience miraculous healing of physical problems after doing this process, as many physical ailments such as cancer and arthritis are directly related to accumulated anger and resentment.

2. *Now write down everyone you can think of in your life whom you feel you have hurt or done an injustice, and write down what you did to them.*

Again close your eyes, relax, and imagine each person in turn. Tell him or her what you did, and ask them to forgive you and give you their blessing. Then picture them doing so.

When you have finished the process, write at the bottom of your paper (or across the whole thing) "I forgive myself and absolve myself of all guilt, here and now, and forever!" Then tear up the paper and throw it away.

---

* I recommend reading Catherine Ponder's *The Prospering Power of Love.*

One final clearing process:

Go through your closets, drawers, basement, garage, or desk – wherever you have accumulated "stuff" that you don't need, and throw it out or give it away.

This vigorous, concrete action on the physical level is symbolic of what you are doing on mental, emotional and psychic levels – clearing out old, useless stuff, getting the energy flow moving, and getting your "house in order." It will make you feel great, especially if you do affirmations while you're doing it, such as:

"The more I outflow, the more space I create for good things to come to me."

"I love giving and I love receiving."

"As I clean up and clear out my physical space I am cleaning up and clearing out my life in every way."

"I am now putting my life in order, preparing to accept all the good that is coming to me now."

"I give thanks now for all the good that I have and all the good things to come."

Writing Affirmations

The technique I'm about to describe has brought some of the fastest and most dramatic changes in my life on many different occasions. It is a combination of writing affirmations and a clearing process, neatly rolled into one. I love it because it is so simple and easy to do, yet it gets down to a very deep level.

Writing affirmations is a very dynamic technique because the written word has so much power over our minds. We are both writing and reading them at the same time, so it's like a double hit of energy.

Take any affirmation you want to work with and write it 10 or 20 times in succession on a piece of paper. Use your name, and try writing it in the first, second, and third persons. (For example: I, John, am a gifted singer and songwriter. John, you are a gifted singer and songwriter. John is a gifted singer and songwriter.)

Don't just write it by rote; really think about the meaning of the words as you are writing them. Notice whether you feel any resistance, doubts, or negative thoughts about what you are writing. Whenever you do (even a slight one) turn the paper over, and on the back write out the negative thought, the reason why the affirmation can't be true, can't work, or whatever. (For example: "I'm really not good enough"' "I'm too old" "This isn't going to work.") Then go back to writing the affirmation.

When you are finished, take a look at the back of the paper. If you have been honest, you will have a good look at the reasons why you keep yourself from having what you want in this particular case.

With this in mind, think of some affirmations you can do to help you counteract these negative fears or beliefs, and begin to write out these new affirmations. Or you may want to stick with the original affirmation if it seems effective, or modify it slightly to be more accurate.

Keep working with writing the affirmations once or twice a day for a few days. Once you feel that you've really looked at your negative programming, discontinue writing it out, and just keep writing the affirmations.

My experience with this process is that whatever I have been affirming often manifests within a matter of a few days or even a few hours. And I have usually gotten many valuable insights into my own patterns this way.

Setting Goals

Possibly the trickiest part of getting what you want in life is just figuring out what you really want! And yet it is certainly the most important part of all.

I have found this to be unfailingly true in my life: As soon as I have a very clear, strong intention to create a particular thing, it manifests almost immediately (often within hours or days of getting clear about it) with very little effort involved. I experience this as a kind of "click" in my consciousness, when I suddenly get a very strong experience of what I want, and an equally strong experience that I'm going to get it . . . It usually takes a certain amount of time and energy spent in processing before I arrive at that point of clarity. And very often the "click of clarity" has been preceded by feelings of confusion, despair, hopelessness and so on, which I have had to work my way through. So don't worry . . . the darkest hour is truly just before the dawn.

Discovering what you want in your life can be facilitated by the process of setting goals. I often find it helpful to do some exercises with pen and paper, which I will share with you. When you are working on setting goals it's important to keep a few things in mind.

Remember that setting goals does *not* mean that you are stuck with those goals. You can change them as often as you want to and feel that it's necessary.

Remember also that setting goals does *not* mean that you have to pursue them through effort, striving or struggling. It does not mean that you have to become emotionally addicted to achieving them. On the contrary, setting goals can help you flow through life more easily, effortlessly and pleasurably. The nature of life is movement and creativity, and goals give you a clear focus and direction in which to channel your natural creative energy, thereby helping you to outflow and contribute to the world, which enhances your feeling of well-being and satisfaction in life. Goals are there to help you and support you in your true purpose.

Goals can be made in the spirit that life is an enjoyable game to be played, and one that can be deeply rewarding. They are not to be taken too heavily or seriously. At the same time, you must give them enough weight and importance so that they are of real value to you.

You may find that the very process of choosing goals will bring up a certain amount of emotional resistance in you. You might experience this in various different ways, such as feeling depressed, hopeless, or overwhelmed at the thought of trying to set goals. Or you might feel the desire to distract yourself by eating, sleeping, or whatever. These emotional reactions (if you should have them) are clues to the ways in which you avoid getting what you want in life. It's important to go ahead and experience these feelings and reactions, to go through them and proceed with the process. Once you get into it you will find it of value.

Then again, you may thoroughly enjoy the whole process and find it very expansive, fun and enlightening. I hope so!

Don't make the choosing of goals too complicated or significant. Start with simple, obvious things. Remember you can always change and develop them as you go along.

Exercises:

1. Sit down with a pen and paper and write down the following categories:

Work/career

Money

Life style/possessions

Relationships

Creative self-expression

Leisure/travel

Personal growth/education

Now, keeping in mind your present life situation, write down under each category some things that you would like to have, to change, or to improve in the near future. Don't think too hard about it, simply write down any ideas that come to your mind as good possibilities.

The purpose of this exercise is to loosen you up and get you thinking about what you want in the various areas of your life.

2. Take another piece of paper and write at the top: "If I could be, do, and have everything I want, this would be my ideal scene:"

Now list the same seven categories, and after each one, write a paragraph or two (or however much you want!) describing your absolute ideal situation in life, as far as you can fantasize about it.

The purpose of this exercise is to stretch and expand you beyond your present limits, so let your imagination take over, and really let yourself have everything *you could ever want.*

When you have finished this, add one more category – world situation/environment. Describe the kinds of changes you would like *to see happen in the world in your lifetime, if you could have the power to change things – world peace, the end of poverty, people becoming conscious of each other and the earth, schools transformed into exciting learning centers, hospitals becoming true centers of healing, and so on. You can be as creative as you like with this category, and you may find that you have all kinds of interesting ideas you never thought of before.*

Now re-read the whole thing and meditate on it awhile. Create a mental picture for yourself of a wonderful life in a beautiful world.

3. Again, take a fresh sheet of paper. Based on what seems most meaningful from the ideal scene you have created above, write a list of the ten or twelve most important goals for your life, as you feel them to be right now. *Remember you can change and revise this list at any time (and you should do so from time to time).*

4. Now write down: My Five Year Goals, and list the most important goals you would like to achieve within the next five years.

It's great to write your goals in the form of affirmations, as if they had already been achieved. This helps to achieve a clearer, stronger effect. For example:

I now own 20 acres of land in the country, with a beautiful house, orchards, a creek, and lots of animals.

I now support myself easily and abundantly through singing and playing my own songs for enthusiastic and appreciative audiences.

In writing your goals, be sure to put down things that are real and meaningful to you, things that you actually want, *not* what you think you *should want.* No one else need ever see your goals unless you want them to, and this process requires that you be totally honest with yourself.

5. Repeat the process above with your goals for one year. Don't make too many; if you have a lot at first, eliminate all but the five or six most important ones. Check to see that they are in alignment with your five year goals. That is, make sure they are moving in the same general direction so that when you accomplish your one year goals, you will be a step closer to your five year goals. For example, if one of your five year goals is to own your own business, one of your one year goals might be to have a certain amount of money saved toward that end, or to have a job in a similar business where you are getting a certain type of experience you will need.

Now write out your goals for six months from now, one month, and one week from now. Again, keep it simple and choose the three or four that are most important. Be realistic about how much you can accomplish in the shorter range goals. Again make sure they are in alignment with your longer range goals.

You may find it difficult to be so specific about events so far in the future, and you may have an uncomfortable feeling about planning your life ahead. However, just making a plan does not oblige you to follow it; in fact you are bound to change considerably. This exercise is for the purpose of:

a) getting practice in setting goals,

b) acknowledging that some of your fantasies *can* become reality if you wish them to, and

c) getting in touch with some of the important purposes and directions in your life.

I suggest that you keep your goals in your notebook. Every now and then, perhaps every month or so, or whenever it feels like a helpful thing to do, sit down with your notebook and do some of the processes again, revising and reshaping your goals as needed. Be sure to date your paper each time you do this, and keep them in order in your notebook, as it is very interesting and informative to look back and see how they gradually evolve.

Some general rules:

1. For short range goals (one week, one month) be fairly simple and realistic — choose things that you are pretty sure you can accomplish, unless you especially feel like taking on a big challenge (which can be very good sometimes too). The further range your goal, the more expansive and imaginative you can be, so that your horizons are constantly extended.

2. When you find that you have not accomplished some of your goals (which will inevitably happen) do not criticize yourself or assume that you have failed. Simply

acknowledge clearly to yourself that you have not accomplished that goal, and decide whether it is still a goal for you; that is, decide whether you want to set it again for yourself, or whether you want to let it go. It is *most* important that you acknowledge unaccomplished goals in this way. Otherwise, they may accumulate in the back of your mind and you will feel unconsciously that you have "failed," which will eventually make you tend to avoid goal setting.

3. When you find that you *have* accomplished a goal, even a small one, be sure to acknowledge yourself for that. Give yourself a pat on the back and enjoy at least a moment of satisfaction about it. All too often, we accomplish our goals, and forget to even notice or enjoy the fact that we have done so!

4. Don't take on too much at once. Set goals that feel good to you. If you feel overwhelmed, confused, or discouraged . . . simplify. You may want to work on goals in one area of your life only, such as your job or your relationships. This process is ultimately to help you enjoy your life more.

If you set a lot of goals that you don't accomplish you are probably either setting them unrealistically high, or setting goals that you don't truly desire and therefore have no real inner intention of pursuing. Choose goals that you genuinely like and want.

Your goals should make you feel *good* — uplifted, expanded, pleasured, challenged. If not, find ones that do!

Ideal Scene

Creative visualization can take the form of mental imagery and words, of spoken words (affirmations), of written words, or of a physical image or picture (treasure map). Anything that helps you to create a clear "blue print" to put out in the universe is an aid in creative visualization.

This exercise will help you to create a clear picture through written words. The process of doing it will help you get clearer about what you really want, and it will help you to manifest it. I use it for all my important goals.

Exercise:

Think of a goal that is important to you. It can be a long range or short range one.

Write down the goal as clearly as possible in one sentence.

Underneath that, write Ideal Scene, *and proceed to describe the situation exactly as you would like it to be when your goal is fully realized. Describe it in the present tense, as if it already exists, in as much detail as you wish.*

When you have finished, write at the bottom,

"This or something better is now manifesting for me in totally satisfying and harmonious ways,"

and add any other affirmations you wish, and sign your name.

Then sit quietly, relax, visualize your ideal scene at your meditational level of mind, and do your affirmations.

Keep your ideal scene in your notebook, in your desk, near your bed, or hang it on your wall. Read it often, and make appropriate changes when necessary. Bring it to mind during your meditation periods.

One word of warning . . . if you put it away in a drawer and forget about it, you are very likely to find one day that it has manifested anyhow . . . without your consciously putting any energy into it at all.

I have often looked back through my old goals, ideal scenes, and treasure maps, surprised to find that things I had completely forgotten have magically come into being in my life, almost exactly as I had originally pictured them.

Treasure Maps

Making a "treasure map" is a very powerful technique, and fun to do.

A treasure map is an actual, physical picture of your desired reality. It is valuable because it forms an especially clear, sharp image which can then attract and focus energy into your goal. It works along the same lines as a blueprint for a building.

You can make a treasure map by drawing or painting it, or by making a collage using pictures and words cut from magazines, books, or cards, photographs, lettering, drawing and so on. Don't worry if you're not artistically accomplished. Simple, childlike treasure maps are just as effective as great works of art!

Basically the treasure map should show you in your ideal scene, with your goal fully realized.

Here are some guidelines that will help you make the most effective treasure maps:

1. Do a treasure map for a single goal or area of your life, so that you can be sure to include all the elements without getting too complicated. This enables the mind to focus on it more clearly and easily than if you include all your goals on one treasure map. You might want to do one treasure map for your relationships, one for your job, one for your spiritual growth, and so on.

2. You can make it any size that's convenient for you. You may want to keep it in your notebook, hang it on your wall, or carry it in your pocket or purse. I usually make mine on light cardboard which holds up better than paper.

3. Be sure to put yourself in the picture. For a very realistic effect, use a photograph of yourself. Otherwise draw yourself in. Show yourself being, doing, or having your desired objective — traveling around the world, wearing your new clothes, proud author of your new book, etc.

4. Show the situation in its ideal, complete form, as if it already exists. You don't need to indicate *how* it's going to come about. This is the finished product. Don't show anything negative or undesirable.

5. Use lots of color in your treasure map to increase the power and impact on your consciousness.

6. Show yourself in a real setting; make it look believable to yourself.

7. Include some symbol of the infinite which has meaning and power for you. It could be an "om" sign, a cross, Christ, a Buddha, a sun radiating light or anything that represents universal intelligence or God. This is an

acknowledgement and a reminder that everything comes from the infinite source.

8. Put affirmations on your treasure map. *"Here I am driving my new Datsun truck with a camper top. I love it, and I have plenty of money to maintain it."*

Be sure to include also the cosmic affirmation *"This or something better now manifests for me in totally satisfying and harmonious ways for all concerned."*

The process of creating your treasure map is a powerful step toward manifesting your goal. Now just spend a few minutes each day quietly looking at it, and every once in a while throughout the day give it a thought. That is all that's necessary.

Some Sample Ideas for Treasure Maps

To stimulate your imagination, here are a few possible ideas for treasure maps:

Health: Show yourself radiantly healthy, active, beautiful, participating in whatever activities would indicate perfect health.

Weight or physical condition: Show yourself with your perfect body (cut a picture from a magazine that looks like *you* would look in your perfect condition, and paste a photo of your head on the body!), feeling wonderful about yourself. You can make statements with balloons around them coming out of your mouth like in cartoons, to indicate how you are feeling, i.e., *"I feel wonderful and look fantastic now that I weigh 125 lbs. and am in great physical condition."*

Self-image and beauty: Show yourself as you want to feel about yourself . . . beautiful, relaxed, enjoying life, warm and loving. Include words and symbols that represent these qualities to you.

Relationships: Put photos of yourself and your

friend, lover, husband, wife or child in your treasure map, with pictures, symbols, and affirmations showing that you are happy, loving, communicating, enjoying a deep, wonderful sexual relationship, and so on.

If you are looking for a new relationship find pictures and words that represent qualities you desire in the person and the relationship; show yourself with the ideal person for you.

Job or career: Show yourself doing what you really want to do, with interesting, agreeable co-workers, earning plenty of money (be specific about how much you want), in the location you desire, and any other pertinent details.

Creativity: Use symbols, colors, and pictures that indicate your creativity is really opening up. Show yourself doing and manifesting creative, beautiful, interesting things and feeling great about it.

Family and friends: Show members of your family or friends in totally harmonious, loving relationships with you and each other.

Travel: Show yourself wherever you want to be, with plenty of time and money to enjoy it.

And so on. You get the idea. Have fun!

Health and Beauty

There are so many ways that creative visualization can be used to maintain and improve our health, physical fitness and beauty. Like everything else, our health and attractiveness are created by our mental attitudes, so changing our beliefs and the way we tune into ourselves and the world can have profound physical effects.

I have already mentioned the value of doing treasure maps in these areas. Here are a few other techniques that I like to use. I'm sure you'll find many more of your own.

Physical exercise

No matter what type of physical exercise you do, you can use creative visualization and affirmation to help you get maximum benefit and enjoyment from it. You can use visualization both while you are doing the physical exercise, and also at other times, while sitting in meditation or relaxing.

For example, if you like to run, picture yourself running very swiftly, smoothly, and tirelessly. While you are running, imagine that you are taking a huge leap with every step, covering vast territory effortlessly, almost flying. During relaxation periods, affirm to yourself that you are daily growing faster, stronger, and in better physical shape. Picture yourself winning races, if that is one of your goals.

If you do dance or yoga exercises, while you are doing them put your consciousness in your body, in your muscles, picture them relaxing and stretching, see yourself becoming more and more limber and flexible.

Use creative visualization to improve your abilities in your favorite sport; imagine yourself becoming more and more accomplished until you are truly excelling.

Beauty treatments

Do things for yourself regularly that make you feel that you are taking special care of.yourself and doing nice things for your body. Using creative visualization can turn a daily routine into a beauty treatment ritual.

For example, take a hot bath or shower, and visualize the hot water totally relaxing, soothing, and healing you. Picture any problems melting or being washed away, and nothing remaining but your natural radiance, shining from within.

Put lotion or oil on your face and body, giving yourself lots of loving attention, affirming that your skin is becoming smoother and more beautiful all the time. When you wash your hair, put your attention in what you're doing, and affirm that your hair is thicker, shinier, and healthier than ever before. When you brush your teeth, mentally affirm that they are strong, healthy, and beautiful. And so on.

Eating rituals

Many people have negative concepts relating to food. We are afraid the food we eat is going to make us fat, or make us sick (unhealthy). Yet we tend to compulsively continue eating the very foods we fear, thus creating inner stress and conflict, and eventually creating the feared effects — fatness and illness.

Also, many people are very unconscious while they eat. We are so busy talking and thinking of other things, we fail to tune in to the delicious, satisfying taste and nutrition of our food.

Eating is really a magic ritual, an amazing process in which various forms of energy from the universe are transformed into the energy that forms our bodies. Whatever we are thinking and feeling at the time is part of the alchemy.

Here is a ritual to practice at least once a day if possible, no matter what you are eating:

Sit down with your food in front of you. Close your eyes for a moment, relax, and take a deep breath. Silently thank the universe for this food, and thank all the beings who helped provide it, including the plants and animals, the people who grew it and prepared it for you.

Open your eyes and look at the food; really observe what it looks like. Observe how it smells. Slowly begin to eat it; really be aware of and enjoy the taste. As you are eating, talk to yourself silently in your mind, and tell yourself that this food is being transformed into life energy for your use. Tell yourself that your body is using everything that it needs, and easily eliminating anything that it doesn't need. Picture yourself becoming healthier and more beautiful as a result of eating the food. Do this regardless of any other previous concepts you may have of how good or bad the food is for you.

If possible, eat slowly, and take a moment or two after you finish to enjoy the pleasant warm glow that emanates from your stomach when it is satisfied and happy.

The more often you remember to tune into your food this way, the more beauty and good health you will create for yourself.

Here is another ritual that is even simpler:

Before going to bed, when you arise, or sometime during the day pour yourself a tall glass of cool water. Sit down, relax, and drink it slowly. As you drink, tell yourself that this water is the elixir of life and the fountain of youth. Imagine that it is washing away all impurities and bringing you energy, vitality, beauty and health.

Here are some good affirmations for health and beauty:

Every day I am growing more beautiful and more radiantly healthy!

Everything I do adds to my health and beauty.

Everything I eat adds to my health, beauty, and slender attractiveness.

I am good to my body, and my body is good to me.

I am now slender, strong, and in perfect condition no matter what I do.

I am growing stronger and more powerful everyday.

I now desire to eat only those things that are best for me at any given time.

The more I love and appreciate myself, the more beautiful I am becoming.

I am now irresistibly attractive to men (or women).

Creative Visualization in Groups

Many of the techniques that I have given in this book can be easily adapted for use in groups. Creative visualization is especially good when used by a group, because the group energy automatically gives it a lot of power. Each person's energy tends to support the others, and in this case the whole becomes more than the sum of its parts.

No matter what the group you are involved in, whether it is your family or a group of friends, a work group, social action group, church or spiritual group, or a workshop or class, you may find that creative visualization provides you with tools for achieving your group's goals, or just for tuning into each other in a deeper way.

Here are some of the ways you can use creative

visualization in a group:

Singing and chanting. Choose songs or chants that express a feeling, an idea, or an attitude that you want to create or cultivate in yourselves and in the world. Music is very powerful in effecting change.

Meditating and imaging. Choose a goal or image, and have everyone sit in silent meditation, visualizing and affirming it together. You may be amazed at the results.

Treasure mapping. Have each person create their own treasure map for a group goal, or as a group create one treasure map together. Or you can even appoint a committee to make a treasure map!

Affirmations. Do affirmations in partners, as I described in the section on how to use affirmations. Or have the whole group speak affirmations aloud together.

Healing. Healing in groups is a wonderful experience. See the section on healing meditations.

Creative Visualization in Relationships

One of the most valuable ways we can use creative visualization is in improving our relationships. Because human beings are so sensitive to each other on so many levels, we are especially susceptible and receptive to the thought forms that we hold about each other. It is these thought forms and the underlying attitudes that they reflect which form our relationships, and cause them to work or not work.

In relationship, as in everything else, we get exactly what we believe in, expect, and "ask for" on our deepest levels. The people we are in relationship with are always a mirror, reflecting our own beliefs, and simultaneously we are mirrors, reflecting their beliefs. So relationship is one of the most powerful tools for growth that we have; if we look honestly at our relationships we can see so much about how we have created them.

Take an attitude of total responsibility about your relationship. Assume for a moment that you alone are responsible for creating it the way it is, no matter how much it may look to you like the other person is responsible for certain things. If there are certain things about the relationship that are unsatisfying to you, ask yourself why and how you have created it that way. See if you can discover what core beliefs you have that cause you to create a less than satisfying, happy, loving relationship. What is the payoff for you in keeping yourself in an unhappy space? (There is always a payoff in everything we do; otherwise we wouldn't do it.)

If you truly *desire* to have deeply fulfilling, happy relationships in your life, if you *believe* that it is possible for you to have them, and if you are willing to *accept* that happiness and satisfaction, then you can and will create relationships that work for you.

Here are some things you can do to help you with your relationships:

1. Look at your goals in the relationship. What do you truly want out of this relationship? Consider all levels — physical, emotional, mental, and spiritual. Write out an ideal scene, or do a treasure map that expresses your perfect visualization in this relationship.

2. Take a good honest look at what beliefs and attitudes are keeping you from creating what you want. You can use a clearing process to help you get in touch with your limiting attitudes. For example, you can write "The reason I can't have a perfect relationship with __________ is. . . ." or "The reason I can't have what I want in this relationship is. . . ." Then write all the responses that come up for you.

3. Use affirmation and visual imagery to change your negative beliefs, and to start visualizing and creating beautiful, loving, fulfilling relationships.

4. The technique of saying affirmations to each other can often help to improve relationships dramatically. Of course it's very important to communicate with each other honestly from your true feelings about what you like and don't like, and what you want. But instead of continuously complaining about each other's shortcomings and weaknesses, try making an agreement to *affirm* to each other that you are improving and making progress in your growth and development. So instead of "George, why do you always interrupt me when I'm saying something" you might agree to say to George at appropriate moments "I appreciate the way you are becoming a good listener." In this way you not only remind George in a friendly way to be a better listener, but you also begin to change your image of George, as well as George's image of himself.

Remember that the potential for perfection lies within every relationship, just as it lies within each individual. It is already there, we simply have to uncover it by removing the layers of "stuff" we have put on top of it.

All too often in ongoing relationships we have gotten stuck in certain roles and images with each other which we find it difficult to change. It's as if we've put ourselves and each other in a certain box with certain labels on it. We find this very limiting and confining, but don't always know how to step out of it.

Creative visualization provides us with a wonderful tool for expanding out of our roles and stereotypes. Begin to visualize and affirm new images for yourself and for the other person; see the potential for positive change within every person and every situation, and give energy and support to that positive change through creative visualization.

Part Five

Living Creatively

The only successful manifestation
is one which brings about a change
or growth in consciousness;
that is, it has manifested God,
or revealed him more fully,
as well as having manifested a form . . .

David Spangler
in *Manifestation*

Creative Consciousness

Creative visualization is not just a technique, but ultimately it is a state of consciousness. It is a consciousness in which we deeply realize that we are the continuous creators of our universe and we take responsibility for that at all moments.

There is no separation between us and God; we are divine expressions of the creative principle on this level of existence. There can be no real lack or scarcity; there is nothing we have to try to achieve or attract; we contain the potential for everything within us.

Manifestation through creative visualization is the process of realizing and making visible on the physical plane our divine potential.

Discovering Our Higher Purpose

A basic need of all human beings is to make a positive contribution to the world and to our fellow beings, as well as to improve and enjoy our personal lives. We all have a great deal to offer the world and to each other, each in our own special and unique way. To a great degree, our own personal sense of well being is a function of how much we are expressing this.

We each have a significant contribution to make in this lifetime. It may involve many things, or it may be something very simple. I call this contribution our higher purpose. It always involves being yourself totally, completely, and naturally, and doing something or many things that you genuinely love to do, and that come easily to you.

We all know in our hearts what our higher purpose is, but we often do not consciously acknowledge it, even to ourselves. In fact, most people seem to go to great lengths to hide it from themselves and from the world. They fear and seek to avoid the power, responsibility, and light that comes with acknowledging and expressing their true purpose in life.

As you use creative visualization, you will find that you become more and more attuned to and aware of your higher purpose. Notice the elements that tend to recur in your dreams, goals, and fantasies, the particular qualities that are there in the things you find yourself doing and creating. These are important clues to the underlying meaning and purpose of your life.

You will find in using creative visualization that your ability to manifest will work to the degree that you are in alignment with your higher purpose. If you try to manifest something and it doesn't seem to work, it may not be appropriate to the underlying pattern and meaning of your life. Be patient and keep tuning into your inner guidance. In retrospect you will see that everything is unfolding perfectly.

This is a time of great transformation on our planet. We all have a part to play, just by being willing to be our true, magnificent selves.

Your Life is Your Work of Art

I like to think of myself as an artist, and my life is my greatest work of art. Every moment is a moment of creation, and each moment of creation contains infinite possibilities. I can do things the way I've always done them, or I can look at all the different alternatives, and try something new and different and potentially more rewarding. Every moment presents a new opportunity and a new decision.

What a wonderful game we are all playing, and what a magnificent art form . . .

Recommended Reading and Study

Books

Living in the Light by Shakti Gawain. Whatever Publishing 1986. Shows us a new way of life – becoming a channel for the creative power of the Universe by developing our intuition. Offers practical guidance in expanding our perspective on who we are and what we have the potential to become.

The Creative Visualization Workbook by Shakti Gawain. Whatever Publishing 1982. A large format book, especially designed to go with *Creative Visualization,* leads you step-by-step in planning your goals.

Work With Passion – How To Do What You Love For A Living by Nancy Anderson. Whatever Publishing/Carroll & Graf 1984. Career consultant Anderson guides you through the nine steps that show you how it *is* possible to do what you love for a living and get well paid for it.

Friends and Lovers – How to Create the Relationships You Want by Marc Allen. Whatever Publishing 1985. Includes a six-step process that is *guaranteed to settle arguments* at home or at work.

Prospering Woman by Ruth Ross. Whatever Publishing 1982. This fine book presents an entirely new way for women to view themselves and effectively take charge of their own lives. Men as well as women benefit from this book.

The Nature of Personal Reality (A Seth Book) by Jane Roberts. Prentice Hall 1974. An excellent explanation of how we are each totally responsible for creating our own reality. Very highly recommended.

The Silva Mind Control Method by Jose Silva and Philip Miele. Simon and Schuster 1977. Contains explanations and practices in creative visualization by one of the modern pioneers in the field.

Pray and Grow Rich by Catherine Ponder. Parker Publishing Co. 1968. Also many other books by Catherine Ponder, including *The Prospering Power of Love, The Dynamic Laws of Prosperity, The Dynamic Laws of Healing.* These books have sensationalistic covers and a Christian orientation which may not appeal to some, but I have found them to contain deep understanding and a wonderful variety of techniques and affirmations.

The Art of Spiritual Healing by Joel Goldsmith. Harper and Row 1957. Also many others by the same author, such as: *The Art of Meditation, The Infinite Way, Practicing the Presence.* Written by a great healer, these books are channeled from a place of deep understanding. I have found them profoundly helpful and inspiring.

I Deserve Love by Sondra Ray. Les Femmes 1976. Contains many good affirmations dealing with our attitudes about love and sex.

Kinship With All Life by J. Allen Boone. Harper and Row 1976. A unique and beautiful book. Although primarily concerned with human relationships with animals, it contains deep wisdom and insight about the use of visualization and affirmation in all relationships.

The Findhorn Garden by the Findhorn Community. Harper and Row 1975. One of the most beautiful and inspiring books I've ever read; it's about how we can communicate and cooperate with all forms of life and all of nature.

Handbook to Higher Consciousness by Ken Keyes, Jr. Living Love Publishing 1975. A very clear explanation of how our own "programming" creates our experience of reality. This book is especially helpful in learning to flow more easily through life.

Mystic Path to Cosmic Power by Vernon Howard. Prentice-Hall 1967. Channeled wisdom from a high, clear perspective.

Rebirthing in the New Age by Leonard Orr and Sondra Ray. Celestial Arts 1977. An explanation of how our basic beliefs are often adopted at the moment of birth.

OTHER BOOKS AND TAPES FROM WHATEVER PUBLISHING

Books

Living in the Light by Shakti Gawain. Shows us a new way of life — becoming a channel for the creative power of the Universe by developing our intuition. Offers both practical and inspirational guidance in expanding our perspective on who we are and what we have the potential to become.

The Creative Visualization Workbook by Shakti Gawain. This companion volume to *Creative Visualization* provides a convenient format in which to write down and practice many creative visualization techniques. The Workbook is designed to be fun; in addition to the exercises, there are pages on which to record your dreams, creative ideas, inspiring quotes, and more.

Work With Passion*—How To Do What You Love For A Living* by Nancy Anderson. This highly effective guide will help you master the secrets of finding your niche in life — doing what you love to do and getting paid well for it. *Work With Passion* is filled with inspiring stories of ordinary people who have achieved extraordinary results by following the nine-step program of the author, developed during her years as a highly successful career consultant. This is *the* career book of the 1980's!

Friends and Lovers*—How to Create the Relationships You Want* by Marc Allen. An upbeat, knowledgeable, and contemporary guide to living and working with people. Contains a six-step process that is *guaranteed to settle arguments* at home or at work.

Anybody Can Write *— A Playful Approach* by Jean Bryant. A delightful, humorous, and *effective* new book for non-writers, beginners, and writers who are "blocked." It will inspire you to learn to "fingerpaint with words," and encourage you to experience the pleasure and fulfillment of writing.

Cassettes

Creative Visualization. Shakti Gawain guides you through some of the most powerful and effective meditations and techniques from her book. An inspirational cassette.

Living in the Light. In this exciting hour-long interview, Shakti Gawain reveals the main principles and techniques from her book of the same title, showing us how to connect with our intuition and become a creative channel for personal and planetary transformation.

Stress Reduction and Creative Meditations. Marc Allen guides you through a deeply relaxing, stress-reducing experience on the first side. Side Two contains effective, creative meditations for health, abundance, and fulfilling relationships. Soothing background music by Jon Bernoff.

Friends and Lovers*—How to Create the Relationships You Want.* In this dynamic cassette companion to his book, Marc Allen gives an interview highlighting the most important ideas and techniques from *Friends and Lovers.* Inner work and core beliefs are stressed.

Anybody Can Write. Jean Bryant highlights some of the writing techniques and ideas from her book: trusting yourself, writing without thinking, escape writing, writing with passion, fingerpainting with words.

ORDERING INFORMATION

We invite you to send for a free copy of our full-color catalogue so that you can see our complete selection of books and cassettes.

Whatever Publishing, Inc.
P.O. Box 13257, Northgate Station
San Rafael, CA 94913
(415) 472-2100

ORDER TOLL FREE WITH YOUR VISA/MC
(800) 227-3900
(800) 632-2122 in California

About the Author

Shakti Gawain has a gift for blending the rational approach of the Western mind with the deep, intuitive wisdom of the East. She studied psychology and dance at Reed College and the University of California. After graduation she traveled for two years in Europe and Asia, studying Eastern philosophy, meditation, and yoga.

When she returned to America, she continued to delve deeply into her own personal growth, reading extensively and studying with many well-known teachers in the human potential movement. Her continuing exploration of philosophy and psychology culminated in the writing of her best-selling book, *Creative Visualization.* There is also a companion volume, *The Creative Visualization Workbook,* which provides a convenient format in which to write down and practice many creative visualization techniques.

Her second book, *Living in the Light,* which shows us how to use our intuition and become a channel for the creative power of the universe, created much excitement. During its first year of publication, *Living in the Light* was translated into five languages.

Shakti Gawain conducts workshops and retreats throughout the U.S., including Hawaii, as well as her Creative Leadership Program in Marin County. For a complete schedule of classes, please write: The Shakti Center, P.O. Box 377, Mill Valley, CA 94942, or phone (415) 927-2277.